Swamp Doctor

OTHER BOOKS BY THOMAS LOWRY:

The Story the Soldiers Wouldn't Tell

The Attack on Taranto

Tarnished Eagles

Don't Shoot That Boy!

Tarnished Scalpels

SWAMP DOCTOR

*The Diary of a Union Surgeon
in the Virginia and North Carolina Marshes*

Edited by Thomas P. Lowry, M.D.

STACKPOLE
BOOKS

Published by
STACKPOLE BOOKS
5067 Ritter Road
Mechanicsburg, PA 17055
www.stackpolebooks.com

Printed in the United States of America

10 9 8 7 6 5 4 3 2 1

FIRST EDITION

Library of Congress Cataloging-in-Publication Data

Smith, William Mervale, b. 1825
    Swamp doctor : the diary of a Union surgeon in the Virginia and North Carolina marshes / [edited, and with an introduction and commentary by] Thomas P. Lowry.—1st ed.
        p. cm.
    Includes bibliographical references (p.) and index.
    ISBN: 0-8117-1537-X
        1. Smith, William Mervale, b. 1825—Diaries. 2. United States. Army—Surgeons—Diaries. 3. United States—History—Civil War, 1861–1865—Medical care. 4. United States—History—Civil War, 1861–1865—Personal narratives. 5. Virginia—History—Civil War, 1861–1865—Medical Care. 6. Virginia—History—Civil War, 1861–1865—Personal narratives. 7. North Carolina—History—Civil War, 1861–1865—Medical care. 8. North Carolina—History—Civil War, 1861–1865—Personal narratives. 9. United States. Army. New York Infantry Regiment, 85th (1861–1865)—Biography. 10. Surgeons—New York (State)—Diaries. I. Lowry, Thomas P. (Thomas Power), 1932- II. Title.

E621 .S665 2001
973.7'75'092—dc21
                                                                              00-054744

The morning he left us, the regiment was drawn up in line, at dress parade, and bade him goodbye with a sorrow and depth of feeling seldom felt, and still more rarely manifested by veteran soldiers. We all felt that we were losing a royally good man—one whose place it would be difficult to fill.

Illustrated History of Allegany County

CONTENTS

THE FORMAT OF THIS BOOK

This book is an annotated diary. Each chapter of diary text is followed immediately by the footnotes relevant to that chapter. This is a happy compromise between having the notes and comments at the bottom of each page (which has an ugly, pedantic, and Teutonic look) and putting the notes at the back of the book (where the reader needs several fingers to keep track of the explanatory text).

The Introduction and Chapter 1 are entirely the words of the editor, as are Chapters 10 and 11.

Chapter 2 has several pages of lead-in, and then the diary proper begins.

Chapters 4 through 9 have a brief lead-in before the diary text recommences.

The entire intent is to give a flow, a setting, and a historical-geographic perspective, both to the Civil War aficionado and to the newcomer to this field and era.

To this final end, there are a considerable number of illustrations and maps.

ACKNOWLEDGMENTS

There would be no book, had not our neighbor in Woodacre, California, Mrs. Cecelia Smith Donahue, asked, "I have my great-grandfather's Civil War diary. Would it interest you?" All else stems from that wonderful question.

The labor of transforming the diary, with the editor's notes and commentary, into a finished manuscript, fell upon Beverly Lowry, whose patience and accuracy have no equals.

For technical help on numerous historical points I give heartfelt thanks to John Ball, Raymond Barber, Edward Boots, Conrad Bush, Sue Greenhagen, Robert E. L. Krick, Robert K. Krick, Wayne Mahood, Benedict Maryniak, and Debbie Schriver.

Any errors in opinion or interpretation rest, as always, upon the editor.

FOREWORD

Army surgeons got strongly mixed reviews during the Civil War. Limited by the primitive knowledge of medicine in that age, at first ignorant of how to treat traumatic injuries such as gunshot wounds, besieged by thousands of soldiers with illnesses not fully known and/or not fully curable, field physicians in the 1860s labored under every form of adversity.

Few soldiers in the ranks were aware of such hindrances; and the more they suffered, the more they blamed the surgeons. On Christmas Eve, 1862, an Illinois soldier wrote his wife: "The Damned Surgeons are not worth a Curse. They dont no any thing." Nine of every ten army physicians, a newspaper correspondent believed, "scare their patients by long faces . . . and dosing them with quinine and ipecac. The first makes you deaf and dumb, the other turns you inside out."

Of course, charges of neglect and incompetence tended to be widespread in the calmness of camp life. When troops shifted to the chaos of battle, many of them recognized—and some empathized with—the handicaps under which army surgeons labored. A Massachusetts soldier badly wounded in battle later said of the surgeons: "Their sympathetic devotion, their professional skill, their unselfish, untiring energy, saved many a poor, mangled sufferer from an untimely grave."

Wartime diaries and letters by these surgeons are difficult to find. For one thing, the demands of war were such that medical officers had little time for personal writing on a regular basis. Further, physicians of that day rarely described either to colleagues or loved ones their patients or the treatments administered.

Surgeon William M. Smith is a marked exception to those standards. His regiment, the 85th New York, spent more time on garrison and patrol duties behind the lines than was the case with most Civil War units. Smith's medical duties were therefore more concentrated on daily sick-calls and less consumed by battlefield medicine. Yet more important than those factors were Smith's powers of observation and exercises in philosophy.

His diary of military service is unusually lengthy and refreshingly personal. Smith made daily entries on the countryside, marches, the army to which he belonged, camp life, morale, individual officers and soldiers, plus medical problems both present and feared. The surgeon never presumed to be a military man. An ongoing feud he had with the major of the 85th New York was a clash between personalities rather than policies. Smith's many references to God reaffirm the inspirations of faith at every level of Civil War armies.

Other comments are highly unique. At one point Smith had to face charges of fraud made against him by civilians back home in New York. Throughout the journal runs an unbreakable fear that his fiancée was not waiting faithfully for his return. Smith also provides the only known written account of a physician going to a brothel to treat an ill prostitute.

As thoughtful as he was observant, Smith's running narrative tells us much about Civil War army life in general and medical life in particular. Statements in the diary provide evidence that the physician had a greater understanding of the surgical techniques of amputation, the prophylactic qualities of quinine, and the potential benefits of vaccinations.

This is an extraordinary memoir by an extraordinary participant in the midst of America's most defining hour. It underscores once again that the Civil War was a contest filled with the full range of human emotions.

James I. Robertson, Jr.
Virginia Tech

INTRODUCTION

A ll the witnesses are dead. No living man or woman has seen the Civil War. Our sole source is the written word (plus a few thousand photographs), and these words are not always reliable.

Like any other commodity, historical information comes in four grades: dubious, good, better, and best. The best are primary sources: documents created on the spot, by people who saw and heard the events and recorded their experiences while those moments were still fresh in their memories.

The next grade of information is "better": books and articles by historians attempting to be objective, fair, and coherent. A close reading of even the most renowned historians tends to show unspoken assumptions, hidden biases, and personal judgments. The authors, of course, begin with primary sources, but in their selection of what to include or exclude, in the choice of adjectives, in the placement of emotionally loaded words, in the insertion of value judgments, the meaning of the primary material can be transformed. Such alterations are inevitable, and it is the reader's duty to make adjustments for the geographic and familial influences that shape the author's thoughts and words.[1]

The next lowest grade of historical writing is found in high school textbooks. The presentations are based mostly upon secondary sources and are further influenced by publisher's guidelines, which reflect the current tenor of school boards and curriculum committees. They, in turn, are influenced by a wide spectrum of political, religious, and "heritage" groups, with a variety of axes to grind. These tertiary sources, which are the major exposure of most citizens to the great issues of our nation, are useful as a general outline of events but tend to lack the accuracy, the human drama, and the interplay of motives that are the reason for history in the first place.[2]

The fourth category of historical reliability is the dubious. Thousands of families have word-of-mouth tales of great-grandfather in the Civil War: his heroic deeds, his encounter with Robert E. Lee (or Abraham Lincoln), his painful war wounds. Every consultant at the National Archives can recall at least one descendant who refused to believe that the actual records did not confirm the family myth. Other myths belong to the general public. Everyone "knows" that the Virginia Military Institute cadets at the battle of New Market captured six Yankee cannons, and that Dan Butterfield composed "Taps." Other stories, equally mythic, are Abner Doubleday's invention of baseball, John Metcalf's shooting of a Confederate general from a mile away, and the champion myth, that of the young girl made pregnant by a Minié ball that had first struck a soldier's testicle.[3]

The beginner in Civil War history would do well with a balanced menu of some of the famed writers: perhaps Bruce Catton paired with James M. McPherson, or Douglas Southall Freeman (who emphasized the war in Virginia) paired with Richard McMurry (who places greater stock in the Western theaters). But the writings of even these luminaries, though based on primary sources, lack the immediacy of the primary sources themselves. And even in the universe of the primary, there are the issues of self-censorship.

Soldier letters are good examples. Bachelor privates often wrote to their male friends of the blood and horror of the battlefield and of the wild leisure times with whiskey and fallen women.[4] The same soldier would write to his sister or mother a much different letter, omitting the shocking details of combat and immorality. Some soldiers wrote letters for publication in the hometown newspaper; here, his words would be read by an entire community. Such correspondents were even more prone to stringent self-censorship.

Diaries are another prime source of fresh material. Some diaries are truly personal, written for self-remembrance of the titanic events of that national conflict, and come to light only by accident. Other diaries were meant for later public consumption, sometimes reflecting the political ambitions of the diarists.

That great foundation of Civil War scholarship, *The War of the Rebellion: A Compilation of the Official Records of the Union and Confederate Armies* (the OR), fills 131,000 pages (not counting the later Navy and Supplement volumes) and is the basis for much Civil War writing. But even these primary sources are official correspondence—reports of subordinates to commanders and reports of battles by ranking officers. They can hardly be expected to emphasize errors, misjudgments, or emotions, much less the views of the common soldier. Even the famed *OR* must be taken with its grain of salt.

Another widely used semiprimary source is *Battles and Leaders of the Civil War*, a multivolume work based upon a series of articles that appeared in the *Century* magazine between 1884 and 1887. Most of the authors were generals and admirals. While these sources, and their accompanying maps, are invaluable, one could hardly expect a commander, writing twenty years after the war, to recall his errors as clearly as he did his triumphs.

In brief, it seems clear that documents written at the time of a Civil War event, and not intended to be read even by family, much less the general public, are rare and wonderful finds. Such seems to be the case of the diary of William Mervale Smith, Surgeon of the 85th New York Volunteer Infantry. Many of his entries are of such a personal and self-revelatory nature that we can reasonably conclude that he wrote to himself alone, as a sort of a spiritual exercise, a self-communication.

What do we know of the authenticity of the diary? It has been in the family since it was written. After Dr. Smith's death in Redlands, California, in 1902, it was in the possession of his widow until her death in 1922. So far as is known, the diary has been in the family home at 916 West Olive Street until the present day. Dan Clarence Andrew Smith, Dr. Smith's grandson and a lawyer, had his secretary, Miss Adeline Amundsen, transcribe the diary around 1955. A chance encounter between myself and a neighbor, Mrs. Cecelia Smith Donahue, Dr. Smith's great-granddaughter, brought the diary to my attention. I have compared twelve pages of the original, handwritten version with the typed version and found no errors. On any point in the typescript where there might be confusion, such as the spelling of proper names and places, I have referred again to photocopies of the original handwritten text.[5] From the style of handwriting (I have read over thirty thousand Civil War court-martials) and the chain of ownership, there seems little reason to question the diary's authenticity or the accuracy of the transcription.

It might be good here to consider that this diary is that of a *doctor*, not a military man. While it is true that most line officers in the volunteer forces (95 percent of the Union army) were men with no formal military training, they were expected to function as combat officers, and they were judged as such. Their bravery in battle and their competence in maneuver and leadership were the standards by which they were judged. Their standards were success on the Field of Mars. What were the standards for doctors?

Today, one expects that a doctor will have a state medical license, based on four years of premed, four years of medical school, and one to eight years of postgraduate training. He or she will have passed the National Board examinations. If the doctor is a true specialist, he or she will be board-certified and most likely be a fellow of the relevant specialty society, such as The American College of Surgeons. In 1861, things were much different. Medical training consisted of a nine-month course of lectures; to obtain the M.D. degree, one attended the same lectures a second time. The newly hatched doctor with money went to Europe for a few months and visited famous clinics; their poorer colleagues apprenticed with a doctor already in practice.

Most states had abandoned licensure, since the doctors themselves could not agree on the standards. In the realm of the visible, all doctors agreed on the location of the clavicle, the knee joint, and other such anatomical features. There was fair agreement on the physical maneuvers of delivering babies. There was a consensus on the indications for amputation and the need to tie off the arteries and veins as part of the procedure. There was even considerable understanding of the meaning of heart sounds and their relationship to heart valve disease.

But when it came to the invisible, or at least those things that could be seen only with a microscope, doctors everywhere were on a par with the Egyptians of five thousand years ago. Diseases caused by bacteria, viruses, and protozoans were utterly beyond the ken of medical men in 1861. However, there were five areas of medical knowledge that any competent doctor in those years should have known. The first was pain control. For millennia, it had been known that derivatives of the opium poppy will sooth pain. For the acute pain of surgery, general anesthesia with chloroform or ether had been perfected a decade before the war, and most surgery in the Civil War used one of these wonderful additions to the battle against suffering.

A second pillar of medical practice was the use of mercury compounds in the treatment of syphilis. (There were eighty thousand *reported* cases of syphilis in the Union army.) Several centuries of experience had shown that mercury, in spite of its ferocious toxicity, had some benefits in suppressing this ailment that so often flowed from the rites of Venus. A third area of useful knowledge was the use of quinine in suppressing the manifestations of malaria. Cinchona, Peruvian bark, and Jesuit's bark had been in medical books for three centuries, and it was a rare doctor who did not know of quinine's near-miraculous aid for sufferers with the "the chills and fever" and "the ague."

Seventy years before the Civil War, Edward Jenner had demonstrated the use of vaccination in immunizing men against smallpox. Smallpox, often fatal and always disfiguring, could not be treated, but it could be prevented. Added to this fourth medical boon was the fifth and final item in our list of things every doctor should have known: the prevention of scurvy, another discovery of the 1700s. The Royal Navy had shown clearly that fresh fruits or vegetables could both prevent and cure scurvy. While most doctors today have never seen a case, it was sadly familiar to travelers a century or two ago. The profound weakness, the loosened teeth, the bleeding around the bones, the reopening of long-healed wounds, and the decreased resistance were all part of the miseries of sea voyages, and the addition of antiscorbutics to the diets of soldiers and sailors was a true blessing.

As we follow Dr. Smith in his self-recorded adventures, we may look for evidence of his knowledge in amputation anatomy and in the five useful medical treatments of mercury, quinine, antiscorbutics, vaccination, and anesthetics. In doing this, we can fairly judge him *by his own standards,* not by our wholly unearned retrospective omniscience, but by what was known in 1861–65.

The diarist himself seems to have been in five wars simultaneously. The first, of course, was the Civil War itself. The second was conflict with the major of the regiment, while the third was with political enemies at home in New York, who accused Smith of theft and fraud. The fourth was his constant struggle with his fears that his fiancée might be unfaithful to him, and the final combat was with his obsessive doubts about his relationship with God.

Who was this doctor who brought his medical skills and his worried conscience to the low country of North Carolina? His family origins and his prewar politics will tell us much.

NOTES: INTRODUCTION

1. My own possible bias may be judged by the following: of my five family members who served in the Union army, two were killed at

Fredericksburg, one was killed at New Market, one survived prison at Andersonville, and one was crippled for life pushing a wagon out the mud.

2. James W. Loewen, *Lies My Teacher Told Me—Everything Your American History Textbook Got Wrong*. The New Press, New York, 1995.

3. William C. Davis, "Tall Tales of the Civil War," page 48, *Civil War Times Illustrated*, Vol. XXXV, No. 4, August 1996.

4. My as-yet-unpublished collection of nearly fifty Civil War soldiers' letters amply confirms the scandalous nature of many such communications.

5. Personal communications, William Melbury Smith and Cecelia Smith Donahue, 1999.

CHAPTER ONE

The Gathering Storm

The Civil War did not appear overnight in April 1861, born of a sudden thunder of cannon fire across Charleston's harbor, but had, instead, ancient roots, whose fibers and tendrils extended deep into the murky layers of the nation's history. The growing tension 'twixt North and South was nourished by the shadow side of America, by a dark blot on the radiant shield of Liberty herself. Long before the founding fathers broke the New World's ties with England, inspired by ideals of liberty and self-determination, an internal contradiction in the nation's moral corpus loomed large and was, at the same time, veiled in reticence, not to be mentioned in polite conversation.

There were many differences that formed the wedge between Yankee and Southerner—a different climate, a different range of crops to be grown, a different self-concept of British origin, a different view of the impact of tariffs, and a different emphasis on industrialization, but the single most divisive fact was one that the drafters of the Constitution could not even bring themselves to name. They would not even place the evil word on paper. The documents that drew their strength from the proposition that all men are created equal did not once use the word "slavery." To give it its true name might have alienated many illustrious citizens of the new nation, not the least of whom were George Washington and Thomas Jefferson. And so, in the end, in our Constitution, the children of Africa became "persons held to service."

It was not as though the Northerners had no acquaintance with the great blemish; indeed, slavery, in some form or other, had reached from Canada to Tierra del Fuego. Nor were blacks who had obtained their freedom universally welcomed in the North. Lincoln's home state barred free blacks from settling there. Yet in spite of the fear and sense of difference felt by most persons of north European stock when they encountered their darker brethren, slavery fell out of favor in the North, and state after state abolished slavery entirely or set schedules of gradual emancipation.

True, the Yankee industrialists may have merely substituted the labor of children and desperate immigrants, but the concept of an intrinsic evil in human beings as property was one that hardened into the rhetoric of the abolitionist.

The evolution of the Southern agricultural economy away from nutrition and into cash crops such as tobacco and cotton increased the planter's reliance upon slavery as a perceived necessity. As the 1800s progressed, the wondrous human capacity for rationalization promoted slavery from a necessary evil to a positive good, and Southern theorists described their "peculiar institution" as a system that benefited the slaves: It brought them to Jesus and away from the false gods of central Africa; it taught them habits of industry; it gave them housing, food, and free medical care. Without the beneficent supervision of the owner and his overseer, the slaves would have fallen into habits of idleness, intemperance, and idolatry, lost to this world and to the next. Or so it was said.

The stage was set for a dialogue of the deaf. The abolitionists wished all the slaves freed, but had not a clear plan for what to do with four million people with no land, no formal education, no financial assets, and no legally recognized family structure.

The defenders of slavery saw themselves as misunderstood benefactors, providing home and structure for a benighted race. (They also deeply feared a revolt by the slaves and had ample historical reasons for such fear.)

The white Southern farmers and mechanics who did not own slaves were the subject of several conflicting forces. In their daily lives, they competed against unpaid labor. They were not invited to the big house on the hill, with its imported pianos, mirrors, and porcelain. They were not invited to participate in the Southern legislative institutions, dominated by wealthy planters, who had the time, money, education, and leisure to become politicians. These same leaders explained to the poor white folk that their real enemy was those distant Yankees who would take away their cherished "way of life" and deprive them of their ill-defined "rights." (This chicken of xenophobic feather came home to roost late in the Civil War, when Southern troops began to sense the conflict as a "rich man's war and poor man's fight," an insight that was the motivation for thousands of desertions.)

By 1861, the stage was set for the most dreadful of wars, a civil war, brother against brother, with each side convinced of the evil of the other.

When our diarist was born, in 1825, the cauldron of regional differences was not yet at full boil. The stories of Dr. Smith's contemporaries and the political turning points that shaped all their lives will shed light upon the man whose newly found words form the body of this work.

In a way, the Civil War started with the French. In 1803, Napoleon, needing money to finance his almost-endless wars, sold Louisiana to the United States. The territory as then defined included most of the drainage of the Mississippi and Missouri Rivers. In 1812, out of these vast new lands, the territory of Missouri was organized. Five years later, Missouri applied to Congress to be admitted as a state—a slave-holding state. Until then, the U.S. Congress reflected a careful balance between free and slave states. To admit Missouri as she requested would have given added power to the South. Three years of fierce debate resulted in a compromise: Missouri entered the union as a slave state, counterbalanced by the admission of Maine as a free state. This was the Missouri Compromise of 1820, which, for a generation, delayed the apocalypse. As the ink dried on the final documents, William Mervale Smith was a boy of five.

That same year, the titans of his future life were already assuming their places on the stage of history. Robert E. Lee had just graduated from West Point, where he exhibited the forbearance and self-discipline that he learned from his mother. Robert, of all the Lees, had not disgraced the family name. His father, "Light Horse Harry," had ruined the fortunes of two wives and was a fugitive from creditors. Robert's half-brother, Henry, lived off the inheritance of his morphine-addicted wife and begat a bastard child upon his teenage sister-in-law. Meanwhile, Carter, Robert's full brother, spent the last of the family money on high living. The self-control and calm demeanor that Robert learned from these disasters served him well and inspired his men during the coming conflict.

Jefferson Davis, the future leader of the Confederacy, completed West Point when Smith was still a toddler and was a lieutenant at a frontier post in Wisconsin as Smith learned his ABCs.

Abraham Lincoln was a volunteer in the Illinois militia that same year, serving in the brief Black Hawk War. Two years later, in 1834, as Smith turned nine, Lincoln was elected to the Illinois State Legislature.

The year of Smith's birth, 1825, had seen several momentous events. John Quincy Adams was elected President; the future Omaha, Nebraska,

The New Jersey medical license of the diarist's father, Dr. Reuben Smith, issued May 12, 1829. SMITH FAMILY COLLECTION

was founded as a trading post; the first wave of Norwegian immigrants reached New York, many of them Quakers fleeing persecution by the state church of their homeland.

Ulysses S. Grant was a three-year-old boy at Point Pleasant, Ohio, when Smith was born. The future general grew up loving horses and became a master handler of those indispensable beasts. Thomas J. Jackson was born at Clarksburg in what is now West Virginia, the year before Smith's birth. The home of the future Stonewall was not a happy one. His father, Jonathan, was an unlucky poker player, an alcoholic, and a cosigner of many loans that went bad. These misfortunes were compounded by typhoid, which left Stonewall's mother a destitute widow when the future tactical genius was only two. When he was seven, tuberculosis carried off his remaining parent. The many burdens of orphanhood were compounded by an attack of malaria when Jackson was twelve.

As these household names marched forward to their rendezvous with destiny, Smith was growing up to manhood in the mountains of southwest New York State.

He had been born in Paterson, New Jersey, the son of Reuben H. and Orpha Van Blarcom Smith. The thirty-year-old Reuben, an 1829 graduate of Rutgers Medical College, moved to Granger, in Allegany County, New York, when William was five.

For the next twenty years, William's life centered around four New York counties: Cattaraugus, Allegany, Wyoming, and Steuben. The town of Granger was first surveyed in 1807. The hilly countryside was covered with pine and hemlock, and the clay hillsides and gravelly valleys were unsuited to agriculture. Grazing of sheep and dairy cattle were the early industries. When the Smith family settled there, it was still a wilderness, the only transportation being on horseback or on foot. Reuben supplemented his medical income with surveying. Before his arrival, what medical care existed in Granger was provided by Capt. Isaac Van Nostrand, who owned a tooth-pulling instrument and bled those citizens who wished such a "restorative."

Thirty years after being settled, Granger contributed its bit to history by providing a major station on the Underground Railroad. Reverend A. Richmond was the chief agent in helping escaped slaves on the way to Canada. Simeon Thorp of nearby Short Tract had become superintendent of public education in Kansas and was shot dead on his own doorstep by one of Quantrill's infamous bushwhackers. Even the isolated hills and hollows of southwest New York were not far removed from the issue of slavery.

William M. Smith attended the primitive district schools until age fifteen, when he was ready for Middlebury Academy. He paid part of his tuition by teaching school during the winter. At age seventeen, he sought a business career in New York City, but without capital or influence, he was soon back at Lima, New York, where he completed his academic education at Genessee Wesleyan Seminary.

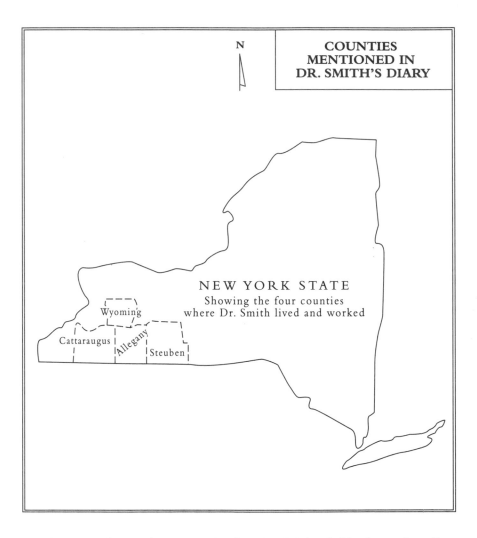

N

COUNTIES
MENTIONED IN
DR. SMITH'S DIARY

NEW YORK STATE
Showing the four counties
where Dr. Smith lived and worked

Wyoming

Cattaraugus

Allegany

Steuben

At age eighteen, he apprenticed to Dr. Richard Charles at Angelica. This practical training plus the course of lectures at Castleton College, Vermont, rewarded him with the degree of Doctor of Medicine. At the age of twenty-one, he opened his practice at Short Tract, where he stayed for three years. In 1851, he joined the practice of Dr. William F. Cooper of Cayuga County for two years, followed by a four-month visit to the hospitals of New York City to see the latest in modern medicine. With this refresher, he returned, in 1853, to his original practice at Short Tract and was soon involved in politics.

National politics in the 1850s was more complex than today's two-party system. The Democratic Party that is ancestor to today's Democrats traces

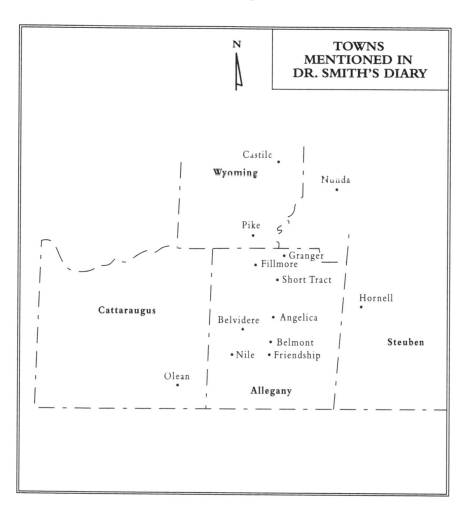

N

TOWNS MENTIONED IN DR. SMITH'S DIARY

Castile

Wyoming

Nunda

Pike

• Granger
• Fillmore

• Short Tract

Hornell

Cattaraugus

Belvidere • Angelica

• Belmont
• Nile • Friendship

Steuben

Olean

Allegany

its origins to the supporters of Thomas Jefferson. They advocated personal freedom and limitations on the Federal government. The party rested on a coalition of Northern city-dwellers and Southern agrarians and was deeply weakened by the Civil War.

The Whigs, who favored high tariffs and a loose interpretation of the Constitution, began in 1830 as opposition to the Democratic policies of Andrew Jackson. Dissension within the Whig party (it was formed from such divergent groups as the National Republican Party and the Anti-Masonic Party) was present from the beginning and was furthered by a split between the "Northern Whigs" and the Southern "cotton Whigs," represented respectively by Daniel Webster and Henry Clay. In spite of internal dissension, at least three Whigs made it to the White House: William H. Harrison, Zachary Taylor, and Millard Fillmore.

The Kansas-Nebraska Act of 1854 repealed the Missouri Compromise and set the stage for the bloody warfare in Kansas between the antislavery "free-soilers" and the proslavery settlers. The act also killed the Whig party: The cotton Whigs went to the Democrats and the Northern Whigs formed the nucleus of the new Republican Party, founded in 1854, just seven years before the Civil War. The Republicans' first presidential candidate was John C. Frémont, who lost the election of 1856. The 1860 candidate, Abraham Lincoln, fared better at the polls.

Parallel with these two parties was the now-obscure Know-Nothing Party, officially termed the Native American Party, founded around 1843. The party's chief motivation was a violent hatred of Roman Catholic immigrants; its platform required twenty-five years of residency for citizenship and restricted eligibility for elected offices to native-born Americans. Organized and conducted in secrecy, party members answered, "I know nothing," when queried. In alliance with a faction of the Whigs, the Know-Nothings almost captured New York State in 1854. Where did Dr. Smith stand in all this conflict?

The first Republican convention in New York State was held in 1854 in Allegany County at the Angelica courthouse, just across the town square from Smith's future home. By now, the Know-Nothings held a majority in the county, but a coalition of Whigs and Democrats put Dr. Smith forward as a candidate for the 1856 county supervisor's race. He won and six months later was also elected to the State Assembly as a Republican, a victory he repeated in 1859.

His intense involvement in these issues is shown by his appointment as a delegate to the 1860 Republican convention. There, in Chicago, he cast one of the votes that propelled Abraham Lincoln into the presidential race and snapped the final links that held the extremist South Carolinians (dubbed "fire-eaters") to the Union.

Medicine and politics were only part of Smith's life. Love, marriage, and parenthood were essential to his nature. In 1848, at the age of twenty-three, he married Adaline Weeks. Their one child, Frank, was born in 1851; when Frank was four, Adaline died. In 1857, he married again, this time to nineteen-year-old Emma Spinks. In April 1859, their son, Clarence, was born; five months later, Emma died. In April 1861, when the

Civil War began, Smith was relying upon a Sarah Daggett to care for his two motherless boys.

In September 1861, Dr. Smith raised Company E of the 85th New York Volunteer Infantry and marched off to war. With him went his brother, 1st Lt. Andrew W. Smith. Behind him he left his two boys, a new fiancée, and his elderly parents.

His regiment was first stationed in the defenses of Washington, D.C., where, in January 1862, he was in charge of the Porter Mansion Hospital at Meridian Hill, District of Columbia. In late March, Smith's regiment and tens of thousands of other Union troops joined the grand flotilla that carried them to Fort Monroe, Virginia. It was the beginning of Maj. Gen. George B. McClellan's Peninsular Campaign.[1]

NOTES: CHAPTER ONE

1. Local history information is based on *History of Allegany County,* Anonymous, F. W. Beers & Co, New York, 1879; an article in the January 4, 1889 *Allegany County Republican;* and *Contemporary Biography of New York.* Dr. Reuben Smith's medical diplomas, as well as the diarist's papers, are still in the Smith family archives. The famous generals and prewar political history are from standard biographical sources, such as Ezra J. Warner's *Generals in Blue,* William C. Davis's *The Confederate General,* and John S. Bowman's *Who Was Who in the Civil War.*

CHAPTER TWO

The Peninsula

D r. Smith's diary will make little sense without a description of that campaign. The summary presented here may tell some readers more than they wish to know; the Civil War specialist may find the matter oversimplified; with those caveats, the principal themes are these.

During the Civil War, both sides placed great importance upon the capture of the capital city of the opponent. Such a stroke, by either side, would have had enormous economic, psychological, political, and strategic importance. If the South could have seized Washington, D.C., the Confederacy would have surely received diplomatic recognition by France and Great Britain, and have been in a position to dictate the terms of peace, which would have included recognition by the Union of the Confederate States of America as a separate nation.

On the other hand, if the Union were to capture Richmond, diplomatic recognition of the Confederate States by the European powers would almost certainly have never come. The economic repercussions, too, would have been enormous. The Tredegar Iron Works at Richmond were the South's largest manufacturing establishment, turning out armor plate, railroad wheels and axles, gun carriages, and artillery projectiles. A mile away were the Virginia Armory, which delivered five thousand rifles a month, and the Confederate States Laboratory, which produced millions of cartridges and percussion caps. Without these factories, the south would have been almost weaponless. Further, Union capture of Richmond would be a shattering blow to Southern morale.

The initial Union attempt to march on Richmond came to utter ruin on July 21, 1861, at the First Battle of Bull Run (Manassas). The defeated boys in blue retreated in confusion back to Washington, D.C. Six days later, Maj. Gen. George B. McClellan was given command of the troops in the

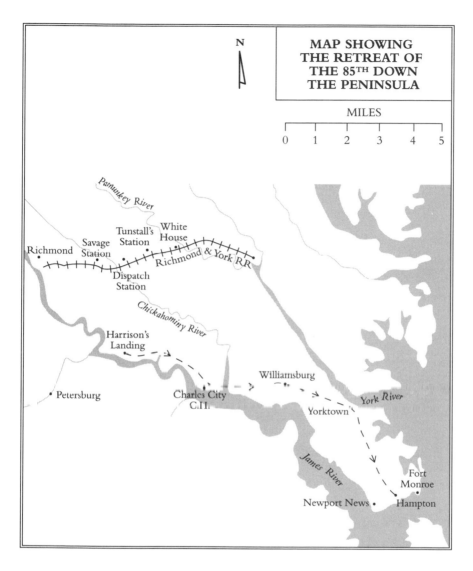

MAP SHOWING
THE RETREAT OF
THE 85TH DOWN
THE PENINSULA

Washington area. Oceans of ink have been spilled on the subject of McClellan's personality, strategic vision, and political machinations. His strategy for the war, reduced to its simplest outline, was that he would capture Richmond by way of the Peninsula.

This great spit of land projects roughly seventy-five miles southeast from Richmond. The Peninsula is an extended triangle, about forty miles wide at its base near Richmond and ten miles across at its tip, where the Peninsula rounds off and then terminates at Fort Monroe. The body of water that forms the northern boundary is the York River; along the southern edge runs the James River, swarming with sturgeon back then, and giving entry to the docks and wharves of Richmond itself.

McClellan's plan was to land his army at Fort Monroe, march the seventy-five miles to Richmond, and put an end to the war. His plan took advantage of the Union superiority in water-borne transport and the impregnability of Fort Monroe. The York and James Rivers would guard his flanks. He could muster around one hundred thousand men for this campaign. Those were the bright sides of his plan.

On the negative side of the ledger were half a dozen key factors. With the Army of the Potomac *south* of Richmond, Confederate forces could more easily attack Washington, D.C.; this led to a tug-of-war, in which Lincoln wanted to keep more troops near him to defend the capital, while McClellan wanted more troops to attack Richmond. Each man deeply distrusted the other, and the Confederates exploited this rift by a series of attacks in the Shenandoah Valley, which terrified the politicians in Washington, D.C.

Further problems vexed McClellan. His intelligence reports had told of good roads on the Peninsula. The reports were wrong. Coupled with record rainfall, the roads that did exist were nearly impassable seas of mud. McClellan's chief source of military intelligence was the reports of Detective Allan Pinkerton, who wildly overestimated Confederate strength. Another weakness of the Union effort was the failure to follow enlightened medical opinion regarding the use of quinine as a preventive for malaria. Epidemics of "remittent fever" swept the Union ranks; combined with scurvy and the fatigue of marching in knee-deep mud, Yankee strength was rapidly and deeply depleted. And finally, there was the unique personality of McClellan himself. He was a superb organizer of armies and inspirer of men, but his obsessive caution, mixed with an apparent paranoid egomania, caused him to feel outnumbered everywhere and to generate enemies both real and imagined.

In late March 1862, Dr. Smith and his regiment received the order that brought them into McClellan's grand scheme. The regimental trunks and valises went into government storage in Washington; much of this luggage would be reclaimed only by the heirs of soldiers, men who slept the long sleep under Virginia's soil.

On March 28, 1862, the 85th New York Infantry moved to Alexandria, Virginia; on the 31st, they were packed aboard steamboats for the overnight trip to Fort Monroe. That afternoon, moving down the Potomac

River past Mount Vernon, the regimental band played "The Star Spangled Banner," in honor of the father of our country. The next morning, they landed on Virginia soil and marched six miles to their camping spot on the road to Newport News, where they took their place as part of McClellan's left wing on the long march up the Peninsula.

The first line of Confederate defense was a series of fortifications extending from Yorktown, on the York River, southward to the banks of the James. McClellan, convinced by Pinkerton, by initial skirmishes, and by his own caution, did not use his great superiority to break through the Confederate lines, but instead set about conventional siege warfare. He had imported a vast array of siege guns and powerful mortars. Hauling these ponderous weapons along the muddy ruts of Virginia's primitive roads strained to the limit the aching muscles of men, mules, and horses. McClellan used an entire month preparing his grand assault. When he unleashed his thunderbolt, the Confederates were gone. Having gained their objective—time—the Confederate forces, commanded by Maj. Gen. Joseph E. Johnston, moved north toward further defensive positions.

And what of Dr. Smith's regiment in that probably wasted month of siege preparations? Ninety-seven men were dead of malaria or too sick to move. The left wing of the Union army at the tail end of the supply line, had no tents for the sick, nor beds, nor medicine, nor means to move these helpless men to the hospital ships at Fort Monroe. A brief reconnaissance to Lee's Mills, in the swamps of the Warwick River, had done little harm to the regiment, but the long delay in the fever-ridden swamps had ruined a tenth of the regiment before it even began to fight.

The retreating Confederates paused briefly to engage the Union in a rear guard action at Williamsburg. This confused, two-day conflict was conducted in a sea of mud. The Union suffered twenty-two hundred casualties, the south, five hundred less. Each side claimed victory, McClellan because he held the field, and the South because they had delayed the progress of the bluecoats.

On and on, they all trudged in the mire and muck, the Confederates keeping ahead of their pursuers, the Union unable to move faster because of fatigue, sickness, and the slow advance of the supply wagons.

On May 14, at 2:00 in the morning, the 85th New York marched past New Kent Courthouse. Three days later, the whole left wing of the Union army had passed Baltimore Cross Roads, just fourteen miles due east of Richmond.

The geography of the upper Peninsula had two physical features important in this discussion. The first was the Richmond and York Railroad,
which ran thirty-five miles eastward from the capital to the port town of
West Point on the upper reaches of the York River. Its little country train
depots form a litany of crucial Civil War sites: Fair Oaks Station, Savage
Station, Tunstall's Station, and White House.

The second feature is a natural one, the Chickahominy River. Its
mouth is a five-mile-long estuary, oriented north and south, emptying into
the James River at a point halfway between Fort Monroe and Richmond.
After the Chickahominy reaches the center of the Peninsula, it angles
northwest and runs parallel with both the York and the James. Its upper
drainage is a vast territory of swamps, made worse in the spring of 1862 by
the hardest rains in twenty years.

Here, almost within sight of the spires of Richmond, the Union
received its first setback. McClellan had placed most of his army north of
the flooded Chickahominy, with his smaller IV Corps on the south bank at
Fair Oaks (also called Seven Pines). The Confederates noticed this isolated
segment and launched a three-pronged attack on the IV Corps, hoping to
destroy it, and then turn and concentrate on McClellan's forces north of the
river. This set the stage for the battle of Fair Oaks, May 31–June 1, 1862.

In these two days of bloody confusion, the South lost 6,000 men. The
85th New York, which formed part of Casey's Division, was in the thick of
the fight. In two hours, this division lost 1,842 men, out of less than 5,000
engaged—37 percent casualties between lunch and midafternoon.

As the sun went down on the second day of the battle, the men of the
85th counted up their losses since they had landed, bands playing, at Fort
Monroe: 220 men out of 900; 72 had been killed or badly wounded at Fair
Oaks; 148 others had been killed by bullets or by malaria or left behind, too
sick to walk.

General McClellan and some of the Northern newspapers placed the
blame for the difficulties at Fair Oaks onto the forces under the command
of Brig. Gen. Silas Casey. This enraged Dr. Smith, who wrote home to a
friend, W. Van Nostrand, on June 11, 1862, saying, in essence, "I was there.
I know who did their duty, and McClellan's criticisms have discouraged my
men." (See Appendix A.)

At Fair Oaks, the Confederates lost, not only 6,000 men, but also their
commander, Major General Johnston, who was wounded in the chest and
right shoulder. He was replaced by Maj. Gen. Robert E. Lee, whose very

different concept of warfare would shape the lives of the 85th New York and all other Union soldiers. And very soon.

In addition to the officers and men lost at Fair Oaks, the 85th New York lost all of its baggage: wagons, tents, food, ammunition, knapsacks, and regimental papers. Among the many items never seen again was Dr. Smith's first diary, which documented his regiment's passage from Fort Monroe to Fair Oaks. He began a second diary on June 13, 1862. Eight days after his first entry, there began the series of battles known today as the Seven Days before Richmond, seven days that left McClellan confounded, confused, angry, outfoxed, puzzled, and penned to the narrow confines of Harrison Landing on the James River.

Just before the beginning of the Seven Days, Dr. Smith had been granted a thirty-day leave of absence. He, like all of us, had no knowledge of the future. His new diary begins as he is about to take the Richmond and York Railroad east to the Union supply base and medical center at White House, on the Pamunkey River, which flows into the upper York River.

Our diarist is on his way to New York State, to see his parents, his motherless children, and his fiancée. Smith, like many Northerners that day, seemed to assume that Union victory lay just ahead, and so his thoughts were of home—and of love.

June 13, 1862. I left camp this P.M. (about 3:00 o'clock) for a few days rest from the toil which I have for several months past undergone without an hours rest. My health has come to imperatively demand it. For many years, I have not been so entirely sick and never so worn out as now—let me but lose thought of sick and wounded men a few weeks, and I shall be able to return to my duties with renewed strength and zeal. My journal containing jottings of my experiences during the war, was lost at the battle of the 31st of May [Fair Oaks] and has doubtless ere this amused, if not instructed, its rebel captor whoever he may be. It will be a source of pleasure in coming days to draw from the recollections of these passing hours, through the simple instrumentality of my journal. It will therefore occupy some future leisure hour, before their memory becomes dim, to re-record them on a subsequent page of this, being hopeful that a less unfortunate fate will be the lot of these pages. I reached Savage's Station on the railroad from White House to Richmond in time for the train, but my valise, which was entrusted to an ambulance man, got on a bye road, and so did not arrive in time for me to leave on that train;

which, though I was greatly annoyed by it at the same time was probably for the best, as this very train on reaching "Tunstall Station" was fired into by a large force of the Rebels and several killed and wounded. [Two days before this first entry in Smith's new diary, he wrote a long letter home, denouncing McClellan's telegram that had blamed Casey's division for the loss at Fair Oaks. See Appendix A.]

June 14, 1862. I got aboard a train about 12:00 at night and went as far as Dispatch Station, when we heard the news of the attack on the train that preceded us. I concluded to wait for daylight—it was a tedious night for me; too weak to sit or stand, there was nothing but a filthy car bottom on which to lie; but there is a virtue in necessity which sometimes compels—I laid down and got up alternately until the glad morning broke when, no news of the condition of the road being received, I got into a sutler's wagon and made the best face possible at the 20 miles of horrid roads before me. Came near running into rebels at Baltimore House and should but for a contraband who warned us—we turned off, and by another road reached White House in safety about 12:00 M. I sought an asylum on the <u>Elm City</u>, in care of the U.S. Sanitary Commission. Every needed comfort and luxury was provided—I soon was made very comfortable and refreshed. I met Dr. Lewis this P.M. He came on board— found Captain Noble on board quite ill—Dr. Elisha Harris was also here.[1]

Sunday June 15th. Had a refreshing night's rest—so cool and comfortable were the clean sheets and sweet couch. I feel greatly refreshed. I took a light breakfast and bade the Good Samaritans on the <u>Elm City</u> goodbye. God bless the "Sanitary Commission." Tens of thousands way-worn, sick and wounded soldiers have already cause to invoke blessings on them. Went aboard the mail boat at 7:00 A.M. for Fortress Monroe—the trip down the Pamunkey and York River is delightful—reached the Fortress at 2:00 P.M.—had an excellent dinner at the Hygiea Hotel and at 5:00 P.M. took the mail boat for Baltimore. The Chesapeake Bay was very rough, the wind blowing almost a gale—there were many seasick, but to my surprise I was not in the least affected. Had a filthy berth in the lower cabin, but a good sleep.

Monday 16 June. Reached Baltimore about 7:00 in the morning and put up at the Eutaw House. This is a very fine house, well kept and charging prices high enough to satisfy the most aristocratic purse. At 1:00 o'clock P.M. I took the cars for Philadelphia, where I arrived about 6:00

P.M. The country traversed by this route is rich and interesting. I put up at the [blank in original manuscript] one of the most luxurious and best-appointed hotels in the United States. Being in company with Dr. Charles Winne of Buffalo, I yielded to his invitation to attend the Walnut Street Theater, though feeling very worn and ill.

Tuesday 17 June. Rose early this morning feeling little refreshed. Having no appetite for breakfast I took the early (5:00 A.M.) train for New York City via New York Central Railroad to Amboy and thence by steamer to NY where we arrived about 10:00 A.M. I employed a portion of the day shopping—replenishing my wardrobe exhausted by service in the field and loss in the battle of "Fair Oaks." In the afternoon, I called on Dr. Taylor (corner 6th Avenue and 38th Street) and was warmly welcomed and invited to make my home there while I remained in the city, which I was fain to do, for I was greatly wearied and worn out. A few errands about the city was all I felt inclined or able to undertake, and for the remaining part of the time, for the two or three following days, kept close to my room enjoying the luxury of quiet and rest for the first time in many days and months—O, how much I enjoyed it.

Thursday 19 June. I bade my new found but excellent friends, Dr. Taylor and Lady good bye. Mrs. Taylor is a superior Lady. At 5:00 o'clock P.M. I was on board the train on the N.Y. and E. Railroad bound for home.

Friday 20 June. I reached Hornellsville about 7:00 o'clock A.M. and stopped at the Osborne House until the evening train for Buffalo. Several friends called on me in the course of the day. Ira Cutler and lady and Miss Cora took tea with me, also Mr. Durfy and other friends. Miss Cora is a young lady of more than ordinary intelligence and not unprepossessing in personal appearance. At 5:00 o'clock P.M. I left for Castile, this being the only station from which I could reach friends the same night, as the train did not stop at Nunda. At dusk, I reached Castile and immediately chartered a horse and carriage to take me to Pike, where I arrived before my friends had retired for the night. I was very cordially welcomed by my dear friend, Miss L.[2]

I found her the same warm and affectionate woman I left nearly a year ago. She has been one of the bright places in memory and one of the sunny spots in my future, that has encouraged and stimulated me through the many toils, exposures and privations of the past few months. My visit this evening was pleasant, and I was very happy until the shadow of my friend's strong will, I cannot call it less harshly, I would not call it more, clouded the pleasure of the passing moments.

Saturday June 21. Rose early this morning, feeling feverish and unrefreshed—indeed, did not sleep at all and rested but little. The morning was dark and cloudy, threatening rain. I expected to have started for Granger quite early, but the coming rain prevented. But about 12:00 N. I started with Miss L. in company and Mr. Frank L. and lady (wife) in the "rear." At, or near, Fillmore, we met Mr. Luron Van Nostrand and wife, and Mrs. Lyon, on their way to Pike. Mrs. Van Nostrand is in failing health and being on her way to Pike to stay some days and wishing very anxiously that I should see and examine her case induced me to return to Pike. Not, however, until I had the assurance that my loved ones at home were quite well this A.M.[3]

Sunday June 22. I was greatly refreshed and improved this morning—I feel much stronger than when I left camp the 13th instant. I am compelled to confess to my own heart that my dear friend can bend her will to the dictates, perhaps I ought to say, to the intercessions of a love that equals, if it does not exceed, her own. Oh, for the assurance that she would always do this if our lives should be more intimately associated in future years. After breakfast this morning, I left with Mr. V.N. for home, where I arrived shortly after M. I found all well—thanks to a kind and good Providence that has preserved my Household Treasures thus far.[4]

My dear babe has very greatly improved since I parted from it. The embryo mind has rapidly developed; where was but sparks of intelligence I now see the unmistakable light of a fine intellect; scarce able to articulate when I gave him one last kiss for his sainted mother, and another for the last consolation of my own lonely heart, he now rattles on with a volubility that surprises me. He seems sorely perplexed with the idea of his "other pa" as he calls me; but a few hours passed, however, before, as if by instinct he clung to me, all his coyness and timidity gone. Frank is rapidly improving in many respects, but I cannot fail to see how much he needs my own firm hand and paternal love. God grant I may soon be with you, to protect and guide you, my dear son, through the devious paths of youth.

Monday June 23. Rose early this morning and enjoyed the sweet songs of birds and the rich fragrance of the summer flowers in my yard. How much I appreciate the quiet luxury of my home. I have not tasted of Spring or Summer until now—the seasons have passed almost unheeded among the bustle and din of a great army, and the luxury is appreciated fully now—the luxury of birds and flowers—of the fragrant shrubbery, the green growing grass, the fruit-laden trees that embower me, and of home and its <u>loved ones!</u> This P.M. I rode up to see my parents, taking with me Mrs. D. and the boys—had a very pleasant visit. My dear father and mother are hastening to the end—the valley and shadow of death lies just before them—let me learn a lesson from their life—a lesson of wasted opportunities, of years lost to themselves and society. Oh, my mother, why have circumstances always crushed that warm and loving heart of thine.[5]

Tuesday June 24. Set about getting workmen to repair and build my yard fences—am feeling much improved; my strength is returning as if by some magic art. I am determined to give myself a few days breathing time and rest, then business for a few days and then again try the chances of life and duty in camp.

Saturday June 28. I worked pretty hard today, with thankful heart that I am once more able to work. Thursday evening, I went to Angelica to attend to some business—after its hasty transaction took a horse and buggy and drove over to Friendship to see my friend Lt. Col. Wellman, who being severely wounded at the battle of Fair Oaks had been sent north and then to his home.[6] He had gone to Richburgh and I was disappointed—I rode over to Belmont and called on J. Whitcomb, Esq.—did not get there until after dark and to my great surprise found Mrs. Emily Fenno there. I have not desired to meet her, and yet felt compelled to improve this opportunity to say some plain things in a plain way. She is a dangerous woman and more dangerous to her friends than to her enemies. Towards evening, I rode over to Pike, reaching there shortly after dark, a pleasant visit [with Frances] was marred by unpleasant feelings before it terminated. Shall such experiences be repeated? I am losing faith in our future!

Sunday June 29. I left Pike very early in the morning for home— arrived in time for breakfast. Attended the M.E. [Methodist Episcopal] service this morning. The funeral sermon of Richard Groves, who fell at the battle of Fair Oaks, was preached by Reverend J. Duncan. A great number was in attendance. Richard fell near the close of the struggle at the front of Casey's Line, just as the 85th was compelled to fall back before the overwhelming numbers of the rebels—he was always a willing soldier in the discharge of his duties and proved himself in this terrible battle a cool, brave man.[7]

Tuesday July 1. Was very busy yesterday and today about the farm and in assisting the workmen. In the afternoon, Mr. Frank Lyon and wife and Miss F.A. Lyon called and took tea with me. Frank has made choice of a very pleasant woman for a wife, but she has neither personal or intellectual attractions of a superior order—but it matters little, only so that mind mates mind and heart weds heart—life is one weary, toilsome march, but if there be that one green, bright spot a warm affectionate-hearted wife, to which the soul can retire when almost discouraged and worn out, there is, even under the infliction of so much toil and tears, enough to live for.

Friday July 4. Independence Day! Dreary and storm-like looks the future of my beloved country this anniversary of its birth. Many rumors come to my ears within the last few days from the Army of the Potomac, which I interpret to be a reverse of our arms and our cause. I am impatient to be able to return to my post, to share the perils and the fortunes of the brave men there. I spent a good part of the day at Angelica, not to see the crowd that was there, but to meet a few friends who I expected would be there. Was gratified at seeing Lt. Col. Wellman and many other friends. Late in the afternoon, I returned to Granger.[8]

Saturday July 5. The heat today, as yesterday, is oppressive; I have hurried forward my business matters this week as rapidly as possible for time at home is now very limited.

Sunday July 6. It was a bright and warm day. Rode over to Luron V.N. this A.M. with my boys. Mrs. V. is rapidly passing away with tuberculosis. In parting with her, I felt sure I should not meet her again in the shores of Time. In losing her, the family will lose a faithful wife and mother, and society a quiet, unostentatious woman, whose heart has ever been more susceptible of noble and good purposes than society has given it credit for. Many friends called on me in the course of the morning, which delayed my preparations for departure. At 4:00 P.M., however, I was ready and Mr. F.L. having arrived to take me to Pike, enroute for the early train from Hornellsville, I bade good-bye to my home, but not just yet to the loved ones there—they accompanied me as far as Mr. William Van Nostrand's and to the humble graveyard nearby where lie entombed so many of my hopes. A brief prayer—an unspoken vow and my steps are turned from the narrow house of those I have loved so well.[9] And then came the most bitter of the parting moments. My dear babe! Little do you know the trial it cost the father to leave you again in the hands of strangers. And you, my Frank, through the tears that streamed down your cheeks gave token of the affectionate sensibilities of your little heart, and yet you could not understand how great a loss is the loss of a father's care. My memory will not cease to dwell, through all the long days and months of absence, on that tearful little group with which I parted on the wayside. But for the assurance in my heart that my noble-hearted friend, Mrs. Sarah Daggett, would be a mother to my motherless boys in my absence, I could not have left them. As it was, only a sense of duty—from which I did not feel at liberty to think of escaping enabled me to bid them goodbye. I did not fail to recognize the full extent of my obligations to those who are looking to me alone, for care and protection; and when I am assured that their safety, or mine for their sake as in the event of failing health, depends on my return to them I shall not hesitate to make a sacrifice of the duties I owe the brave men with whom I have cast my lot in this unhappy struggle. A rapid drive to my father's and a hurried good-bye to them (father and mother) and I set my face toward the home in yonder village, where my heart already was. Arrived there just before the sun went behind the western hills—<u>she</u> was not there; tired of waiting for me, perhaps, for I promised to come early—or was it to punish me for my delay! But soon she came, smiling, as usual, and the hours went by on swiftest wing, toward that hour of final parting—final, did I say? Ah, who can say that it is not? My heart could find a refuge here, I feel assured!

Monday July 7. Rose very early—had a good precious visit last night—the moments came and went on eagle wing. 5:00 o'clock A.M. I bade them all good-bye—and she, who I loved so well, a long, long good-bye. What matters it, though I did leave her in "sadness and tears," if we shall meet again. Perhaps the heart of each will be exalted with the trials of separation and the bonds which unite our heart made more strong by time. But I cannot subdue the fears which have taken possession of my mind—I cannot for one moment endure that she should toy with any, or receive the attention of any, other than as the bride she is affianced to be—my heart is too proud, and my position is too public, not to be compromised by the least attempt of this kind. It will be comforting and reassuring to believe that she has pride and faithfulness enough to resist any and all temptation to take one step that shall wrong a heart devoted to her above all others. But I will try and not anticipate evil, or borrow unnecessary trouble; it comes fast enough truly. A furious drive of 35 minutes and Frank L. set me down at the portage depot in time for the train. At 11:00 o'clock A.M., I was in Elmira—remained until the early train next morning for Williamsport—the transaction of business for the most part consumed the afternoon; but found time to call on the family of Mr. Farnum and Mrs. Arnott. I had a very pleasant call at Mrs. A.'s. Mrs. A. and "Maggie" are very excellent and very interesting ladies. A little before 5:00 P.M., a severe thundershower drenched the ground and cooled the heated atmosphere.

Tuesday July 8. Before 5:00 o'clock A.M., I was enroute for Washington via Williamsport and Harrisburgh[*sic*]. Reached Baltimore too late in the afternoon for the last train for Washington—stopped at the Eutaw House with my friend H. Brown, who goes to Washington in behalf of his brother-in-law, Capt. John Brown, 85th New York, under sentence by court martial for buying a mule on the march from Hockaday Springs to Roper Church for $10.00, knowing it to be stolen from a rebel Virginian. The sentence, to be disgracefully discharged from the service and imprisoned in the penitentiary at Washington for three years, is one of the most atrocious on record. The mule was purchased by the captain to assist in carrying his baggage and that of some feeble men of his company. The heat today was most oppressive—particularly to my friend who has more adipose tissue to encumber him and has never before been subjected to the influence of a southern climate—but with the assistance of a servant to fan him, he survived the ordeal of a warm supper.[10]

Wednesday July 9. Took the early train for Washington—arrived about 8:00 A.M. and took rooms at the National. I was very poorly today—scarcely able to leave my room on account of a return of my previous difficulty. Being better late in the P.M., I called on my friend Major Richardson, who arrived in town this A.M. from a long visit to his family. The day is very fine—the heat oppressive.

Thursday July 10. I am feeling much improved—in working order again. Yesterday P.M. I removed my quarters to the Ebbett House, a more quiet but excellent hotel. Here, I have the luxury of a large, fine room and an excellent table. I was very busy all day in pursuit of the "ways and means" to secure the pardon and reinstatement of Captain J. Brown—the President is out of the city on a visit to the "Army of the Potomac." General Van Valkenburgh and Theodore Pomeroy and several other of my friends in the House have gone home, which considerably embarrasses my success in securing the influence necessary to obtain the Capt's pardon.[11]

Friday July 11. Called on Senator King this morning with Major B. and Mr. H. Brown. He has not returned (called on Sec. War).[12]

Saturday July 12. The senator volunteered to accompany us to call on the President, who arrived in the city yesterday P.M. We found the President having a conference with the senators and representatives of the Border States—access to him was of course impossible. Augustus Frank kindly volunteered to accompany us (Senator P. King and H. Brown and myself) in our call on the President. Finding the effort to see him this morning fruitless, we called on his private secretary, Mr. Nicolay, and then on the Judge Advocate, Major Lee.[13]

We ascertained here that the case of Captain Brown had already attracted the attention of the President, who had referred the case to the Judge Advocate and that he had made a report on the case, deciding the sentence to be illegal, whereon the President had already issued a pardon, for so much of the sentence as related to the imprisonment. The captain was supposed to be somewhere in the city in charge of the authorities, as he was taken from camp by order of Gen. McClellan some days ago. At 2:00 o'clock P.M., he was found in the Old Capitol Building Prison. I regard the sentence of Captain Brown one of the most severe in the records of military tribunals. There is no doubt in my mind that he was designedly made the scapegoat in all this made. Many other officers and men were arrested for similar offenses, but none of the sentences were carried out or attempted to be, except in this instance. And a greater number of cases were never brought before the court martial. I cannot but believe that political capital, or the hope of it, had much to do with General McClellan's course in these arrests and the sentence in the case of Captain Brown. Suppose the General should succeed to the extent of his wishes in the defeat of the Rebel force before Richmond, and the border states are reclaimed in time to bear a part in the political campaign of 1864, his course in the treatment of Rebels and in the protection of their property would very naturally incline them to regard George B. McClellan with more favor than many others, some of whom may be candidates for the presidency. This careful attention to the preservation of the property of rebels and traitors has been carried too far. Our brave men have been constantly employed, through the burning suns and the nights poisoned by the malaria that pervades the swamps of the Peninsula in guarding the property—the fences, the fields, the houses, the poultry and onion patches of rebels who were in the Confederate Army.

Sunday July 13. Met Captain Brown, for a moment, this P.M. He was released yesterday P.M. His triumph will be complete if he shall be

Dr. Smith made several trips to Washington, D.C. During one such trip he visited the photographic studio of the famous Mathew Brady, whose staff took this portrait. SMITH FAMILY COLLECTION

restored to his command. Governor Morgan can alone do this by com-
missioning him again. I left Washington at 3 o'clock this afternoon, in
company with Major Richardson, for the Peninsula via Baltimore at 5
P.M. and proceeded immediately to the steamer for Fortress Monroe. The
passage up the Chesapeake Bay was very pleasant engrossed in the last
"Atlantic Monthly" and by my friend R. by turns, the time flew by very
swiftly until a late hour in the evening.

Monday July 14. Reached camp of the 85th New York Volunteers
late in the afternoon. The trip up the James River was very pleasant, in
spite of the rebel riflemen who saluted our steamer and the gun boats acting as its convoy, with several shots from the bank of the river near Fort
Powhatan. [The fort is on the south bank, four miles down river from the
mouth of the Chickahominy.] A material change has taken place in the
circumstances and situation of the Army of the Potomac since I left the
Peninsula 30 days ago. Instead of lying before Richmond, in a threatening
attitude, we are stretched along the eastern bank of the James River in a
strongly <u>defensive</u> position. The army then rested its right at Hanover
Court House on the Virginia Central Railroad and its left at Seven Pines
on the old Richmond and Williamsburg Road—since then, the whole
right and center has fallen back across the Peninsula, making our base
entirely the James River and lying under the protection of the gun boats.
This movement was the only one that could have saved the army, after the
many delays on the part of General McClellan had enabled the Rebels to
bring a large part of Stonewall Jackson's and Beauregard's forces to Richmond and with the overwhelming forces thus concentrated, sweep down
our right flank. This change of our front in the face of an active foe, is one
of the most brilliant retreats or maneuvers on record. But it seems to me
that it would have been more brilliant, dashing and would have read better
in history had we entered Richmond two months ago, as we might have
done. One of the largest, best and most munificently appointed armies
ever led into battle has been wasted in the poisonous swamps of the Peninsula and digging the eternal ditches that the Commander never seems to
be at ease without having, between his army and the enemy. <u>Forty percent</u>
of the "Grand Army of the Potomac" was hors de combat before the
series of battles commencing with the 26th of June, upwards of 15,000
was our loss in killed, wounded and missing in these battles, and thousands
more date the commencement of a serious illness to the exposure and

fatigue during and immediately subsequent to this trying retreat. So we must wait here, until the loyal men of the north rally to reinforce us.

Tuesday July 15. I find the regiment encamped in a dense wood, in very low, wet ground, some 40 rods to the rear of the line of our entrenchments, near the left of our position. I rode over to the camp of the 27th and 33rd NY Volunteers this forenoon. Captain McNair of the 33rd informs me that cousin Norton Bardwell is probably a prisoner to the Rebels—he fell out of the ranks with a sick comrade on the last day of the retreat (about 30 June) between Savage's Station and White Oak Swamp Fords and has not been seen since.[14] My friend Major R. called and dined with "our mess"; the day is oppressively warm. Tomorrow shall put on my harness again, and set to work again among the sick in earnest. I find a general feeling, I may truly say, a <u>universal</u> feeling of pleasure & gratification among the rank & file of the regiment, at my return. I think they expect more of me, than I am capable of. Certainly I could not desire more unbounded confidence in my professional skill & ability than the Officers and men bestow on me.

Friday July 18. <u>My birthday!</u> And a beautiful day it is—a little too warm for comfort, but the dense foliage of the woods in which we are encamped—the fly of my tent extended in front for an awning, and the sides of the tent looped up all around, gives a refreshing coolness to my quarters which those encamped on the open plain may well envy. One year ago today I was with my household Treasures, away yonder at my quiet home in Allegany. When shall I be with them again, to leave them no more for the camp & the battlefield—ah, I might better have asked when this bloody war would end—when will the sacrifice of life and blood be sufficient to satisfy the insatiate Demon that rules the hot blood of the south?

I wrote my dear friend Miss L. today, for the first time since I bade her good-bye. It never occurred to me as possible, until my last visit with her, that I should ever have the occasion for feelings which would prompt me to write her as I did today. If she has done, as I fear she has, and as I learn, there has, then, an impossible barrier come between us. It has cost my heart more suffering than she will ever know, to believe she could forget her position, and relations, even for a moment, with one who has sacrificed so entirely his hopes of the future to love of her as I have. If it be true, I learn from it, that she does not—that she <u>cannot</u> appreciate or value, the heart I have given her, or the proud position in society it has been my fond occupation that she should occupy as my <u>wife</u>.[15]

Sabbath, July 20. I have tried several times today to realize that it was the Sabbath day. It is so unlike the quiet of this day at home that I have to "think twice" before I can realize the day.

Sunday July 27. The beautiful morning has been but the herald of a pleasant day. A smart shower late yesterday but makes the morning look more glad—just as joy makes more beautiful the human countenance, when it smiles through tears.

We removed from our camp yesterday morning to a much more pleasant and healthy camp, but a short distance to our rear. I have not seen so beautiful a camp since we were on the Peninsula. No persuasion of the colonel could induce Gen. Wessells to

Brig. Gen. Henry Wessells, a veteran of the Seminole War, the Mexican War, and skirmishes in the Dakotas, was one of the few men Dr. Smith seemed to admire.

GENERALS IN BLUE, EZRA J. WARNER, LOUISIANA STATE UNIVERSITY PRESS, 1964

give leave for the regiment to occupy the ground. And only after I made an official report, setting forth the imperative necessity of a change in order to secure the health of the regiment would he yield; and then, rather ungracefully. The week has not been productive of any particular event except, the agreement entered into between the Union & Rebel forces for a general exchange of prisoners—many of our wounded have been liberated in consequence & taken North.[16]

Monday July 28. The morning has been cool—refreshingly so; but before midday a tropical heat again pervades the atmosphere. I have had the sick of the 92nd New York Volunteers on my hand for a number of days—there is no position in the army more arduous—whose duties are more incessantly taxing, than those of the Regimental Surgeon; particularly when in the field in the prosecution of an active campaign. I shall be very happy when I can with honor retire from the service, to the quiet of my loved home.

Tuesday July 29. I rose quite early this morning, considering that I did not turn into my blankets until 2:00 o'clock in the morning—I read until quite late in the evening, then my mail was brought—some letters which I received required an answer at once—not least among them one from Miss L. I should be happier if my mind was at ease concerning her—I cannot banish suspicion—and I must not let suspicion haunt my soul. The toil, the exposures & the dangers of my condition are quite enough without the heartache which I have felt for some days past. The resolve of last evening, which dictated my reply to her letter, must be my guide. It is an alternative I would have escaped; but my peace, especially with my pride, demand it. If she lives for herself, and pleasures which the society of others yield—in plainer words, if she is unworthy the heart that has lived for <u>her</u> through the many long and weary months of the year past more than for any other object in the wide world, it is far better that my heart be schooled to forgetfulness, before the certainty of it is realized; and if she lives for me, like a true & faithful <u>affianced</u> wife, denying herself to all others, I shall learn it of those who surround her, and bid her welcome to the heart that will admit no other, however long this separation may last—and, shall I confess it, to a heart that has not, and cannot, displace her until her unworthiness is beyond the possibility of doubt.

Wednesday July 30. About noon today, we received orders to be in readiness to march at a moment's notice. Many guess we march to the valley of Virginia—but it is all speculation. Yet my own opinion inclines to believe that may be our destination. The Division was out for review when the order came—all were sent back to their camps (17 regiments) and ordered to be in readiness. Later in the afternoon—several orders have been received, which go to show that there is an attack by the Rebels expected—and the preparations along the entrenchments indicate an expected attack instead of a march. There is a rumor that the ironclad vessel which the Rebels are understood to have been building at Richmond is on its way down the river (James)—if this be true there is undoubtedly a heavy land force to cooperate & take advantage of any success by the Rebel craft, if not attack us independently of it—this however I do not believe they will undertake. But I think the greater probability is, that it is but a feint to prevent a detachment of our force to the assistance of General Pope. The day has been <u>very</u> warm.[17]

Thursday July 31. The morning has been pleasantly cool, for a wonder; about noon the rain commenced quietly falling, and late in the afternoon assumed the proportions of a regular storm. Early in the afternoon, the thunder was sharp & frequent in the distance. I have often been startled here, by the artillery-like reports of the thunder—the intensely charged clouds peculiar to latitudes where the heat of Summer is long or steady and severe, affords an explanation. The time hangs heavy on my hands—fly away with winged swiftness, and hasten the restoration of loved Ones far away. My spirit chafes at this idleness and procrastination. I cannot see the benefit to our cause, or triumph to my beloved country in it.

Friday August 1. Another month is gone—another month has come. The past with fruitful record has gone with ages past to posterity—it is no longer the property of the present age exclusively. The future of the month we have entered on is pregnant with events of absorbing interest to the present & the future—those who are part of the present and those who will be part of the future.

We are making history with a rapidity which no other nation ever surpassed. And this month will not pass away until there has been many eventful issues decided—much blood spilled & many noble lives sacrificed to this bloody demon that rules the hot blood of the South. The day has been fine & very warm—rode over to the river to procure hospital supplies of the Medical Purveyor—called on Surgeon Judson at General Emory's quarters.[18]

The evening has closed in very beautifully. In the quiet twilight, the shadows of the forest in which we are camped have a solemnly grand look, not incompatible with my own feelings. If I was sitting on the verandah of my own beautiful home this evening, it seems to me I should be happy. But that quiet home and its loved ones is a long ways off and the long, uncertain distance of a bloody war lies between me and them.

Sunday August 3. Cloudy and comfortably cool this morning. The atmosphere feels like rain. The routine of the soldier's life in camp may have much of dullness, but there is also much of activity & clockwork. This morning reveille beat at daylight and every soldier rallies at the beat and falls in line for roll call, and immediately after roll call, falls into line by battalion. Then they stack arms and are dismissed for breakfast. At 5:00 o'clock the Surgeon's Call is sounded and the sick "in quarters" are marched to the place designated by the surgeon, generally in front of the hospital tent & receive treatment. The sick in hospital tent are now also examined and prescribed for, and those in quarters unable to come to the call are visited. The average number of men applying at Surgeon's Call is now about 60 to 80 each morning—this is exclusive of hospital patients, which now number 13.

At 5:00 o'clock 30 M.,—Breakfast is sounded. At 8:00 o'clock, the companies form for the Sunday inspection of arms and men. At 12:00 N. the Dinner call is sounded. 4:00 P.M. dress parade and inspection of arms again, so as to be prepared for service at a moment's warning. At 9:00 P.M., the tattoo sounds the hour for retiring. This constitutes the main features of our Sunday life in camp at present. Weekdays, Company, Battalion or Division or Brigade drills fill up the time, and at present very fully, for the men are drilled several hours each day. Those exercises and that quiet which is so refreshing & grateful to me at home on the Sabbath day, these peopled solitudes never have known since the advent of the Army of the Union. Had a refreshing shower about noon, but the heat seemed increased rather than abated by it. Two divisions of the army crossed to the other side of the river last night. I do not think anything intended, but to hold the opposite bank of the river against any force which may attempt to repeat the experience of shelling our shipping & camps such as brought us all to our feet at 1:00 o'clock A.M. the first of August. Without a note of warning, suddenly, 15 to 20 field guns operated on the (our) camps situated on and near the bank of the river and on the large fleet of our transports in the river. It was an incident of much interest, and speculation, while the cannonade was kept up. As soon, however, as our artillery on this bank, & guns of the gun boats got ranges of the rebel batteries, they were silenced. I have believed since I returned, that it was not only possible, but very probable, that the rebels would be able to very seriously annoy us, if not entirely cut off our supplies, by a blockade of the river, within a short time.

Monday August 4. At break of day, the deep boom of the morning gun from one of the fleet of gun boats in the river awakened me with a start. The shrill notes of the bugle, from the different brigade headquarters instantly echoed the call, which was immediately followed by the reveille of the regiments. Surgeon's call being at 5:00 A.M., there is little more than time after the morning gun to get ready for the sick.

Evening—the day has been very warm. The evening is very pleasant. I find no mind to mate with mine among the officers of the regiment. There are most excellent men among them, but none with whom my mind can hold that communion & fellowship for which I so much long. I walk in restless idleness the grounds in front of my quarters every evening—lonely & weary of the slowly passing hours. This isolation may serve me well, in bringing my thoughts nearer to Him who sees all with equal eye. Orders were received late this evening to be in readiness to march at a moment's notice. Five days rations are ordered to be drawn immediately.

Tuesday August 5. This has been the warmest day of the season. At this hour, 10:00 P.M., the heat is oppressive—it is hardly possible to eat, drink, or sleep, much less study or work, it is so warm.

Early this morning, a heavy cannonade commenced on our front— some four or five miles out—probably in the vicinity of Malvern Hill. Troops were moving all the forepart of last night in the direction of Malvern Hill, and a large number of field guns accompanied. It is now known that Hooker's and Kearney's Divisions went out with a part of Porter's. And it is pretty generally understood that the battle which was announced to excited ears by the continuous thunder of the cannon for several hours, has resulted in the rebels being driven at all points with the loss of two or three batteries and several hundred prisoners. The loss to our troops engaged, is understood to be considerable. While I write, the rumble of moving artillery comes to ear, and I learn that Couch's Division is moving toward the battlefield. I have removed our sick today, to general hospital, except the invalids and convalescent, preparatory to the order to march and our men have two days rations in their haversacks. Perhaps before I make another record here, I shall face again the perils of the battlefield and perhaps—but I will not anticipate. He who sees even the sparrow's fall will preserve me for the sake of my loved ones far away. I commit myself to His holy keeping, and every night beneath the starry sky, will continue to renew my vows & entreat His guardianship & direction.[19]

Friday August 8. In the cool & early hours of this morning, I once more find leisure to make a brief record. The past two days have not been particularly eventful—on Monday the 6th inst. about 3,000 of our soldiers returned from Richmond—exchanged prisoners. Several belonging to the 85th. One Harmon Sortore belonging to the 5th New York Cavalry brings news of the death in prison at Richmond of Jefferson Parker, Company E, 85th NYV. Poor fellow, he left a good home and many comforts for the service of his country. The troops sent out to Malvern Hill have mostly returned. The movement in that direction was evidently intended to be a diversion for the benefit of Pope in central Virginia. Late last evening, (10:00 P.M.) I received a letter from Miss F. L. Her letter breathes a spirit of love, & sadness withall. It has not the same warmth and devotion in its tone as her letters used to have—she seems not to have received my letter of the 18th last at the writing of this letter. I have felt much depressed in spirits for a few days past—it seems as if some impending ill is hanging over me. God is my refuge whatever may betide me. Oh, for a more complete communion with Him. Guide me, O, Thou Great Jehovah! In mercy guide me, in all my ways.[20]

Saturday August 9. It has been very warm again. This steady warm weather is very trying to our northern soldiers. I nearly sick all the afternoon with headache. I rode over to General Keyes's quarters pretty early in the morning to see Prof. Hamilton. Colonel Belknap accompanied me, & from there we rode over to the encampment of the contrabands, hoping to find two good housemaid girls to send to our Northern homes. Poor creatures; of the hundreds grouped around in idleness, not one could I find that seemed to possess the qualities and characteristics necessary for a good house-maid. I nursed my aching head until late in the evening, reading what I could & waiting for the mail, with the hope and expectation of a letter from Pike. I was disappointed—none came. I am very anxous to hear from my Dear Friend there; that her heart is faithful and true I cannot but believe; but that she has been inconsiderate, I fear. I would not wrong her for all the world. I do most earnestly pray for direction and wisdom in this matter.[21]

Sunday August 10. The morning is cool and pleasant, but there are indications of another warm day. My sleep was feverish & disturbed last night until 2:00 or 3:00 o'clock in the morning. My pillow was too hard for my aching head & I woke again and again from a troubled sleep, to gaze out into the moonlight straying in fitful gleams through the leafy canopy of the camp; for it is too warm during the night to close my tent front. My mind has been ill at ease for a few days, but I feel more assured this morning and confident that I, and all my friends far away, whom I value as my life, will be in mercy-guided & kindly-cared-for by my Heavenly Father. A thousand images filled my imagination during my feverish sleep last night; and all but one were forgotten as they passed—it was my sainted Emma; just as I have seen her a thousand times—the same sweet smile welcomed me, with which she always met me. Oh, with what joy my heart was filled, as with hurried step I went to clasp again my lost treasure in my arms. And then, how sank my heart within me, as the bloom faded from her cheek, quickly as the summer cloud sweeps over the landscape, and I realized that she was not of the living, but the Dead! Oh, my dear, dear Emma, it is not long before I shall indeed see you as you are—clothed in a blessed immortality, and that other Blessed Presence, too.

Evening. The heat has been intense—thermometer over 100 degrees in the shade. About 8:00 P.M., orders were received to march at 1:00 o'clock P.M. tomorrow. I waited until very late before I retired to my couch of poles, for the evening mail—it came & I was rewarded only with disappointment. It is probably the last opportunity for a long time that I shall have to hear from home friends. It is something strange that Miss L. does not write me. Can it be that she chooses to express her resentment in this matter, because I have expressed to her my grief that she has held too familiar terms with another, for an affianced wife? Oh, I will try and not believe it. A smart shower last evening cooled the atmosphere into an enjoyable condition.

Monday August 11. The day awoke in smiles. While the dawn was just creeping up the Eastern horizon, the band of the 85th, drawn up before the quarters of the Field & Staff played several beautiful airs. It was the farewell of our band. They were mustered out of service last evening, agreeably to the late law of Congress. Right glad were they to turn their faces homeward. I could have wept while I lay & listened to the music. My heart was full of pent-up emotions. The day has been very warm —no event of importance has transpired. The order to march today at 1:00 o'clock was countermanded, but the regiment ordered to be in full readiness to fall in at a moment's notice, quietly and without noise. The movement in progress is evidently one of magnitude & great importance. No less, I think, than the removal of the whole army from the Peninsula. Several thousand men have been thrown out three or four miles beyond our works in the direction of Malvern Hill, as if to threaten the approach to Richmond. The attack on the Rebel position at Malvern was part of the plan. A strong force of our troops was thrown across the James River some day since, and cavalry reconnaissance pushed well out toward Petersburg.

These movements are doubtless intended to answer the twofold purpose of preventing the approach of the enemy sufficiently near to make any observations, and to deceive the enemy as to our real intentions. Everything is, of course, conjecture; but the great amount of baggage, artillery & cavalry that has been shipped within the past few days can have no other explanation than our entire evacuation of this position and of the Peninsula. All extra baggage is ordered to the landing, including the knapsacks of the soldiers, to be shipped. A great many troops have been shipped down the river within the last few days. It is impossible, in my opinion, that the whole army can be shipped down the river; the last few thousand would inevitably be sacrificed. There is no other way, then, than for a sufficiently

large force to march down the Peninsula to Yorktown & with such rapidity
as to escape an overwhelming force of the enemy sent in pursuit or resist
attack, if necessary. In this view of the case, it becomes not only a matter of
speculation, but of interest, to know what portions of the army will be
selected for the fatiguing, hazardous march down the Peninsula. I have
thought we might go to Acquia Creek on the Potomac, and thence to
Fredericksburg. One thing has become very certain. The policy that
divided the Army of the Potomac and transferred more than 130,000 of
the men that composed it to the Virginia Peninsula, instead of moving the
whole force upon Richmond through central Virginia, was a bad one. It
remains to be seen if the error can be retrieved. Certain it is, the 50,000
noble, brave men sacrificed, cannot be recovered.[22]

Tuesday August 12. The order to march yesterday at one o'cl PM was
countermanded. We wait impatiently for the order to move. No news of
importance from our own lines. The news from General Pope in central
Virginia is stirring. His advance met the rebel forces under Stonewall Jackson the P.M. of the 9th instant. A severe engagement commenced about
5:00 P.M. & continued until after 7:00 P.M. The artillery continued much
longer. Both parties held their ground. The enemy withdrew the next
morning, and asked permission under a flag of truce to bury their dead.

The day has been the warmest of the season. The atmosphere is fur-
nace-like. About noon, the gun boats roused us a little by some practice
firing on a point on the opposite side of the river, supposed to cover the
progressing erection of a rebel battery. I sent about 30 sick and invalids to
the general hospital today; from which they were immediately shipped
down the river. The order to send all that could not march was imperative. This would indicate that we were to move by land. But there are
many officers who believe that the whole of <u>our</u> corps will be shipped—
probably to Acquia Creek. But their opinion has probably no better foundation than conjecture; though it may be true. If General McClellan has
no other quality of a good commander, he certainly has that of secretive-
ness. The feature of <u>my</u> day was the reception of a letter from Miss L. I sat
up late with small hope of hearing from her; but I was not disappointed.
Her explanation seems frank and <u>truthful</u>. I cannot but believe she is
truthful; and this belief disarms my resolution, and bids me trust and love
her with undiminished affection.

Wednesday August 13. As usual, was up with the earliest dawn. I
wrote to my much-loved friend before breakfast; after breakfast, I

mounted "Kit" and rode to the "landing" and deposited my letter in time for the mail boat to Fortress Monroe. I feel well repaid for the trouble with the consciousness that she (Miss L.) will receive it one day earlier, and her affectionate heart be unburthened so much sooner. The day has again been very warm—sent six more men to general hospital—so as to be unburthened if we have to make a rapid march.

It is impossible to understand which way, or how, with any degree of certainty, we are to leave here—but it is very certain we are going <u>some-where</u>. Yesterday it was ascertained that the baggage of the whole division was under water. It has all been stowed into an old, rotten canal boat & in towing it out into the stream, the old hulk sank. I rode to the scene of the disaster, about 5:00 P.M. It was really a disaster to me—all my clothing except what was on my back and many mementos of value to me were four feet under water. A large force of contrabands were at work. I had the satisfaction of rescuing a few of the choicest articles of my clothing and some mementos and returned to camp late in the evening (8:00 P.M.). Today, I have been busy a part of the A.M. priming up my sorry-looking "regulation suit," which was so unfairly and unceremoniously submitted to a baptism by immersion in the James River—I say unfairly because of the loss of everything the 31st of May (Battle of Fair Oaks) which I suffered, it seems to me, was my share of contribution, whether to the Rebels or to the elements.

Thursday August 14. I took an early gallop to the landing this morning and mailed an "Atlantic Monthly" to Miss L. Perhaps it will afford her an added pleasure to follow the footprints of my mind in those articles on which I have annotated. Certainly, she cannot read the articles in the "Atlantic" without improvement of her mind. Last night was the coolest night I have known for the last two months, and the day has been quite cool and comfortable, when compared with the past five days. Still, there are no further indications of our moving—war is a game; the soldier is but part of the machinery employed in it. It must not be expected that these automatic machines can question the objects and purposes of him who plays the game.

Captain [Peter] Regan of the 7th New York Light Artillery called on me this evening, and we had a pleasant chat. The captain was a fellow member of the NY Legislature of 1860. He was a member from Orange, and greatly interested in the defeat of the bill for the erection of Highland County from parts of Orange and Ulster, with the county seat of the

proposed new county at Newburgh. He was successful in defeating the
bill. My relations with him was very pleasant during the session, and the
renewal of the acquaintance at Washington last winter was as unexpected
as it was agreeable. The captain fought his battery bravely and well at "Fair
Oaks" the 31st of May. He is esteemed as an efficient & brave officer.

The question recurs to my mind again, has the experiences of the day
improved my moral & mental understanding, or have they retrograded? I
think not; I have been able to conquer and resist temptation. Oh, for
power to conquer all the sins that so easily beset me. I have courage and
hope that He will enable me to live for the future a life of devotion to my
Creator, who I have so much forgotten and of love and usefulness to my
fellow man. Word comes to me as I write, 9:00 PM, that the troops are
embarking at the Landing.[23]

NOTES: CHAPTER TWO

1. An excellent description of the hospital steamboat *Elm City,* Dr. Harris, and the work of the Sanitary Commission at White House, Virginia, can be found in *With Courage and Delicacy,* by Nancy Scripture
   Garrison (Savas Publishing, El Dorado Hills, CA, 1999). Smith men-
   tions dozens of ships in his diary; for convenience, information about
   each ship is compiled in Appendix C.
2. "Miss L." is Frances Lyon, his fiancée. She lived at Pike, about five miles
   from Granger. Dr. Smith's ruminations regarding her fidelity occupied
   his mind nearly every day.
3. The Van Nostrands were early settlers in Allegany County. Isaac,
   William, and Lewis all served as county supervisors. James, Jerome, and
   Timothy were officers in New York regiments. Aaron was one of
   Smith's patients in North Carolina.
4. His "Treasures" were Frank, age eleven, and Clarence, age three.
5. "Mrs. D" was Sarah Daggett, who took care of the two boys. Dr.
   Smith's father was sixty-seven; his mother was fifty-four. The issue of
   "wasted opportunity" is unclear.
6. Lieutenant Colonel Wellman was Abijah Wellman of the 85th New
   York, a native of Friendship. He was wounded at the Battle of Fair
   Oaks (Seven Pines). Dr. Roderick Stebbins noted on June 30, 1862,
   "A considerable portion of skull is still bare and there are some tenden-
   cies to miasmatic disease [malaria?]." After the Battle of Kinston, Dr.

Smith wrote that Wellman had not recovered sufficiently for active service, and he recommended further sick leave because of "brain congestion and vertigo."

7. "Casey" was Brig. Gen. Silas Casey (1807–82), an 1826 West Point graduate, who commanded a division of the Union IV Corps at Fair Oaks.

8. June 25 through July 1, 1862, were the "Seven Days before Richmond," when McClellan snatched defeat from the jaws of victory, outgeneraled by Robert E. Lee in the suburbs of the Confederate capital.

9. This would be the burial site of his first two wives, Adaline Weeks and Emma Spinks.

10. "Capt. Brown" was John A. Brown of Company H, 85th New York, a forty-two-year-old native of Wellsville; he was indeed the subject of unusually harsh punishment. He had been too sick to carry his baggage and had bought a mule for this purpose. The full trial is in Record Group 153, folder II960, at the National Archives. After reinstatement, Brown was captured at Plymouth, North Carolina, and imprisoned at Camp Asylum, Columbia, South Carolina. Smith's speculation about the hand of McClellan in the trial, and its possible role in a future Presidential election campaign, is fascinating, though without proof.

11. Robert B. Van Valkenburgh (1821–88) was a three-term New York assemblyman and served in the U.S. Congress as a Republican from 1861 to 1865; he was chairman of the Committee on Militia. He organized seventeen regiments for the Civil War and served as colonel of the 107th New York, which he commanded at the Battle of Antietam. Theodore M. Pomeroy (1824–1905) served four terms in the U.S. House of Representatives. Before the war, he had been district attorney for Cayuga County, New York, and was elected to the state assembly. In 1860, he was a delegate to the convention that nominated Lincoln. After the war, he was general counsel for the American Express Company.

12. Preston King (1806–65) served in the House of Representatives as a Free-Soiler, from 1849 to 1853, and was elected from New York to the U.S. Senate as a Republican in 1856. At the time of his suicide (he leaped into New York Harbor), he was Collector of the Port of New York. (It is interesting to note Dr. Smith's easy access to influential political figures.)

13. This would be John G. Nicolay, Lincoln's private secretary and a future U.S. Consul in Paris. John F. Lee, an 1834 graduate of West Point,

served in the Seminole Wars and was Judge Advocate of the Army from March 1849 to September 1862. He was later a member of the convention to amend the constitution of the State of Maryland. Augustus Frank had been a delegate at the Republican convention that nominated Frémont and represented his district in the Congress from 1859 to 1865. Frank was a director of two railroads and later president of the Bank of Warsaw in Wyoming County, New York.

14. Capt. James M. McNair served two years with the 33rd New York. Maj. R. is probably Richardson, regiment not known.

15. The nature of her offense is unknown.

16. Henry W. Wessells (1809–89), who graduated from West Point in 1833, had served in Florida, Mexico, and on the frontier. At Fair Oaks, he commanded a division of Keyes's Corps and was slightly wounded. He was captured at Plymouth, North Carolina, the following year.

17. Smith probably refers to the CSS *Richmond,* a 180-foot armored steamboat, mounting four seven-inch Brooke rifles. See *Capital Navy,* by John Coski (Savas Publishing, El Dorado Hills, CA, 1996). Maj. Gen. John Pope was the newly appointed commander of the Union Army of Virginia; his disastrous defeat just weeks after Smith's diary entry ended Pope's active service in the war.

18. Oliver A. Judson was a prominent physician in Philadelphia before the war. He served with Brig. Gen. William H. Emory's brigade on the Peninsula. Diarrhea ended Judson's active field service, and he was assigned the next two years to Carver Hospital in Washington, D.C. Emory, an 1831 West Point graduate, had a long career mapping the far West and was the only officer in that area to bring all his troops east, when so many were defecting to the Confederacy in 1861.

19. Dyer's *Compendium* describes this action as a skirmish. Kearney is, of course, Philip Kearney, a tough old soldier, who wrote of his commander, "McClellan is no General, for all his talents. He has not the remotest aptitude for war." See Indianapolis *Daily Journal,* October 12, 1864. Kearney was killed at Chantilly, Virginia, a month after Smith's note.

20. Depressive and obsessive thinking seem to come easily to our diarist.

21. Erasmus Keyes graduated from West Point in 1832 and was a favorite of Winfield Scott. Keyes commanded the IV Corps on the Peninsula. Prof. Hamilton is not identified. Jonathan Belknap commanded the 85th New York until his resignation in June 1863. His troops regarded

him as a "dandy" and a "coward." See *The Plymouth Pilgrims,* by Wayne Mahood (Longstreet House, Hightstown, NJ, 1991). "Contrabands" were newly freed slaves.

22. Here, Smith's disillusionment with McClellan is growing.
23. Peter C. Regan, age thirty-seven, enrolled in the volunteers at Buttermilk Falls, near West Point. (The falls were the scene of some rowdy cadet picnics, which led to court-martials.) In December 1862, Regan requested a leave of absence, as he had not been paid in eight months and the family business was in trouble. He was shot in the left tibia at Petersburg in June 1864 and discharged six months later for disability.

CHAPTER THREE

An Ignoble Retreat

Friday, August 15. Morning cool and cloudy—about noon sprinkled, but rain was less threatening, at this moment, 1:00 P.M. The great movement is about to take place—orders came an hour since to have the teams of the baggage wagons harnessed, baggage packed ready to start at a moment's notice. I still think we move down the Peninsula via Williamsburg and Yorktown. And this is the end of the great strategic plans of the young Napoleon (?), George B. McClellan. And it about finishes him in the estimation of the public North. So ends the campaign of the Virginian Peninsula, undertaken at a cost, for transportation of troops and material alone, of 23 millions of dollars; and it is well understood, against the opinion of the President and Secretary of War.

It is evident that this movement has been well concealed from the enemy, and the best of plans adopted for its success. Notwithstanding, it is a movement full of peril & may easily prove disastrous to the whole or part of the army. But if successful, will be recorded by the impartial historian as one of the most masterly movements of the campaign, retreat though it be. If, as I think, the design be to unite with, or cooperate with General Pope, and the plan is successful, it will throw an irresistible force upon Richmond through central Virginia. But I must pause here, for the pins of my tent are loosened, the fly removed and packed, my haversack and canteen filled with the rations that must last me the next three days and—in fact, everything ready for the call of the drum, and the word, "Fall into line."

Saturday August 16. We were roused this morning at 3:00 o'clock—by the beat of the drum, & the call quickly followed to "Fall into line." We moved from camp yesterday about 5:00 PM, lay an hour a short distance from camp and then were ordered back to camp. Our camp was

lighted only by the stars and with no canopy but the sky. I lay myself
down on the pole couch, where, notwithstanding its harness and rough-
ness, I have slept as sweetly as ever on my own soft bed at home. But, not
so sweetly last night—it was quite chill and cold; so much so that with my
single blanket, I was quite uncomfortable; others may sleep when their
blood chills, and the biting frosts repel the life current from the surface,
but it never was my good or ill fortune to be able to do so. Consequently,
I had plenty of leisure during the long hours to count the stars, and to
watch the waning moon as she crept up the eastern sky. Our march during the morning was very pleasant; the air was cool and the soldiers
tramped along with an ease and celerity I have never seen them surpass.
Indeed, the whole day's march was made in the best order and with more
ease than I have seen them accomplish the same distance in. At night, we
had made about ten miles, and camped in an open field some three miles
from "Jones Ford" or bridge across the Chickahominy. The enemy was
driven off the ground this morning by our cavalry, and pushed them
across the Chickahominy. A supper made up of a slice of pork broiled on
the end of a stick, a slice of bread from our own bakery, an ear of roast
corn, and a dish of tea, fragrant as a connoisseur could desire, made the
inner man very comfortable. The morrow's march, biding fair to be commenced early, I made proposals to Varius soon after supper for lodging. A
bundle of oats, over which was laid my rubber blanket, and a woolen
blanket to cover, constituted the best accommodation to which he could
invite me—good enough, too, for a soldier. Here I am, then, sitting up in
my humble bed, Lewis already fallen asleep, my candle swales in the night
air and is rapidly wasting through my bottomless candlestick, a bayonet
inverted and stuck in the ground. I have never seen a more characteristic
and grand exhibition of one of the most prominent features of camp life
in the field—the night bivouac!

Behind us, the whole southern horizon was illuminated by the campfires of Couch's Division and as far as the eye could see, on and around
the plains on which we lay, were the numberless fires of our own division
(Peck's); the spectre-like appearance of the soldiers grouped around the
more distant of the fires, the illuminated countenances of the bronzed veterans moving about those nearer me, the hum of thousands of voices,
mingling with the short, sharp words of command, and the incessant
brawl and wail of mules and neighing of artillery and cavalry horses, made
a scene never to be forgotten; yet this evening's experience was but one of

many experienced in the course of the campaign. But never has the deep
blue vault of Heaven seemed quite so impressively beautiful as tonight;
and never have I revered more sensibly my utter insignificance and the
greatness and majesty of Him who ruleth among the armies of heaven.

Sunday August 17. No drum sounded the call, or bugle blast roused
the sleeping host this morning. Quietly, the slumbering soldiers were
roused at 3:00 o'clock A.M. and ordered to be in readiness to move at
daybreak. A dish of coffee, a piece of broiled pork, and a slice of bread
made my hasty breakfast; yet shivering with the chill morning air, I
mounted as Aurora swiftly swept up the eastern sky, and before the eye
could see the whole of the long line, we were again enroute for—who
can tell where? Certainly, we were going down the Peninsula; and if not
greatly mistaken, bound for central Virginia via Yorktown and Fortress
Monroe. All the early morning, the men marched on cheerfully and with
no sign of flagging.

About 9:00 o'clock A.M., General McClellan and staff, attended by a
numerous bodyguard, passed us. The hundreds of baggage wagons composing his "headquarters" train passed shortly before; for these, the troops
gave the road, in consequence, two long and precious hours of the day
were lost. Notwithstanding, the troops would have traveled the distance
which had been determined without unusual fatigue, but for the unrea-
sonable course pursued, in moving them until 3:00 o'clock P.M. without
sufficient halt to allow the troops time to make a dish of coffee. And the
pace at which they marched from 10:00 A.M. until 3:00 P.M. was most
killing. Scarcely half the regiment or of any regiment in the division, was
present when we arrived on the ground designated for camping. It was
the most killing march I have seen, and yet we had not marched more
than 20 miles. But the great amount of dust which filled the eyes and
lungs and the scarcity of water on the route contributed to make the
march more disagreeable and exhausting. About 1:00 o'clock P.M., we
arrived on the bank of the Chickahominy near its confluence with the
James River. A pontoon bridge had been thrown across and several gun
boats were present to overrule any objection any Rebel force might inter-
pose to our crossing. The vast train of baggage wagons attached to the
Army of the Potomac had already crossed and were parked in order on
the opposite bank. Whatever may be said of the success of the general in
this campaign, General McClellan will have the credit of conducting this
retreat in a masterly and soldierly manner.

Our camp for the night was on the estate of a wealthy Virginian about three miles from our crossing at the Chickahominy. A supper of usual simplicity—roast corn, a slice of pork and bread, and a cup of tea, made the inner man comfortable and a couch of straw on the velvet sward, with the luxurious addition of my rubber cloth spread on some rails, supported at one end by a pole resting on a couple of muskets inverted, and the bayonets of which served as stakes (it is surprising how easily our wants are supplied), prepared for a sleep as sound and sweet as a soldier ever need desire.

In crossing from the west to the east side of the Chickahominy, we left the fairest and best part of the Peninsula. In fact, that portion lying east of Richmond and west of the Chickahominy, and in between White Oak Swamp on the north and James River on the south is the garden of eastern Virginia. Other portions of the Peninsula are comparatively barren; the soil is sandy, and its little natural capacity in great degree exhausted. I was again surprised in passing "Charles City Court House" to find the place so utterly insignificant—a court house and jail of seven by nine dimensions, three or four old, dilapidated houses and a miserable apology for a horse shed constituted the town. The absence of churches and schoolhouses is another striking fact evident to the soldiers of the north.[1]

Monday August 18. We broke camp this morning at 4 o'cl. The 85th New York is the rear guard of the division today. The march to Williamsburg was very pleasant and comfortable. The coolness of the night was prolonged far into the morning, and the greater part of the route lay along a wooded road, which greatly added to the comfort of the march. We passed through Williamsburg about 10 o'clock AM and took the direct route to Yorktown. At 4 o'cl PM, we camped about six miles from Yorktown. The most important item in the soldier's life when on a march is his breakfast, dinner or supper. When the order "Break ranks" is given, there is a general rush for the conveniences that surround him. Having bought a pair of chickens of a contraband some miles back, there was a pretty good show for a good supper, if the "fixins" could be supplied. These were not long wanting. Barber brought some new potatoes from an adjoining field—Hall, some apples from a neighboring orchard, and in a short time, we sat down to a supper which an epicure might envy—to be sure, the table service was not very abundant, but good appetites supplied the means of gratifying them. Pocket knives & crotched sticks whittled to points made good enough substitutes for knives and forks—a stick to stir

Above: Virginia's Charles City County courthouse. Dr. Smith compared it very unfavorably with his hometown Allegany County courthouse (below). The artist's drawing of the latter is, of course, somewhat idealized. ABOVE: LIBRARY OF CONGRESS #916805, B8171-409. BELOW: HISTORY OF ALLEGANY COUNTY

the coffee, and one iron tablespoon supplied all the dishes and all plates. I have rarely enjoyed, even when surrounded by the luxuries of home, a better meal; and so they all said, and the adjutant, who was an invited guest, in honor of the unusual supply to our table, returned thanks for the same—not to God, for that would have been so unusual as to seem almost unsoldierlike. Ah, how little the men who surround me, reverence, or seem to acknowledge that the Hand that preserves them, and dispenses all their mercies, is Divine. My couch tonight is spread on the leaves beneath a thick copse of bush—weary and sore with travel, by allowing exhausted soldiers by turns to ride my horse, I covet the hard bed beside me, for there is rest and comfort in the temporary forgetfulness of sleep.

Tuesday August 19. Rose this morning at 2:00 A.M. The camps were astir at this time. The men busy in preparing their breakfast in expectation of an early march. Chicken broiled on a stake, potatoes, green applesauce, bread and coffee made us a sumptuous breakfast. At an early hour, Couch's Division took up the line of march, followed by Franklin's Corps. This made it evident that we of Peck's Division would not move for some hours. All day the road has been filled by passing troops, artillery, cavalry and baggage wagons. Franklin's Corps, then Kearney and Hooker's Division.[2]

Dinner found us still luxuriating on broiled chicken, boiled corn, green pear sauce, et cetera. But dinner consumed all our stores—only six hard crackers, one ration of coffee, ditto sugar, I find by a careful inventory of my haversack. Something must be done—can't draw anything from the commissary until we get through to—well, Yorktown, Fortress Monroe or some other place where providence & General G. B. McClellan sees fit to send us—guess we must forage a while; so, Patterson, Hall & Barber start out—and they are not the boys to come back empty-handed.

Wednesday August 20. We broke camp this morning at daylight, and took up our line of march for Yorktown. Where we arrived about 11:00 A.M. After a few moments rest, the troops resumed their march, reaching camp two miles below Yorktown, a little after noon.

Thursday August 21. Our camp was arranged today as if for a considerable stay; but do not believe we shall remain here long. Heintzelman's Corps embarked from Yorktown and today Porter's has gone to the Fortress. Franklin has gone to Newport News, and Sumner is hastening on toward the Fortress to embark. The day has been very fine, not uncomfortably warm, and the soldiers have enjoyed it greatly, fishing, clam hunting & bathing in the York River.[3]

Friday August 22. The day has been warm but cloudy. At evening the clouds broke away, and lay in gorgeous, massive piles in the southern horizon—it was a scene of beauty I have scarcely beheld. This morning, I received a number of letters from absent friends. It has been a week or more since I heard from them, and their letters refreshed me very much. But there was <u>one</u> letter missing; there will remain a void until <u>her</u> loving words come to fill it.

Saturday August 23. Nothing of importance has happened today. But the movement of positions of the corps indicate the intention to keep this corps on or near the Peninsula. The First Brigade has been ordered to garrison Yorktown and Gloucester. Howe's Brigade of Couch's Division is ordered to Williamsburg. Ferry's Brigade (Second of Peck's Division) to Suffolk, and just at sunset, the order for our own brigade (Wessell's) was received to march tomorrow morning at Daylight for Hampton.[4]

Sunday August 24. The Sabbath has passed without my once remembering that it is our day of rest. I do not recall that this ever happened before. But there is, practically, no Sabbath here. By order, the reveille sounded at 2:00 o'clock A.M. The troops were breakfasted & were in line at the earliest daylight. Last night, the rain fell in torrents for an hour or two, and this morning everything looks drenched and sorry. The sky is leaden, the roads saturated, but at the appointed moment, the long line moved out on the road to Big Bethel. This place, they reached about 11:00 o'clock A.M. and halted three-quarters of an hour for dinner. But scarcely requires that length of time to eat a soldier's dinner if, as is generally the case, it is as plain as my own—a slice of raw pork, one hard cracker and a bit of onion & salt. We marched 14 miles before making this halt, almost the entire distance of which I walked to let feeble soldiers of the regiment ride. Big Bethel has a history, like 1,000 other blood-stained spots in our bleeding country. It was here that the unfortunate mistake of firing into each other occurred by the troops under General Pierce and General Schenck. Approaching by different [routes], which converged at this point, Gen. Schenck mistook the troops under Gen. Pierce for the enemy and delivered a terrible volley into his ranks. This was before the light of morning. But the bloodiest part of that day's drama had yet to be enacted. The history of that brief, but bloody, struggle, has been written. In it fell that brave and accomplished young officer of artillery, Lieutenant Greble and here, too, the manly form of the talented Major Winthrop, so full of hope and promise, was stricken down.[5]

Soon after we resumed our march, a drizzling rain commenced falling and it continued until we reached Hampton. This has been one of the best days marches I have known the troops to make. They left camp near Yorktown at 6:00 o'clock in the morning and stacked arms one mile beyond Hampton (two miles from Fortress Monroe) at 3:00 o'clock P.M. The wind was blowing chill and the men were thoroughly wet & tired out. They had marched 25 miles in nine hours inclusive of the time spent in halting for dinner and rests. Our camp is situated on the plain between Hampton and Fortress Monroe, immediately in the rear of the Chesapeake Hospital (formerly a ladies seminary), but is separated by a bayou which can be crossed dry-shod at low tide.

Thus ends the march of this grand Army of the Potomac <u>down</u> the Peninsula. It has retraced its bloody pathway up the Peninsula in five days march without any extra effort—it was eight long weeks in marching from the Fortress to Fair Oaks; and such weeks as never since the retreat of the French from Moscow has been experienced. The campaign of the Virginia Peninsula will be one of the most memorable in the history of modern wars. My record and jottings of it up to the 31st of May were carefully made, but unfortunately lost in the battle of that day. I will then briefly recapitulate the principle circumstances and dates of our march up to that period, while my memory is not forgetful, and the events seem but as the dream of last night; and <u>such</u> a dream I would not like to dream again— much less would I like to pass through the terrible reality again. My heart is filled with sorrow at the recollection of the great and profitless suffering of the noble army which landed here last spring, the greatest and best-appointed army that ever assembled or was beheld on the continent. Proud, confident, even defiantly, it commenced its march up the Peninsula. Since then, it has fought many bloody battles, tens of thousands have been slain, and thrice the number that have fallen on the battlefield have wasted and died of disease. Who can write a faithful and true history of this campaign—who can depict the untold human suffering and the swamps and pestilential atmosphere which sweeps this Peninsula from shore to shore, or who will know, or if they know, will presume to record the criminal neglect which did not provide sufficient transportation for the troops, but loaded them with packs of 40 to 60 pounds and, when sick and enfeebled, provided no ambulances for weeks after landing at the Fortress to transport the sick; and worse than all, but two hospitals on the Peninsula, and they already crowded with sick from the soldiers of the post garrison.

Again, the "circumlocution office" through which all our requisitions
were compelled to go, rendered it impossible to procure medicines for
weeks after such requisitions were made. In Casey's Division, not one
ounce of that indispensable medicine, quinine, could be procured through
or from the Medical Purveyor, by any of the surgeons of the 14 regiments
composing that division; (and the same was true of other medicines)
without sending the requisition to be approved by the Surgeon of
Brigade, the Surgeon of Division, the Surgeon of Corps, & His Mogul-
ship, Surgeon Tripler, "Medical Director of the Army of the Potomac,"
and from thence must be sent to the Medical Purveyor and take its turn
for being filled. And all of this must be done through official channels. It
was in vain that surgeons asked to be permitted to carry their requisitions
in person to the Medical Purveyor and plead their wants and necessities.
The slain in battle is not the gloomiest and darkest page of the history of
the Peninsula campaign—the darkest is that which will record the needless
suffering of the victims of the pestilential swamps, in which, for long
weeks, General McClellan encamped them, digging and entrenching
behind the flying rebels.

The mind is overwhelmed with the contrast of what that army was,
with its promises, its hopes, and the expectations reposed in it, and what it
is now, what it has done, what it failed to do, what it is now doing—
returning with less than half its numbers, along the route by which it
advanced, every mile of which is marked by many graves of fallen heroes.
But this part of the campaign is over—the Army of the Potomac goes
hence to meet our Rebel foes on other fields.

[Dr. Smith was not the only person to notice the shortcomings of
Surgeon Charles S. Tripler, Medical Director of the Army of the
Potomac. While Tripler was an improvement over the even more senile
and obsolete surgeons of the old army, such as W. S. King and Clement
Finley, he was still not equal to the task. Tripler had some good ideas, but
he tended to attack his friends as though they were his enemies and
denounced, among other organizations, the Sanitary Commission. On the
Fourth of July, 1862, Dr. Tripler was replaced by Dr. Jonathan Letterman,
whose ideas on organizing the Army Medical Service would eventually be
extended to all the Union forces.]

Thursday August 28. The three days past has been productive of very
little of importance in the history of the 85th, or of my own experience.
The usual dull routine of camp life, with now and then a ride over to the

Fortress, or a stroll to the riverside, & a luxurious bath in the salt water, has in some measure relieved the monotony of my present situation. The interruption of all communication with my friends, at least so far as receiving any from them, makes the time hang very heavy on my hands. For two weeks past, not a word or a line from the friends at home or abroad. I think our mail must be delayed at Washington with the expectation that the regiments of this corps are to be sent to central Virginia, as the main body of the army has been. Since our arrival here, our future destination has been uncertain, the Fortress [Monroe], Norfolk, or Newport News, seemed most probable, however. But last evening the anxiety of all was put at rest by an order to march this A.M. at 8:00 o'clock for Newport News. So we are probably to spend a few weeks in the discharge of the humdrum duties of the garrison. My impatient spirit chafes at the prospect of so much inactivity.

My very soul is oppressed and weighed down this morning, and I cannot tell why. The future, I cannot make seem glad & gay—the shadows of coming events seem to darken it. Surely, I have suffered enough in time past to ask that a cruel fate shall "replace me in a mansion of peace, where no peril can chase me." Yet not because I am worthy or because my struggles and afflictions have made me so. O, no! I have nothing due by merit; it is only through and by the Infinite mercy of a kind Providence that I may hope or ask a kindly shelter from the frowns of misfortune and the shafts of sorrow. The hour appointed for our march is at hand and I must close my simple record. <u>Evening</u>. The regiment arrived at its destination, Newport News, this P.M., an hour before I reached it myself. I remained behind to care for the sick and see them taken to hospital or safely in ambulances, and then galloped over to the post office at the Fortress. After some trouble and delay, I secured the back mail of the regiment—which had just arrived from Washington. The treat I enjoyed in hearing from friends once more amply repaid me for time & trouble— all the regiment seemed to enjoy a feast of soul of the same kind. But I <u>thought</u> I was disappointed in not receiving a letter from my very dear friend, Miss L. But an hour afterward, a friend put the hoped-for <u>precious missive</u> in my hand. It had been at first overlooked. Now the aching void was filled. This is my weakness, I sometimes think—there is no other passage in my present history in which the iron will with which nature has endowed me yields; but the devoted affection of her heart, which breathes in all her words, molds me to her will—God grant that she may never presume on the power she possesses, or disappoint my heart by proving to be less good and loving than she now seems to be. The day has been pleasantly cool and cloudy.

Saturday August 30. Thus far, I am better pleased with our new location than I expected to be. The situation is pleasant and healthy for this Peninsula. Newport's News was so named by the colonists settled at Jamestown, who, being discouraged by privations, their number lessened by disease, and subjected to many unexpected hardships, started on their return to England and were met at this part of the James River by Lord Newport, with a number of colonists and the glad news that other ships were on their way as addition to the settlement & with an abundance of supplies. Hence, the settlers signalized the event by naming the point where they met these good tidings "Newport's News." It is entirely a military post, there being but two or three buildings here until the present war broke out.

Situated on a bluff some 25 feet above the river, a fine breeze sweeps in from the water during the latter part of the day, dispersing in a measure the malarious accumulation, and invigorating the hundreds of invalid soldiers on its banks, for there are now nearly 1500 sick and convalescent in the hospitals. The day has been delightfully cool, yet the sun has been cloudless. [Fifty years later, doctors would understand that the cooling ocean breezes had the additional effect of blowing away the mosquitoes that carried the malaria.]

Sunday August 31. 'Tis the last day of summer! The morning sun rose clear but soon passed under light, filmy clouds which modified this day to a delightful temperature. In contemplating the short-lived summer past, but in which I have endured a thousand hardships and dangers to which I was a stranger, my mind is drawn to the recollection of years gone by; years that have passed so swiftly that the events that mark them in my memory seem as the dream of last night. O, for the past! O, for the hours that will not come again—golden moments of my life, when I was happy in the possession of an unbroken home circle—when my heart was glad in the enjoyment of the virgin love of one whose heart knew no guile, and when my future was full of hopes of enjoyment in the society of my Household Treasures! Evening—the day has been more quiet, Sabbath-like than any I have enjoyed for a long time. The mustering of the regiment for pay was the only businesslike feature of the day. Cool and pleasant throughout the day, the evening closed in less cloudy than in the morning, and the stars came out & hung their bright beacons in the sky.

Monday September 1. The Fall has come, was ushered in this morning with characteristic clouds; but they gave way in part and the day was pleasantly warm until about 4:00 P.M., when there came a violent thundershower, which nearly succeeded in drowning us & the violent wind attending, in throwing down all our tents.

The marked feature of interest of today was my visit to the very celebrated "Monitor," or the "Cheese Box on a Raft," as the rebels not ineptly called it. The courtesy of an invitation was extended by Major Runnyon, was accompanied by Maj. King, Lt. Aldrich, Asst. Surg. Lewis and other officers of the post and several ladies. We were very kindly received on board, and shown through the vessel. In the afternoon, attended the burial of a 1st Lt. of Burnside's command—40 men of our regiment acted as escort & six of our first lieutenants as pall bearers. It was a solemn spectacle—muffled drums & fife, followed by escort; then the ambulances bearing the coffin, followed by the bearers and the promiscuous crowd among which I found Maj. King and other officers of my own regiment. Three volleys—the soldier's tribute, & we left him alone in his glory.[6]

I formed the acquaintance here of Capt. Stevens of the Monitor, Capt. Macomb of the gun boat Genesee and Surgeon Cole of the same vessel. They were all very intelligent gentlemen; Capt. Stevens seemed a stern, resolute iron man, yet courteous and gentlemanly. He will make his mark when the opportunity offers, I predict.

Returned late to supper—found a dearer, more precious offering than my supper—a letter from my dear friend Miss L. It made me a little homesick. I shall be so thankful to Him who heeds the sparrow's fall, for the privilege of meeting friends at home, once more. Fly away, ye tardy hours, with winged swiftness, until I find the golden moments again!

Thursday September 4. Last night was quite cool. This morning very cool, but the sun came up bright and soon infused His genial warmth. Assistant [Dr. Lewis] went to the Fortress yesterday. The work is consequently all on my hands. The health of the regiment is greatly improved. I am impatient that I must remain here inactive. The bloody battles that are daily being fought before Washington makes me feel as if I must and ought to be there—surely I could be of more service there than here; but there must be some here, it is an important post. There are now more than 1500 sick and wounded in the hospital here.

Friday September 5. Cool nights and warm days is the rule of the weather now. The sun is scarce an hour high yet, but it already strikes through my tent with a furnace glow.

My mind is incessantly harassed with anxiety concerning events now transpiring in Va.—in front of Washington. O, my country! Of late, so prosperous and happy, now compelled by traitors & rebels to struggle for existence. But I have this philosophy to support me—the world has never retrograded—all wars and convulsions have contributed to advance the nations in the growth of material prosperity and Christian civilization. In the divine purpose, all is for the best. I may not live to see the good which will grow out of this terribly bloody struggle, but it is nonetheless certain. Order will come out of this chaos and the superstructure which will be erected on it shall be more glorious & beautiful than that which may be destroyed.

Saturday, September 6. I went to the Old Point this morning by the 8 AM boat—settled my hospital account with Commissary Hall, and returned to the wharf at half past 10:00 AM, but the boat had gone— there was no alternative but to wait until 5:00 PM for the return of the boat. In the meantime, through the kindness of Captain Franklin Bates of the 99th New York, Officer of the Day, I obtained a pass to visit the water battery of the Fortress, and the ramparts. Several officers of the 85th accompanied [me]. The Union & Lincoln guns mounted on the beach in front of the Fortress was quite as much objects of interest as anything we found—the last named was cast at Pittsburgh in 1860 and weighs 49,099 pounds. The former weighs 52,005 pounds and carried a ball weighing 600 pounds. A bountiful dinner at the Hygiea Hotel cheered the inner man, after our somewhat tiresome journey around the seventeen acres which walls the Fortress enclosure. At 5 o'clock, we were off—Disappointed again this evening at finding no letter from Miss L.

Sunday September 7. A lovely day today—I have spent it in the quiet of my tent. Received a visit from several of the officers of the Monitor including the Surgeon, Dr. _____ Has a very interesting visit—they were all on board at the fight with the Merrimac. I was surprised at the statement of the surgeon, and which was confirmed by the other officers, the "Monitor" was being withdrawn from action when it was discovered that the Merrimac was, herself, drawing off; the shot which struck the pilot house so severely, wounding Captain Worden, it was supposed had disabled the Monitor far more severely than subsequent inspection proved.[7]

I am disappointed again this evening in receiving no letter from Miss L. What can the matter be? I feel a part of the time very much like revenging my disappointment by a long silence. It is productive of more pain than pleasure to have a loved object, I often think—the pain and anxiety when separated from those we love—the sorrow when they disappoint or deceive, and the keen anguish when lost, goes far to neutralize, if it does not surpass, the enjoyment of their brief presence. I was quite out of sorts tonight—thoroughly homesick. It does not seem as if I could remain all the long months of this fall & the ensuing winter away from my home, my motherless boys, and the dear friend I have learned to love too well. I must set my heart to reflect the influence of this affection for her. It is becoming a weakness in me; if there is a day's delay in her letters, I am worried—if there is two or three, I am quite unhappy, and there seems often to be a tardiness in her correspondence, which her abundant leisure, as compared with mine, gives no warrant for.[8]

Monday September 8. The regiment was paid this forenoon for the months of May & June, by Major Henry. I went to the Fortress this PM—was belated—just one minute too late; the boat was ten rods [165 feet] from the wharf. How many important events in life are decided by the loss of just one minute? There was no alternative but to remain until the 10 o'clock boat tomorrow. The time hung heavy on my hands & I purchased "Guy Manncring" (Scott) to pass away the time. Even this would not suffice, and I sought my room at the Hygiea & retired early, to anything but sweet sleep and pleasant dreams, for the bustle and confusion through the halls, the frequent sharp stroke of the office bell, kept me awake far into the night.

Tuesday September 9. Returned from Old Point—this evening received several letters—from home & one—my friend Miss L. Not very satisfactory from her. I cannot help feeling disappointed when there is not the same rich treasure of love displayed in her communications. The news from my dear boys is cheering—O, that I could be with them—my dear babe kisses its kind protector and tells her to send it to his Pa. Dear little life! How unconscious of the deep hold, the great strength of that love which unites my heart to thine.

Wednesday September 10. Removed today—inside the fortifications; pitched my quarters in tent until arrangements for room can be effected— the surgeon of the U.S. Hospital (Dr. Hand) is sort of dog-in-the-manger—can't like him and won't try. Dr. Shipman of Syracuse is very much of a gentleman—courteous and friendly, and as a man of science far the superior of Dr. H. Dr. H. refuses to give me possession of the regimental hospital of the post—we will see![9]

Thursday September 11. Again received news from Pike. Some things she says & some things she don't say; and the majority of the good things she might say, being left unsaid, the balance is on the wrong side to be satisfactory. Still, the evidence is clear, that the love of a good and pure heart burns brightly on the altar of her heart—and this shall content me for all shortcomings else.

Friday September 12. Took possession of the Regimental Hospital today & very comfortable quarters adjoining for myself, the Asst. Surgeon, the [Hospital] Steward & other hospital attendants—don't feel greatly indebted to Surgeon Hand.

Sunday September 14. The Assistant Surgeon started for home

Lt. Daniel Langworthy brought Dr. Smith the news of Pvt. Jesse Carman Underhill's harsh sentence.

DIVISION OF MILITARY AND NAVAL AFFAIRS, NYS ADJUTANT GENERAL'S OFFICE, ALBANY, NEW YORK

today at one o'clock PM, to visit a beloved sister hopelessly ill with consumption [tuberculosis of the lungs]—a sad visit, you, it will be, my good friend; but the world so goes. Time is the ruthless leveler and spares none—sooner or later, these griefs must come to us all, or we must be the victims for which others mourn. This PM, galloped up to Capt. Smith— some six miles up the James River—had a very pleasant visit with the Capt. & lady & engaged to come back again tomorrow to see the Capt., who is in quite ill health—met several officers here, Lieutenant Langworthy and Mr. Goodrich accompanied me. The day has been very beautiful, as has every day since the severe rain of Thursday—the nights are comfortably cool.[10]

Monday September 15. Visited Capt. Smith this PM and found him much better—had an excellent visit with him & his intelligent lady—she is considerably his junior, and seems to retain all the vivacity, and much of the beauty of former years. Captain S. is an "old salt"; he has followed the sea many years, amassed a considerable property, and four years since purchased this estate, one of the most beautiful locations on the James River, and retired from active duty of his previous life. He is now devoting his time to farming—owns twenty "head" of "niggers," who seem to be better cared for than is usual. Mrs. Smith is somewhat of a genius—she not only feeds all the poor who apply for relief, and they are many, now that the country is so despoiled by army, and bestows many delicacies on her less-favored friends, but doctors half the county. The Capt. thinks the medicine they have given away has cost not less than One hundred Dollars in the last three months. After a refreshingly sumptuous tea with warm invitations to frequently repeat my visit, I bade good-bye to the most inviting and pleasant acquaintances I have formed in Virginia.

Tuesday September 16. Nothing of importance today—save the rumor of a telegram to Fortress Monroe of a great success over the rebels in Maryland—but it is only a rumor. The day has been beautiful and nothing to disturb the monotony of my daily routine. [The telegram must have referred to the battle of Antietam.]

Wednesday September 17. Rose early, & with symptoms of my headache of old. Morning call over, I locked myself in my room, with good resolution to nurse my aching head until it was more quiet. But my dear Frank's letter has been unanswered these two days & I could not but improve the opportunity to write him; and then the letter of my friend Lt. Moses, has been some days on my table. And when I completed them, my poor head was taking on severely—I tried this humble couch for a long time, in vain; but at length, after two or three hours of patient coaxing, I had nearly conquered when a musical voice at the steward's door inquired after Dr. Smith. I knew the game was up, & my poor willful head would have its way, I knew. My visitor was Mrs. Capt. Smith. Mrs. Smith chatted in her own vivacious manner for a half hour, assisted in a feeble manner by Miss Wilbur, and left me in a supremely afflicted condition. The glorious rumors of last night are confirmed.[11]

Thursday September 18. The sun has gone down behind a bank of clouds, but with the full flush of his brightness spreading far toward the zenith. The sky is all lustrous and glowing except just where the King of the Day has veiled his face. There is an ineffable purity and calmness that seems to pervade the world this evening. Even the almost-constant splash of the waves on the sandy beach beneath my window is not heard; scarce a breath of wind ripples the broad bosom of the noble river.

The merry shout of some bathers down the river, & the shrill whistle of the boatswain on the gun boats at anchor a few hundred yards on the river followed by the hoarse call, "All hands," alone, has broken the stillness of the past half hour. It is one of those few, beautiful, quiet evenings, before the rude winds and storms of autumn come. It is just three years ago today that my sainted Emma left me, for a home with the angels. I cannot tell, nor will any mortal ever know, how much loneliness I have suffered, or how desolate my heart has been since then. I have sought to lose myself in the busy world since then; in the hours when I steal away from the throng & confusion to dream of the past, that dear, loving face with all its sweetness and beauty beaming affection is before me. Oh, my dear Emma, thou didst not know how well I loved—I did not know, myself, how closely I had held thee to my heart. These tears that now blind my eyes and relieve this full heart, attest the influence and power of thy gentle, loving spirit over my wayward nature.

I cannot believe that the sunshine will ever come back to gladden this heart of mine as it has been—the sunshine of love! O, I would go to the ends of the earth if I might obtain it there—I would toil and struggle a lifetime, to live over again the few short years that She blessed with her presence and her love—but it cannot, cannot be[.] Thank God she has left me one dear, precious memento—the pledge of a mutual love that shall light my path down into the dark valley—O, thou who seest even the sparrow's fall, spare that little one to this aching heart, until I go to meet its angel mother! Away in the distance, I see another, whom I have learned to love with a deep, unfailing love; oh, that she could understand now, in the morning of her young life, the value of that love which is all the greater for having been strengthened in the purest of earthly affection; I have learned to value hers even more because I have lost all.

Friday September 19. This has been an oppressively warm day—news from the army in Maryland is cheering—oh, I hope the end of this terrible war draweth nigh.

Saturday September 20. There was a fine shower last night, and the clouds still lower threateningly. The good news from the Union Army in Maryland is confirmed, but the battle of Wednesday (17th inst.) was not decisive—Burnside, near the close of the day, & at the critical moment, failed to drive the enemy from their position & though Sumner and Hooker had been successful upon the center and right, Burnside's failure leaves the battle to be fought over again, on that or some other field. Called this evening on Mr. Wilbern's and staid to a late tea.

Sunday September 21. There was a powerful drenching rain last night, and it continued far into the morning. I have had no news from the absent one for more than a week, and I am getting anxious and disturbed—O, why is it, that every pleasure has its pain—to love is but to be anxious & sad.

Tuesday September 23. I have been almost sick these two days—my "call" for the sick and the patients in hospital have hung heavy on my hands. Some 60 to 70 presents themselves each morning for treatment at "Surgeon's Call" and 15 to 20 in hospital. But I managed to go to the Fortress yesterday on business connected with my sick & their comfort. Today, I rode into the country some six miles—out on the Bethel Road in answer to a summons to visit the wife of a Mr. Wm. Wood—the case was urgent & alarming, without immediate aid. I found a country physician in attendance, but he was too ignorant or fearful, or both, and the poor woman was rapidly sinking. In an hour after my arrival, she was relieved—safe; and I left the family amid a shower of thanks to God & blessings on the doctor. This man would, as a large farmer, owning some 400 hundred [*sic*] acres of the sacred (?) soil. A sharp gallop across lots, and through the woods, along bypaths, saved me a distance, & I was in camp again before sunset.[12]

Weak and sick in body and heart, I waited for the evening mail, hoping for tidings from the <u>Absent</u>, but none came! God willing, I will repel these rising murmurs, and all this "winter of my discontent" until the path of duty seems to lead me home—surely, if He will preserve me, there, my loved Ones safe until my time comes, I will hie me from these scenes of war and toil and privation, as happy as the schoolboy when he escapes from the tasks and restraints of the schoolroom. And now, good night, my silent journal! A moment with thee has relieved many, very many moments that have hung as heavy on my lonely heart, as the present does.

Thursday September 25. I have found my hard couch a luxury these two days past, that I could scarce deny myself—from necessity. And my patients, numbering 60 to 80 every day, have taxed all my strength. When we are sick, there is a consolation that we shall be better by and by—yes, even if we go to the hush of the voiceless grave to find it. I waited with anxious hope last evening, for the mail, that some message of love from the <u>loved one</u> would cheer me up a little, but none came; and still today the same silence. She little knows as yet what heartaches are, or she would spare me every pang she might, by every little sacrifice of time and convenience. The day has been cloudy and melancholy as my own heart—a real sour fall day—a premonitory symptom of the darker days to come.

September 30, 1862. This has been a very warm day—so was yesterday. I have rarely experienced warmer days than these in mid-summer. The month of September has gone and still I am here. I thought a few months since, ere this, to be permanently reunited to my family. But the time today seems more distant than it did four months ago. I am greatly anxious concerning my little family at home, now that there is no physician near them. I must return within the next six months to my motherless boys—God preserve them safe & well unto my coming! I have been very poorly since my last record—so as scarce as to be able to discharge all the duties of my post. And they are taxing now that I have no assistant. Late in the evening of my last record, I received letters from several absent ones—from Frank—Mrs. D. & that Dearer Friend. The explanation of her silence relieved my fears.

October 1. It has been very warm and sunny today. The heat is really more oppressive than at any time during the latter part of August. I have been much engaged for some days in making reports—Monthly & Quarterly & Quarterly Requisitions. This PM received another letter from my Dear Friend—she is well and, with heart full of affection, longs for a reunion. O, let my heart realize the fond hopes it has again presumed to entertain—there is yet a green spot in life for me, as her love assures me.

Friday October 3. Yesterday and today have again supplied us with summer days—has been oppressively warm. Rode into the country some six miles on the Bethel road to visit a child of Mr. Wm. Wood—found the child very sick—enjoyed the luxury of relieving the little fellow, and after a hasty cup of coffee, from which I could not escape, left for home amid the thanks of the friends, for my fee-less ride.

Sabbath October 5. Yesterday was another warm summer day—no event of importance in our little world has occurred, except the burial today of Pvt. Foster of Company F. The muffled drums & plaintive dirge of the fife, was his only requiem—the file of his comrades (nine) with reversed arms & bearers (six) was all the procession that followed him to his last resting place—and the volley that announced him laid down in his narrow house, was the last good-bye of those who bore him there.

I finished reading the "Waverly" novels today, which I had taken up to beguile the heavy hours. Have been reading "Edwin of Deira" today, a poem by Alexander Smith. There is little that is original or striking in the style & many of the figures employed by the authors are unnatural. The plot is, however, agreeable and plain.[13]

The sound of congregational singing struck my ears this afternoon, and I walked over to a neighboring barrack from whence it proceeded. I found a congregation of Africans. Their worship was sincere and devout, but of all the primitive and ignorant congregations, this was the most so of any I have ever seen. Not one of the whole 2- or 300 hundred blacks could read a word—almost all were latchy slaves on some of the plantations on the Peninsula or on the opposite shore of the James River.[14]

One of the speakers was a natural orator—his flow of language was excellently free, & many of his figures striking & original; while others were amusingly simple. I shall not soon forget his brief appeal to the soldiers present. In closing, he remarked to them—"In this Rebellion, you have come to subdue, you have left home and friends—fathers and mothers—wife and sisters—brothers and children—you have been hungry and tired—been in dangerous places, slept on the ground and suffered very much." "But," continued he, "remember dat our folks suffered dese tings all de time." I confess my heart was deeply touched. It did, indeed, afflict me to reflect that this Great Republic had for many years, by its local (state) laws, held millions of these ignorant creatures in a condition of servitude which forbade a single ray of additional light, or knowledge, to reach their darkened intellect. The day has been pleasant, but not as warm, as for many days, being there a cool wind—but very comfortable.

[Up to the afternoon of October 5th, 1862, Dr. Smith's life at the tip of the Peninsula had been boring, repetitious, and without adventure. But that evening, all this would change; ahead lay a much different experience.]

NOTES: CHAPTER THREE

1. The courthouse at Angelica, in Smith's home county, appears more elegant but is an artist's idealized rendering.
2. John J. Peck graduated from West Point in 1843. After meritorious service in the Mexican War, he resigned to pursue a lucrative career in business and Democratic politics. Lincoln appointed him a brigadier of volunteers. The complexity of large modern armies is suggested by the

following: The 85th New York was part of the 3rd Brigade, which was part of the 3rd Division, which was part of IV Corps, which was part of the Army of the Potomac.

3. These generals were Samuel Heintzelman, Fitz John Porter, William Franklin, and Edwin Sumner.

4. Albion Howe graduated eighth in a West Point class of fifty-two men. His artillery training served him well in the Mexican War and on the frontier. Orris Ferry had been editor of the *Yale Literary Magazine* and was elected to the Connecticut senate. His service with the Connecticut volunteers led to a general's star.

5. Robert Schenck was an eight-term Congressman, an ambassador to the Court of St. James, and author of a treatise on draw poker. "Pearce" is probably Byron Pierce, a Michigan dentist with an aptitude for military matters. John T. Greble graduated from West Point in 1854. He was brevetted lieutenant colonel for gallantry at Big Bethel, where he was killed. The identity of Winthrop is not known.

6. Maj. Reuben V. King will play a dangerous role in Smith's future life. Chauncey S. Aldrich was later promoted to captain. John D. Lewis, Smith's assistant surgeon, was later promoted to (full) surgeon. These three men were all in the 85th New York.

7. Smith's original manuscript does not name the *Monitor*'s surgeon. Navy records suggest that it was Daniel Logue, Thomas Meckley, or Grenville Weeks. John L. Worden, Lt., USN, commanded the *Monitor* during the historic battle with the *Merrimack*; he was blinded by a Confederate shell and turned over command to Lt. Samuel D. Greene.

8. Here, Smith continues his sensitivity to (probably) imagined neglect by his fiancée.

9. D. W. Hand was surgeon-in-charge of the general hospital at Newport News, Virginia. November 1862 through May 1863, he was medical director for the Union forces at Suffolk, Virginia, and was still in the army as of March 1866.

10. The captain was a retired merchant ship skipper. His home, on the south bank of Watts Creek, six miles northwest of Newport News, appears on Plate XVIII of the atlas for the *Official Reports*. The 1860 census of Warwick County shows Nelson Smith, age forty-five, a farmer, born in England. Others in the household included Margaret, born in New York, Emma age eleven, Annie age eight, and Ruth Smith, age seventy-six. The 1860 slave schedule showed Captain Smith

as owning twenty slaves. (Courtesy of Robert E. L. Krick.) As to Lieutenant Langworthy, two Langworthys served in the 85th New York. Daniel enlisted as a hospital steward, then received a commission. In September 1863, he was sent to his home county to recruit; he reported difficulties in getting men to enlist, complaining that the town of Olean would not pay bounties. In March 1864, Col. Enrico Fardello noted that in eight months, Langworthy had produced no results and must return to the regiment immediately or be declared AWOL. Langworthy came back promptly, was captured at Plymouth, sent to prison camp at Columbia, South Carolina, escaped and returned north, greatly aided by slaves. See *Escape from Dixie,* by John Ball (Goldstar Enterprises, Williamsville, NY, 1996).

11. This may have been Lt. Harvey Moses, of the 91st New York.
12. It is difficult to imagine what life-threatening condition could have been resolved in an hour, considering the state of medical knowledge in 1862.
13. The "Waverley Novels" were a series of very popular romances of Scottish border life, written by Sir Walter Scott between 1814 and 1819. A central theme of these stories was twilight-of-a-nobility, a concept that appealed especially to the Southern gentry. Mark Twain blamed the Civil War on Scott, noting that Scott set "the world in love with dreams and phantoms . . . with the silliness and emptinesses, sham grandeurs, sham gauds and sham chivalries, of a brainless and worthless long-vanished society." Alexander Smith (1830–67) was a Scottish poet; his general style can be seen in this excerpt from *Dreamthorp:* "I go into my library, and all history unrolls before me. I breathe the morning air of the world while the scent of Eden's roses yet lingered in it, while it vibrated only to the world's first brood of nightingales, and to the laugh of Eve."
14. The word *latchy* is not in the 1856 Webster's Unabridged Dictionary.

CHAPTER FOUR

Norfolk to New Bern

After weeks of waiting, Dr. Smith and the 85th New York were bound for a whole new theater of action, traveling through southern Virginia and on into North Carolina, by foot and on horseback, by railroad, and by steamboat, headed for adventure, which will break the monotony of garrison duty. It is said that an idle mind is the Devil's workshop. Will these new challenges divert Dr. Smith from his pattern of rumination and obsession?

Sunday October 5. 7:00 o'clock P.M. We have orders to get ready to move early tomorrow. Our destination is, first, Norfolk—from there, I think we go very soon if not directly to Suffolk, North Carolina, and thence probably towards Petersburgh [*sic*], Virginia.

Monday October 6. By 1:00 o'clock P.M., everything was ready & on shipboard—yet with characteristic delay, we did not leave the wharf until 4:00 P.M. We made a speedy trip to Norfolk, and then again came the usual delays in transferring the troops from the vessels to the cars. But about 10:00 in the evening we were on the way to Suffolk.

There never was a more beautiful night than this. The moon shone with unusual brilliancy; and never did the regiment seem to enjoy a scene more than this. Whoops & yells, laughter & jest rang out far & wide. But the soldiers taken prisoners at Fair Oaks joined just after we reached Norfolk, by the Norfolk boat from Fortress Monroe & this contributed to considerable degree to enliven & cheer the spirits of the men—all seemed in merry mood. It was difficult to suppose that these merry, shouting soldiers were the worn veterans of the Peninsula Campaign—they ran & shouted like raw troops.

The bridge across the Dismal Swamp Canal, night though it was, interested me very much. It is one of the finest iron railroad bridges I have ever seen. We reached Suffolk between 11:00 & 12:00 at night, and the regiment marched to a field adjoining the town and stretched themselves on the ground beneath the starry sky. For my own part, I chose the lee side of a bale of hay, after seeing my hospital tent set up & the sick & invalided comfortably at rest. It was near 2:00 A.M. when I stretched myself beside a bundle of hay & as tired and worn out as I have been in many a day—but I was nearly sick.[1]

Tuesday October 7. The regiment went into camp near where they lay last night. Our position reminds me in many respects of that which we held at Fair Oaks. There, as now, we were at the front; then, as now, we occupied the center of the position & lay, or were encamped, immediately behind the line of works. The abbatis [*sic*] in front of our position & the general make of the ground are also calculated to remind me of that bloody field.

This evening, or P.M., Lt. Col. Wellman arrived in camp—I am greatly rejoiced to see him. He is my most valued friend in the regiment—I shared my blankets with him in our weary march up the Peninsula & until he fell, severely wounded in the head, at Fair Oaks, since which time he has been North, & returns not yet sufficiently recovered for active duty.

Saturday October 18. The past ten days have been very briskly employed in the duties of my Department. I have had Hospital Accommodations to secure for my sick & many other duties necessarily incident to a comfortable arrangement in our new location—so that my record has been neglected. Now, I have my hospital arranged in a fine, large dwelling on the bank of the Nansemond, and my sick very pleasantly & comfortably provided for. It is something more than a mile from camp, but the gallop down there, morning and evening, does me good.[2]

The sad memories which this day brings from the receding past, are among the most painfully sorrowful of my life. "Lured by the sweet persuasion of some angel band, that somewhere in the distance leads thee still." Oh, my Emma, my Emma! Such goodness & sweetness; & affectionate love of him who still mourns thy loss as though it were but yesterday, will never again, I fear, cheer and bless my poor heart. But there is a future & through all the long months & years since I bade my dear Emma a last farewell—through toils, hardships, & dangers, I have looked to that future with eyes of hope, and often with glad anticipation, knowing it would bring a glad hour of reunion! Blessed hope! I know a glad welcome awaits me on yonder shore. Those who loved me in life as she did, will be permitted to greet me when I shall have passed the River of Death, and stand on the peaceful shore of Eternal Deliverance & Rest.

Sunday October 19. A beautiful Sabbath has nearly passed. Sunny and clear as if war and desolation did not stalk through our land once so happy & prosperous. The early morning I employed in writing, while Asst. Surg. Lewis attended the "morning clinic." Soon after breakfast, which as usual was served on some boxes, extemporized for a table, I walked to my hospital, my friend Lt. Col. Wellman in company. After visiting & prescribing for all the sick there, I returned to camp, calling on my way, at the Methodist E. Church. The house was crowded—mostly by the officers & soldiers of the Union. But a very respectable number of the citizens were in attendance. The sermon was by the Reverend Mr. Hedrick, the pastor of the church, from Timothy II, Chapter VIII. It was a very excellent discourse delivered in the very spirit of "Love to all men." This is the first occasion on which I have attended church since I was home in June last, and that one occasion the first in about nine months—truly the sound of these church-going bells is cheering to the soul. 9:00 o'clock P.M. I walked down to my hospital this evening, visiting again all the patients & returned to camp later.

Monday October 20. A warm, bright day today; the smoke of the different camps lingers in the horizon, giving to the atmosphere the appearance it has at the north during Indian summer. I have engaged every leisure moment today, inspecting the sanitary conditions of the camps of this brigade, their police, drainage, et cetera, by order from Headquarters (Medical Director). The Regiments of this brigade (Wessell's) now lie along the front—immediately behind the works. The Brigade is composed of six Regiments.

The new regiments are, for the most part, encamped half a mile to a mile in the rear of the front line. There are now about 21 regiments here, and three or four batteries of Artillery. It is expected the force will soon be further increased. What the purpose of the Government is in gathering such a force at this place, is, of course, only a matter of conjecture. It would seem to indicate an advance toward Richmond via Petersburgh, simultaneously with an advance from other points. But it would seem, if this was the intention, that a force could be landed on the West bank of the James River, at a point some 10 to 15 miles below Petersburg, a better base for operations & a shorter route to Richmond would be opened and the army could be better supplied with munitions & subsistence than from this point. Again, the extensive & strong fortifications nearly completed here, might argue a merely defensive intention on the part of the Government. But the next thirty days will probably solve the problem. The men, particularly of the old Regiments, are making themselves as comfortable as the circumstances will admit, by building log huts covered by their shelter tents or by setting their A (wedge) tents on the logs—then with a little fireplace on one side and poles for a bunk, the soldier is very comfortable for winter frosts & storms.

Sunday October 27. The morning was dark, threatened rain, but after visiting my hospital patients, I attended church at the M.E. Church, and again listened to a very good sermon from the Reverend Mr. Hedrick—Paul's Epistle to the Thessalonians, "Quench not the spirit."

[That same day, a much different discourse, in the form of a letter from Pvt. Lafayette Baird, 67th Ohio, noted how the Union troops at Suffolk were plundering and raping the poor white folk of southern Virginia, while protecting and guarding the houses of the rich Southerners.[3]]

The rain commenced falling before service ended & continued with little intermission for the rest of the day—cold & cheerless, without & little less so within.

Monday October 28. This evening, I find myself within the four walls of a house—a log house to be sure, just ten by twelve covered with the fly of a hospital tent, the gable ends enclosed with "shelter tents," and the light penetrating the camp answers well the place of windows. Small and rough as it is, it is a great improvement on the wall tent. The chill and frosty night air cannot penetrate my castle walls as it does "ducking" [light canvas], however good. My friend Wellman has also built next door on my left a comfortable hut about the same size of my own; we both commence our housekeeping this evening—it is very comfortable, this being alone once more, so snugly and comfortably arranged; and my friend and self have just been exchanging visits of congratulations. A. Owen Taber, orderly in Company E, died in Regt. Hospital today & a most excellent young man. My health is improving—I feel again like my former self—full of energy and work. Thanks to the kind Providence that watches over me.[4]

Tuesday October 29. My respected young friend, Owen Taber, Sergeant in Company E of this Regiment, died at the Regimental Hospital this morning, of Billious Remittent Fever with Gastric complications. "How vain are all things here below," I feel like exclaiming. Here is a

Lt. Col. Abijah J. Wellman, Dr. Smith's closest friend in the 85th New York.
Wellman's noble brow was shattered by a Confederate shell, exposing the
membranes around the brain, a wound from which he never fully recovered.

young man in the morning of life, well educated, carefully nurtured by exemplary parents, with hopes of honor & preferment before him, laid in the unambitious grave when the high hopes & promises of life gave him most to live for; for he was in the daily expectation of his Commission as a 2nd Lieutenant in his Company. The day has been cool but pleasant—the nights have become very chill, and frosts are frequent.

Wednesday October 30. I went to Fortress Monroe today, but could not reach there until 4:00 o'cl P.M.; the boat returned to Norfolk at five. There being no hotel at the Point, the Hygiea being in process of demolition and removal by order of government, I had no alternative but to return to Norfolk. The hour given me for the transaction of business scarcely allowed me to commence it; I resolved to return by the morning boat to the Point. Accordingly, I went back to Norfolk and put up at the "National." In the evening, indeed, it was dark, when I reached Norfolk, I went over to Portsmouth with my friend Dr. (and Lieut.) Langworthy & took tea at his friends, Mr. Whipple. Spent a short evening here very pleasantly and returned to Norfolk about 9:00 P.M. Mrs. Whipple is a very pleasant, rather noble-looking woman. Her daughter, Julia, a young lady of 24 years, is accomplished, and many would call her beautiful—perhaps she is; but there is something that tells me she is vain and self willed—she likes to be admired, I am sure, and there is little of sweetness and affection in that heart of hers, even if an admirer should find one at all.

In the afternoon, before going to the Fortress, and while waiting for the 3 P.M. boat, I called at a bookstore having the sign of Griffith, to purchase some of the monthlies—found what I ought to have known, that to the merchants of Norfolk, the importations of publications of Northern houses, like merchandise, was contraband—but I found a pretty widow—the wife, once, of the former proprietor. I had a long & not-disagreeable discussion with her of the existing political relations of the north & south. While she was strongly attached to the South & its interests, she nevertheless was dispassionate and reasonable. She confessed the Southern ladies were very bitter toward the soldiers & officers of the Union Army & that she had been blamed for treating them civilly.

On my return from the Fortress to Norfolk, I was addressed while on the boat by a very interesting-looking young lady, in that familiar style, that at once showed me that she was a "Nymph of the pave." I amused myself with the acquaintance long enough to draw from her a portion of her history. There is, & has always been, a sort of interest in my mind, one in which I derive satisfaction—I cannot say pleasure, in sifting the history

of those who have fallen. There are so many shades to the picture—some
I have known who were dragged down by the wiles of the Seducer, others who have plunged into their degradation from the mere love of pleasure, & the gratification of passion. Failing to secure from me a promise to
call on her, when the boat touched the wharf, she improved the first offer,
and was quickly hurried into a hack by a man wearing shoulder straps and
doubtless found in his arms, for that night, the satisfaction she craved.

Put up at the National Hotel with my friend Langworthy. It would be
difficult, perhaps, to convince some of the officers of my acquaintance
than an officer ever goes to this city of prostitutes & stays a single night
without yielding to the temptations which they never try to resist.

Thursday October 31. After a good night's rest and early breakfast, I
took the morning boat to the Fort to try & complete the business. I succeeded only in part—the boat returned to Norfolk at half past ten and I
could stay no longer. At about 2 P.M., was on the train bound for Suffolk.
The country through which this road runs, is sparsely settled, the few
plantations there are look very thriftless. Swampy ground characterizes the
whole distance, with only now & then an exception. In fact, the Dismal
Swamp commences here & extends far into the interior of North Carolina. Reached camp about 3 P.M. & found the Regiment had marched on
about an hour before on a reconnaissance to Blackwater.

After getting some refreshment, in company with the Major whom I
found at Norfolk, and who went down there last evening to have a pleasant visit with somebody!—guess he didn't care much who it was, so that
it was a woman! I think on reflection, I have wronged him—he would
want as nice an article as he could find. I said in company with the major,
I then pushed on after the regiment, overtaking it about dark—some
eight miles out. The march during the night was quiet, but wearisome. At
3 o'clock in the morning of Friday, November 1st, we halted at the
Beaver Dam Church, about 20 miles from Suffolk. The 103 PA & 85th
PA Volunteers, several pieces of artillery & the 11th PA cavalry were
thrown forward on the Franklin Road. The remaining portions of the
troop were arranged in line of battle & then allowed to throw themselves
upon the ground for a brief rest. All but the weary sentinel were quickly
sound asleep.[5]

Just as the first faint glimmer of the morning lightened the eastern
sky, the scattering rattle of musketry was heard in the direction of
Franklin. In a few moments, came the boom of a field gun and the scream

of the flying shell was distinctly heard, followed in a few seconds by the less loud but distinct explosion of the shell. Then followed another gun and others in rapid succession. It was evident that the force thrown in front were waking up the Rebels in Franklin. The musketry soon ceased & after a score or more of discharges of cannon, the sounds of battle died away and all was quiet again. In an hour from the time we were roused, the column was in moving toward Suffolk. I cannot see that anything was gained by this movement. The only possible good resulting was the probability that demonstration drew from other points a force to repel our expected attack, sufficient to weaken the Rebel forces at other places— this may serve to weaken the force before Burnside, perhaps. It also had the effect to "season" the men and accustom them to marching.

Marched some six or eight miles, and halted for breakfast. I was never so much annoyed by the conduct of troops as I was on this march by the conduct of the new troops—particularly the 130th & 132nd NY Volunteers, to steal, pillage and destroy was the great work they seemed to think they had in hand. Scarcely a mile of the march was not marked by stragglers from these regiments. Crack, crack, left & right, before & behind were heard their rifles as they fell out of rank & struggled off in pursuit of pigs, geese, sheep, et cetera. Several bullets whined unpleasantly near my head while I was taking my morning cup of coffee, which were carelessly shot by these careless devils. About [?] we halted and rested until about dark and then took up the line of march again for Suffolk. The object of the halt seems to have been to cover the return of the cavalry that had continued the reconnaissance along the Blackwater [River] in case the enemy should pursue. The regiment reached camp about midnight. Found a letter on my table from a much-beloved friend—an affectionate & cheering letter.

Tuesday November 4. The state elections are held today in several of the northern states. I wait with feelings of great interest the result in the State of New York. On her voice in this election depends on many interests dear to my country & its future prosperity. I fear the election of Seymour, and yet cannot believe the people will commit so grave an error. There is no doubt a feeling of mistrust as to the capacity of the federal administration to grapple with and crush this rebellion. Its measures have been too often vacillating, and the direction of the boundless resources which the north has poured into the hands of the government has been too frequently misdirected. There is no saying, therefore, what this lack of confidence on the part of the people may do; in the hands of the traitors and unprincipled demagogues who now control the Democratic party of New York State—of one thing I cannot be convinced—that the people lack patriotism. A large majority of the "soldiers of the Union" from the state of New York are Republicans & would support Wadsworth, if at home. In this regiment, there was an expression taken this morning & all the men present, being some 500, voted for Wadsworth except 47 who voted for Seymour.[6]

Thursday November 6. The day has been dreary, wet above & beneath. This evening the N. York papers announced the election of Horatio Seymour to the gubernatorial chair of the state of New York. I am more completely discouraged by this event than any other in the history of the war—why are we sent here by the almost-unanimous vote of the people, to suffer a thousand hardships & perils, if they are not prepared to stand by us, by electing a loyal governor to assist & cooperate with the Federal government. But the result is not entirely unexpected, yet is nonetheless disastrous.

Friday November 7. The ground was covered with snow this morning. The prospect was well worthy [of] our northern climate. The snow continued to fall until the morning was far advanced—the like of this snow has not been known in the memory of the oldest inhabitant.

Saturday November 8. The weather still continues cold—wind blowing from the North brisk. Patients in hospital are doing finely—have but two that are very sick—these men failed to receive the usual close attention in the early attack of the Fever (Remittent) and they have consequently slipped down into a typhoid condition. It is difficult to raise them out of this, but by faithful, close attention & free use of stimulants & general support, I am able in a great majority of cases to succeed if there is no local complication.[7]

Tuesday November 11. I was much cheered today by the news that Gen. McClellan was removed from command of the Army of the Potomac & Gen. Burnside appointed. The change comes late—I fear too late.

Wednesday November 12. The feature of the day was a review of the whole force in and about Suffolk by Gen. Dix. About 21 Regiments of infantry—two Regts. of Cavalry and three Batteries of Artillery constitute the force. The display was very fine; but I question the judiciousness of thus displaying our strength to the enemy, whose spies were unquestionably mingling in the crowd. The day has been faultlessly fine throughout.[8]

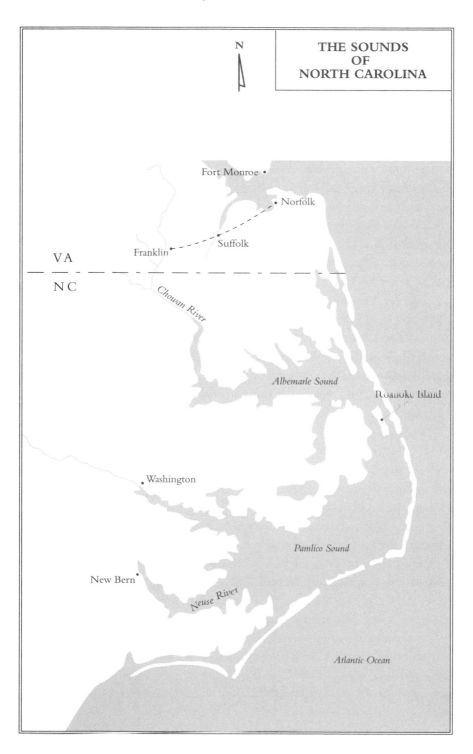

Monday November 17. The day has been very beautiful—feel very unwell this evening. The regiment received orders to be in line for the march at 2:00 o'clock P.M. with three days cooked rations in haversacks— our destination is probably some point on the Blackwater. I am feeling so indisposed this evening that I have determined not to follow the Regt. until early tomorrow morning; it is now several hours on the road, and a few hours of rest will refresh me for the ride.—it is very late—have just returned from my hospital. Aaron Van Nostrand, whom I received into my hospital some days, from the camp of the 130 NY Volunteers, (because he is my neighbor & friend when at home and because, in truth, I fear the conveniences for & management of the sick in that regiment is not what it should or might be); is very, very sick—I have little hope of his recovery. His brother Isaac is also there, himself an invalid and an anxious watcher beside his brother.

Tuesday November 18. I find myself almost used up this evening. Rose at 4:00 o'clock A.M. & was in the saddle at 5:00. Ed Underhill following in my wake, I rode rapidly out on the road to the Blackwater (via the South Quay Road). The ten or twelve picket stations which had to be passed, made the ride for the first five miles very tedious; in the night, the picket compels the advancing horseman to dismount and give the countersign over the point of the bayonet.

The pickets once passed, I dashed on at a speed which few horses beside "Kit" can equal. In the midst of a hostile population, with yet 15 miles between me & the troop, and exposed to the scouts of the enemy in rear & flank of our force, I resolved to make the shelter of the Stars & Stripes as soon as possible. Soon after daylight, I began to pass the stragglers that had fallen out of the ranks. More than a hundred men were scattered along the fence corners & roadside in the last five miles before reaching the army. This straggling is pernicious and destroys the efficiency of the army in which it is allowed. I was gratified in not seeing a man of the 85th NY among the stragglers until the main body was in sight. The march has been very fatiguing, doubtless, but that was no excuse.

It was about sunrise when I rode into the lines of the 85th. They had arrived on the ground but a few minutes before & had scarcely swallowed their coffee. We had reached the Blackwater by a road to the right of the direct road to Franklin, leaving that road at Beaver Dam Church. The pickets of the enemy were driven in a mile before the river was reached. I had not been dismounted an hour when the order to "fall in" was given,

& the whole column began to move out on the road it had come. It was soon generally understood that the intended crossing of the river had been abandoned on account of the unexpected depth of the water—the artillery could not cross without being submerged & the pontoons, made of old boats taken from the Jerico Canal, were not strong enough to support the artillery in crossing. Two miles of our road retraced, & we turned to the right, taking a road that brought us directly in front of Franklin. At this place, the artillery opened up on a body of Rebel cavalry & quickly dispersed them. The guns were then directed upon the town & a brisk artillery duel ensued. The enemy replied mostly with a rocket battery, which threw several shells unpleasantly close to me. Of all the missiles I have heard whir and screech around me, I believe these are the most unsatisfactory—there is something so indefinite in their approach, the sound seems so difficult to locate that they are less desirable visitors than even the solid shot from rifled artillery or the bursting shell.[9]

It was soon evident to me that a serious demonstration was not intended, and feeling extremely jaded & ill, I obtained permission to leave my post & hasten back to camp in advance of the troops. The head of the column had already begun to move, as past the lines in company with Col. Wellman & Adjutant Aldrich, who had resolved to accompany me. The Col. was feeling very poorly—he is very unfortunate; a little excessive fatigue & broken rest, induces symptoms of congestion in that part of the brain (or its membranes, more likely) injured by the passage of the ball by which he was wounded at Fair Oaks. A rapid ride brought us back to camp before it was fairly dark. This reconnaissance is also a failure—how many more such? I do not clearly understand these movements, & can see no good in them except it be to keep as large a force as possible of the enemy at Franklin, which is the best place for them to resist an approach to Weldon. Today, I have ridden 60 miles & spent most of the day in the field, doing that most tiresome of all tasks—nothing at all, but "standing around." The day has been pleasantly cool & cloudy.[10]

Wednesday November 19. The regiment reached camp between one and two o'clock P.M. in good condition & without any straggling. I am feeling so ill that I have not left camp or my bed except to visit the hospital. Poor Aaron V[an Nostrand] is no better. He is doomed—no skill can save him.

Friday November 21. Late in the evening, returned from a complimentary supper given to the officers of this regiment by a company of enterprising mulattos who have erected a boarding house for the purpose

Col. Thomas J. Thorp of the 1st New York Dragoons and his wife. Dr. Smith was convinced that Thorp was an alcoholic and would bring grief to his spouse. Perhaps this photograph, with his aggressive look and her pensive gaze into the distance, reflects such troubles.

ROGER D. HUNT COLLECTION, U.S. ARMY MILITARY HISTORY INSTITUTE of boarding the officers of the Regt. The supper passed off very pleasantly. It was a most elegant & sumptuous affair when the disadvantages of the undertaking is considered. Lt. Col. W. was unable to attend & Maj. King was too sour to do so. My own indisposition had made me resolve to not attend, but the chief of Gen. Peck's staff (Lt. Foster) called & wished the Col. and myself to accompany him.

Thursday November 27. <u>Thanksgiving Day</u> at home in N. York, and in several of the Northern states. And I, an exile from home & friends (though a voluntary one) have occasion to be especially thankful for the blessings I enjoy—thankful that I have been spared by a kind Providence, & preserved amid the dangers of battle, and the terrible pestilence that stalked in our midst, slaying its thousands that the chances of battle had spared—thankful that the illness that has prostrated me for a few days past has passed away, and that I again begin to feel something of my accustomed spirit & energy. And O, I am very thankful that the Dear Ones at home have been preserved, thus far, to encourage & cheer this poor heart that sometimes, for a moment, feels like giving up the struggle, glad to find a refuge, though it be in the cold grave.

It is late—the evening I have spent at the "Officer's Mess" where a sumptuous dinner has been served at the expense of the officers of the 85th (cost $14/.). General Wessels & Staff were present, as invited guests—the chief of Gen. Peck's staff (now Maj. Foster), a Capt. in the Naval Service, Lt. Col. Thorp, Maj. Scott, Capts. Sayles & Brundage, and other officers of the 130th were also present as guests. And I must not forget to mention my sturdy old friend, Dr. Gall, Surgeon of the 13th Indiana, a German of intelligence & ability & formerly consul at Antwerp for several years.[11]

After supper, toasts enlivened the evening—Maj. Foster, Maj. Scott & Capt. Sayles were very happy in their style and spirit in replying to toasts. Lt. Col. Thorp gave us the most rambling and unconnected amount of blarney I have ever had the fortune to listen to on a similar occasion—his chief object seemed to prove his devotion and love of the 85th—fudge! He would annihilate its future, if he could! Col. Wellman was too ill to attend—and the loss to our evening's enjoyment was not a little, for his social qualities are abundant and large. Maj. King stayed at his quarters out of "pure cussedness"—wonder if the service has a more unprincipled & mean man.[12]

Since my last record, Aaron Van Nostrand has died (Nov. 20—night of). The poor wife will be very wretched—ah, poor woman! I know how your heart will bleed, for mine has tasted of that cup.

Sunday November 30. A warm and sunny day has closed again—all is quiet in camp. I wait with much anxiety news of the movements of the Army of the Potomac. Burnside is on the Rappahannock, opposite Fredericksburgh [*sic*], and Lee is prepared to dispute his passage. How swiftly the seasons have passed for a year, & yet how heavy they have hung on my hands.

Monday December 1. The first day of winter! It is as fine a day as September or October can produce. It has hardly seemed like fall. The golden tinge of the foliage has come like the gray hairs in creeping age; slowly, by insensible degrees. The cool & lately the frosty nights have been all there was to herald advancing winter.

Tuesday December 2. This evening's mail brought an Official Notice of the dismissal of Asst. Surg. J.D. Lewis from the service for "absence from camp without leave." I have been convinced for some days that the doctor was dismissed, by information from a friend at Washington (Capt. Clark). It is a grievous affliction & too severe a punishment, as he is dismissed with loss of all pay due him, which will amount to at least $700.00. [$28,000 in today's money.] If a dear friend or sister of mine was lying hopelessly ill & pleading for me to return, and see her once more, I should go, my sympathies are large and free for you, Doctor, & those who know the circumstances will bless rather than blame you for visiting that dying sister.

It is determined that the doctor will leave at once for Washington & seek a revocation of the Order of Dismissal & learn who it was that has informed the government of his absence. He believes it is an enemy at home. I mistrust that it is Maj. King—once, some days since, I suggested the possibility to the doctor, but he did not for a moment entertain the thought. The doctor will go to Allegany from Baltimore to examine a certain box, which I sent home from Washington in July last—said box was packed by Dr. Lewis the day the regiment left Washington; Col. Belknap's effects & mine being put in it by him (Lewis), according to my direction. I obtained an order from Col. B. and sent it home. Rumors have reached me recently that there was a report in circulation in Alleghany County that I had sent home a large number of sheets, towels, pillowcases, et cetera, belonging to the government. On receiving the letter containing the notice of this rumor, I asked the doctor if he was positive he had packed in it <u>only</u> my own & the Col's effects—he seemed not to be positive, but rather thought he had put in his own effects, at least his bedding, in it, and "if there was room, very probably had put in it things belonging to the medical department," his object "being to economize room and pack as closely as possible." The Affidavit of Doct. Lewis on file among my papers will clearly show that if any article is packed in it, that did not belong there, it was done by him, as in it he distinctly declares that he had the entire management & direction of packing all the boxes, & that he has reason to "know that Dr. Smith did not know what articles were packed in the box, only as I told him." And he further affirms that he never told me that he had packed his own effects in the box, or that he might have put articles in it that belonged to neither of the parties mentioned. The Dr. was absent from camp, on service with the sick at Yorktown, or in charge of transports having sick on board, at the time I obtained the order mentioned from Col. Belknap to get the box out of the Government warehouse.

Wednesday December 3. I bade Dr. Lewis good-by this morning with sincere regret. Gave him letters to friends in Granger. Wrote to the Surgeon General in New York in his behalf, and to the Surgeon General of the United States also several letters to other influential friends. I have little doubt he will be restored. The Doctor is an excellent-hearted man. He would not do a wrong to any man, for his right hand. He is very industrious, and always willing to do whatever there is to be done. Intellectually, he is not a great man—morally, there are few who are his superiors. He has attained the age of 36 years, and is as unsophisticated and guileless as the majority of men at 20. His education never seems to have been such as to give to his mind any power of analysis. His perceptions of disease are only superficial—he wants [lacks] the power of analysis to trace cause and effect. But yet he is a very useful & clever man & may the God he tries to serve give him success in the prayer of his friend.

It commenced raining before light & has been dark and gloomy all day. The whole administration of the department now falls upon me—so I attended surgeon's call, and made out the monthly report of sick and wounded—also finished reading "Among the Pines." Read a page in "Perfect Love" this evening—it gives me comfort and strength.

An order has been received this P.M. not to make any more details for guard or picket duty "until further orders." This, coupled with the fact that Gen. Peck has just returned from Norfolk, where he met Gen. Foster, who commands the North Carolina Department, is significant of some movement in which this brigade is to take part.

Thursday December 4. Orders were received this morning to be in readiness to march tomorrow morning at 4 A.M. I embalmed John Chase of the 130th this morning. Poor fellow! Well I remember trying more than a year ago to get him to enlist in the 85th; but maternal love would not consent. I cannot but believe that he could not well have done worse than he did in enlisting in the 130th. I visited the sick of the 130th in hospital when I had finished embalming. My heart bled at the sight. The surgeon in charge does not see the necessity of supporting and stimulating his patients who are stricken with this terrible fever. I found several in the hospital from my own county & with whom I am acquainted.

After dinner, attended to "surgeon's call"—excused an unusual number—some 60, on account of the probability of a long march tomorrow. About 100 men reported on the sick list today. The prospect of marching and fighting is very liable to bring to "call" an unusual number; this makes the surgeon's duties much more disagreeable at the daily clinic. After "call," sent for the Orderlies of the companies, & gave them directions concerning the sick. Accompanied Col. Wellman to Surgeon Hautz (Medical Director) early in the evening & got an approval of my certificate of the "disability" of Capt. Miller, on which his resignation in based.

Captain Hiram C. Miller is a very clever man. In this, consists his chief qualities. As a soldier, he is not efficient, & I am inclined to doubt his courage. With a cheerful, pleasant countenance, well modulated, pleasing voice & finely proportioned physique, he is rather engaging on first acquaintance. Closer contact & intimate relations with him, I apprehend would betray many characteristics less genial than a lesser intimacy could discover. Through the whole campaign, he has not braved the danger of skirmish or battle with his men, and the impression among his men has ripened into a conviction that he would fail them in the hour of danger and peril. He is better out of the service than in, under these circumstances, even though he has no disability, which he has, and sufficient to make it proper and best for him to give his command into more efficient hands.[13]

I then walked to the hospital and prescribed for all the patients there—25. It was 10 P.M. when I got back to camp. Several officers came in & it was late before I could sit down to make my jotting for my journal, so that it will be 12 at night before I can retire. I have been so very busy today that I have had no time for self-improvement today; and I must for a while be content to deny myself this luxury except as the varied experiences of our expedition may supply it.

Friday December 5. Arose between 3:00 & 4:00 o'clock A.M. & packed everything; for though the regiment may return to this camp in 10 or 12 days, as we are told we probably shall, yet all of us may not. It is reported that we go to the confluence of the Blackwater & Chowan [Rivers]. I think we are to embark there, go through Albemarle Sound, perhaps to Charleston. All is kept very quiet, but it seems clear to me that we are to be part of an expedition under General Banks, or to cooperate with it.

I remained some three hours behind the troops, which consists of Wessell's Brigade of six regiments—85th New York, 92nd New York, 96th New York, 85th PA, 101 PA and 103 PA—no artillery accompanied or cavalry, except two companies to act as wagon guard for the return train to Suffolk. Many letters to friends consumed the time until long after daylight. When I mounted, it was 7 A.M. & beginning to rain smartly. Hosp. Steward Goodrich remained to accompany me. A hurried ride of an hour & we came up with the troops about nine miles out on the Summerton Road. [Sommerton is about a mile north of the Virginia–North Carolina state line on today's Highway 13.] Continued to rain all day steadily—it was really one of the most disagreeable marches I have ever made. Between 3 & 4 P.M., we camped about 22 miles from Suffolk & five miles from the Virginia state line in North Carolina. The plantations are more thriving than I have seen in Virginia. The soil, in fact, is better than in the neighborhood of Suffolk. The churches passed this P.M. were of the same schoolhouse pattern so common in the south, but looked more tidy & comfortable. Two in particular had been painted recently, and were neat and modest specimens of country churches.

Our camp was pitched in a dense growth of small pine, which in some measure shielded us from the storm of drizzling rain & mist that continued until late in the evening. Campfires were speedily blazing, & hot coffee served to cheer very much the spirits of our tired & foot-sore soldiers. Before it was fairly dark, I sat down to my own humble but satisfactory dinner. Breakfast before light this morning & only an apple for dinner [the noon meal], made a preparation for supper that left no room for complaint at the fare—the indispensable hot coffee was the only sine qua non. Bread & cheese made up all the deficiencies with an apple, beside, as a dessert. Then a family bed for five was made on the ground; a rubber blanket laid on the ground to shield from the water in the saturated earth, a blanket for a bed & others for a cover and Colonel W., Quartermaster [Lucein] Butts, John and JA Brown and self, turned in a row. Myself the Alpha and the quartermaster the Omega of the row. It is 9 o'clock in the evening, and the quartet of snorers by my side have forgotten all toil and danger; and I only wait to finish this hurried record by the light of my bivouac fire, to join them in the land of forgetfulness.

Saturday December 6. I woke a little after 3 in the morning from a sleep which was broken & disturbed all the night by the complaints of my uncushioned hip bones, and by the ceaseless stir and bustle of the camp, for the soldiers were too thoroughly drenched, & as the night drew on, it was too cold, to allow those who had no shelter tents to sleep. And there were very few who did have them. I had walked half the time yesterday to rest the most weary of the men, by a ride on my horse; this so tired me that it doubtless contributed to my sleeplessness. The sound of the axes in use to replenish the fires & talking, singing & shouting almost entirely denied the benefit of "nature's sweet restorer." Such noise & bustle in camp after the hour for "Taps" is not usually allowed but the condition of the men gave them indulgence.

The clouds were breaking away, and hastening in hurried & heavy masses across the sky. The moon I found in the midst of the "Great Eclipse"; the eclipse had passed off her southern limb when my attention was first drawn to it. This is the only eclipse that will be visible in the United States for several years to come.

Breakfast was disposed of by 5 AM—coffee, bread & butter & cheese constituted our ample repast. At 6, the troops were in line for the march—a few moments after the word was given to "fall in," "take arms!," "shoulder arms!," "right face!," "forward, march!" and the whole column was in motion. The morning was clear, the stars twinkled brightly and the sight as the troops moved off in the shadows of the receding night, the long line of bivouac fires, glimmering in the distance, presented a picture I shall not soon forget. The ground was covered with a hoar frost, and where the water had collected in little pools was covered by a skim of ice.

The march was slow, and no event marred or disturbed the monotony of our progress, if I may except the foolish grimaces or the maniac exhibitions of some of the soldiers who were worse for "Apple Jack." I saw no soldier of the 85th in this condition.

Capt. [Charles] King, of Co. A, yesterday, was in a disgraceful state of intoxication. This habit of the captain is greatly to be regretted. He is a brave man and a thorough disciplinarian, yet is watchful & kind of the interests of his men. He is not communicative, but rather, taciturn—has a very good sense of humor & never stoops from his dignity as an officer, except when he indulges his appetite for drink, or his passion for women. In this last, he has little shame, & can exercise no self-denial when the temptation presents. In intellect, he might have been above the average of men; but he has never cultivated his mind or obtained even the claim to general intelligence, without which, he cannot grace, though he may fill, the position he occupies. In person, he is tall, well-proportioned and looks every inch the soldier.[14]

A little after 10 A.M., we reached Gatesville, three miles from the Chowan. Gatesville is the capital of Gates Co. & has about 300 inhabitants—the county was formed in 1779 & named after Gen. Horatio Gates, of Revolutionary memory who was then in the zenith of his glory. The town seems ancient and dilapidated.[15]

Half an hours halt at this place and on through the town in the direction of New Ferry on the Chowan. A mile beyond the town, we camped for the night. Union sentiment here is much divided. An evidence of this is furnished in the fact that recruits have been supplied to both the Union & Rebel armies from this place. But from the tone and general appearance of the citizens, I have no doubt that sympathy with the Rebel cause largely predominates over Union sentiment. The houses were generally closed & a few inhabitants were to be seen. The whole town has a desolate & deserted appearance.

Our camp was fortunately located in a grove of pines, the fallen leaves of which served a useful purpose in supplying the men with bedding, & the dense growth of trees furnished an admirable screen from the cold North-West wind, which has been blowing with icy coldness all day.

Dinner was served in usual style—sitting on our roll of blankets, the capacious mouth of our haversacks open, and table improvised by laying a newspaper across the lap. Never was dinner more enjoyed than mine beside our cheerily-burning campfire. Supper ditto. The time has passed very socially and pleasant; the indulgence of wit & humor told of spirits good— Col. Wellman is particularly boyish & happy this evening. By 9 o'clock

P.M. the family bed was again spread & in the adopted order, all were soon soundly sleeping but myself—sitting beside the piled-up & blazing logs of my bivouac fire, I indulged in the luxury of waking dreams of the absent Loved Ones far away & noticing thus briefly the incidents of the day.

Sunday December 7. 4 o'clock A.M. All sleep has forsaken my eyes. I have wooed the sleepy God this hour past in vain; I cannot seduce her to my embrace again this morning. Failing in this, I got up and sat beside the fire, still burning before my tent—thoughts of those whom I cherish as my life, far, far, away, now doubtless sleeping sweetly on their soft, warm beds, fill my mind—wonder if they ever dream of him who loves them so well, or in their waking hours, think of the hardships & frustrations he endures. Here & there a soldier, sleepless like myself, replenishes his campfire & seems like a morning specter in the distant glimmering light.

The camp was not stirring as early as usual this morning, as there was no order to move early. It was fully light, therefore, before the soldiers were generally stirring. And breakfast was not served until a much later hour than usual, but in accustomed style & relish. I have never seen the men in better spirits. The morning passed wearily by—there is nothing more tiresome or destructive to the soldier as idleness. Coffee & a hasty lunch served for dinner. Close on our lunch, came the order to move. The horses of the Field & Staff were ordered to be sent to the landing— this looked like moving. The road from the place of our last night's bivouac, to the place of embarkation, is just wide enough for one team, corduroyed and covered with a scanty covering of dirt from the ditch on either side. On either hand is one vast, continuous swamp—unbroken patches of canebrake predominate over every other growth. Here I first saw the cypress tussock, at the root of which the moccasin snake makes his home. Laurel grows here & there on the drier spots of ground. The mistletoe grows vigorously from the limbs of the countless thousands of trees, whose leafless branches bore a striking contrast to the numerous green tufts of the mistletoe.

On reaching the extemporized wharf, I found the 85th PA, 95th NY & 103 PA already embarked. Never have I seen a more dreary and deso- late prospect than presents at the so-called "New Ferry." Not a house, not ten square rods of solid terra firma can the eye rest on—a vast dreary swamp extends on all sides, the turbid waters of the Chowan flow sullenly along between the swampy shores on which alone grow the dense masses of canebrake. The road to the river must have ceased to be traveled years ago—O, ye Champions of the accursed system of slavery—oh, thou land of the "Sunny South," how dearly slavery has cost you.

The 85th New York & the remaining regiments of the Brigade were at the landing by 3 P.M., but did not get embarked until nearly dark. I was hurried off to the "Hussar," the steam transport we were to embark on, about sunset, to attend to a poor fellow whose arm had been crushed in the machinery of the engine the day before.[16]

The last night was very cold for this latitude—water froze an inch thick, and it continued to freeze all day where the direct influence of the sun was not felt. The wind blew as chill from the north as if it had just come fresh from the snow-covered hills of our own North. By the time the troops were embarked, they were almost chilled through. They were made comfortable as possible between decks, and like myself, were tired enough to turn in early.

It is yet all speculation as to our destination, though there are evidences which would point to New Bern, NC, as our next point, but not, I think, our final destination. I have thought our destination was Charleston, SC. Even the officer in command of the vessel has his instructions sealed, which he is not at liberty to open until he reaches the Sound. Our blankets laid upon the cabin floor, made comfortable berths, and gave me promise of sweet sleep, if not of pleasant dreams. Have just been on deck, before committing myself to the arms of Morpheus and find the night is very cold—so cold that the condensed steam falling from the escape pipe has accumulated in a mass of ice that would be a credit to the most hyperborean regions.

[The Sounds of North Carolina are two great bodies of water, stretching nearly one hundred miles north to south and thirty miles east to west. The Sounds are bounded on the east by the Outer Banks, a narrow barrier island, and on the west by the swampy coast of the North Carolina mainland. The northern portion is Albemarle Sound, while Pamlico Sound, three times larger, occupies the southern end. Between the two is Croatan Sound, four miles wide and very shallow. Roanoke Island, site of the still lost Lost Colony, occupies part of Croatan Sound.]

Monday December 8. On going on deck this morning at daylight, all question as to our destination was removed. Roanoke Island was on our left, plainly in sight, the mainland of the North Carolina coast was on the right, and our vessel already among the shoals of "Croatan Sound"—this is the shoal water which connects Albemarle & Pamlico Sounds. The steamer Lancer struck—grounded just ahead of us & we passed her while she was making fruitless efforts to back off. We are now in advance of all the transports except the side wheel steamer Northerner. In a little more than an hour, we were again in deep water, and the waters of Pamlico Sound spread broadly away before, & on either side of us. In passing Roanoke Island, I noticed the wreck of the Rebel steamer "Curlew" lying near the mainland, only her smokestacks visible—she was sunk by the Union fleet a day or two before the attack was made on Roanoke Island.

The whole day was consumed in passing through the Sound—a day of idleness & ennui to me. I have written several letters, but beyond this, the day has been one of unaccustomed leisure for me. If I had anything to read, I could beguile the hours of much weariness—I have never seen the restless tendency of men, & their inclination to be busy at something, better illustrated than I have today in the amusements undertaken by the officers to cheat the dull hours. Some engaged in checkers, some at Euchre; other groups absorbed in "odd and even" & matching dates of coins, with all the zeal & interest of schoolboys. The day has been bright, but chill wind blowing brisk from the Northwest all day and continues—late this evening. Sat up until the cabin floor was covered with snorers, to finish and bring up my humble diary—at 10 P.M., I retire to dream, if I may, of home, sweet, sweet home!

Tuesday December 9. On going on deck this morning, I found we were at the mouth of the Neuse River. The ship was at anchor, waiting for daylight, the channel of the river being so tortuous and shallow that vessels drawing as much water as the Hussar (9 ft.) are very liable to get aground. Soon as it was fairly light, we steamed up the river for New Bern. Then, just past the "blockade" of sunken hulks & ships, about two miles below the city, our vessel grounded strong & fast in the river bed.

No backing off would get us out of the scrape. After two hours of vain effort and it was past 1 P.M., the steam whistle gave one long screech for help—then another, and another—soon a tug was seen coming down, hitched on & tugged and pulled—backed up & pulled again & again, but 'twas no use, fast we were & would remain until lightened. Then came the side wheel steamer "Ocean Wave," which, hauling up beside us, the troops were transferred to her, and then by dint of pulling on the part of the tug & pushing on the part of the Ocean Wave, the gallant, rickety old Hussar got off. Casting off from our late home, we were moored in a few moments beside the wharf, where already our horses were in waiting &

some of the regiments of the brigade already disembarked. The regiment speedily formed on the wharf, marched up to Pollock St.—out on this westward of the town about a mile & a half, and camped in the vicinity of that portion of the brigade already disembarked. The day has been cloudless, but the wind blew chill—returned to the city after getting a hasty dinner.

The city looks antiquated—very little like a Northern city. It is indeed upwards of 100 years old. It derives its name from Bern, the native place of a German baron who settled near this in 1709, having purchased ten thousand acres of land for 100 pounds sterling. The streets of the city are well shaded with the elm, while [*sic*] mulberry and maple, though there are few of these. The town has much more of a business appearance than any other towns I have seen in the South, except Baltimore and Washington. Returned to camp after making a few purchases—found the family bed already made—comfortable and nice.

NOTES: CHAPTER FOUR

1. The Great Dismal Swamp straddles the Virginia–North Carolina border, southwest of Norfolk. Its rich soil and valuable cypress trees attracted many investors and speculators, including George Washington, Thomas Jefferson, Patrick Henry, and Robert E. Lee's father. All lost their money. A web of slave-built canals was dug to drain the swamp. The best known is the Great Dismal Swamp Canal, which runs from the Elizabeth River, at Norfolk, Virginia, to North Carolina's Pasquotank River, and thence into Albemarle Sound. The swamp today is a National Wildlife Refuge.

2. The Nansemond River projects south from the lower reaches of the James River. Suffolk is on the east bank of the Nansemond, about twenty miles southwest of Norfolk.

3. This soldier described in detail the rape and pillage committed upon Southern civilians. The full text is in Appendix E. A copy of the letter is on file at Fredericksburg National Military Park. Courtesy of Robert K. Krick and Joan P. Lowry, Baird's great-granddaughter.

4. Albert Owen Tabor was enrolled in the 85th New York at Granger when he was twenty-eight. In May 1862, he was left sick at Lee's Mills, Virginia, but later rejoined his regiment. His service record shows cause of death as "Remittent gastric fever."

5. Franklin, Virginia, on the west bank of the Blackwater River, is almost twenty-five miles east of Suffolk. The Blackwater and Nottoway Rivers converge to form the Chowan.

6. Not only did Democrat Horatio Seymour get reelected, but his violent denunciation of the Republican-sponsored conscription act lent encouragement to the 1863 New York City draft riots, which killed hundreds.

7. "Stimulants" were usually whiskey or brandy. Remittent fever often meant malaria.

8. John A. Dix was one of America's most remarkable men. He fought in the War of 1812, was adjutant general of New York State, served a term in the U.S. Senate, and was Secretary of the Treasury. Later, he was president of two railroads, a major general of volunteers, our ambassador to France, and finally, governor of New York.

9. Military rockets, designed by Sir William Congreve, were used in the War of 1812 (". . . the rockets' red glare"). An improved British design, the product of William Hale, was introduced in 1840 and saw some action in the Civil War. The Hale-type rockets used by the Union included a six-pounder and a thirteen-pounder. Rockets are mentioned hundreds of times in the *Official Reports*. See *Artillery and Ammunition of the Civil War,* by Warren Ripley (Promontory Press, New York, 1970).

10. One wonders about the effects on the horse of a sixty-mile ride.

11. Alvis D. Gall served with the 13th Indiana until July 1863. In 1864, he was the physician for the two thousand men at the Veterans Reserve Corps camp at Indianapolis, where Col. Allen Rutherford preferred charges against Gall for excusing too many men. Gall retorted that many of these men should not be in army at all. He died of apoplexy in 1867.

12. Thomas J. Thorp began his career with the 130th New York, later designated 19th New York Cavalry and 1st New York Dragoons. He was captured at Trevillian Station, Virginia, and spent the rest of the war in prison. Col. Alfred Gibbs described Thorp as "one of the best officers in the service," noting four wounds and an escape from a Rebel prison camp, foiled only by bloodhounds. In March 1865, Thorp was brevetted brigadier general for "gallant and meritorious service." Nevertheless, our diarist was not impressed with him. (A brevet rank is a semihonorary rank, with no pay or pension increase.)

13. Miller enlisted at Olean in September 1861, at age twenty-seven. He was AWOL two months from the Peninsula in the summer of 1862; his doctor at home certified that Miller was "completely prostrated with typhoid fever, complicated with lumbago and a cutaneous eruption resembling scurvy." Dr. Smith's certificate for Miller diagnosed "General debility secondary to protracted diarrhea and rheumatoid pain in the sacro-iliac articulation."

14. Capt. King was court-martialed for being AWOL in January 1864. He pled guilty but was acquitted on the basis of a surgeon's certificate describing "intermittent fever of four months duration, enlarged spleen and general disability."

15. Twenty-eight years later, Gatesville's population was only 232. In 1998, the population of the entire county was 9,000.

16. For a full description of the *Hussar* (also spelled *Huzzar*), and all subsequent ships, see Appendix C.

CHAPTER FIVE

The Battles of Kinston and Goldsboro

New Bern was about railroads. While the occupation of the town denied one port to the Confederacy, the principal menace of New Bern was its proximity to the major north-south railroad connecting Richmond with the rest of the South and its vital supplies of men and materiel. A glance at the map will show an almost perfectly straight line extending downward from the Confederate capital, through Goldsboro, and on to the vital port of Wilmington. New Bern is less than ninety miles from Goldsboro. An inland thrust would cut this vital artery. Both sides were clearly alert to this possibility, and within hours, Dr. Smith would be caught up in a major Federal attempt to do that very thing—sever the Wilmington and Weldon Railroad where it crosses the Neuse River at Goldsboro.

December 10, Wednesday. It has been a beautiful day—called on Director Snelling—I am much annoyed by the assumptions of Dr. Rush, Surgeon of the 101 PA. He takes upon himself the position of ranking surgeon of the brigade, while he well knows that I am his senior by several months; but I would not for any consideration present my claims, lest it should be supposed that I desire to take upon myself the duties & position of ranking surgeon. I am resolved I will not submit to any direction or exercise of authority toward myself. Returned to camp to dinner & then visited the city again for necessaries for our expected march into the interior.[1]

My comforts for those who may be sick or wounded are very limited—the Medical Director (Dr. Snelling) seems neither kind nor considerate. We have come a long way & are probably going a long way farther, and left Suffolk according to orders, in light marching order. I have consequently not many comforts for myself or necessaries for the sick and

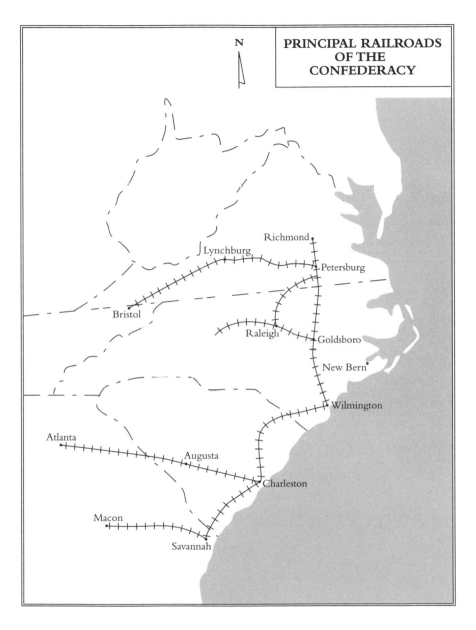

PRINCIPAL RAILROADS
OF THE
CONFEDERACY

wounded. In a measure, I supplied what may be wanted for the sick from my own purse.

On returning to camp, found orders had been received to march tomorrow morning at daylight. Our haversacks were again filled & a scanty mess chest supplied some necessaries. Notwithstanding, the day has been so pleasant, the evening is cold and it is freezing considerably.

Thursday December 11. At 4:00 A.M., reveille sounded—the camps were immediately astir. I slept but little. It was very cold & I found a rubber & one blanket was not sufficient to prevent the cold ground chilling me—I was completely pickled with cold. The lesson learned by my last night's experience is, that the cold ground will conduct off my vital heat in a December night more rapidly than I can manufacture it.

With the first tinge of morning, the troops were in line for the march; but the order to move was not given until the sun was up, & breaking through a dense fog which enveloped us. The scene revealed by the lifting of the fog seemed the creation of some magic wand. Long lines of infantry, artillery & cavalry were suddenly revealed, drawn up in parallel lines while the hundreds of baggage wagons, that were parked in the midst of the regiments whose baggage they contained, gave to the scene a varied and most interesting appearance. As the sun came up, the chill, frosty atmosphere fled as do the dews of a summer morning, and it was a day that would have been no discredit to flowery May. About 1:00 P.M., we had marched about ten miles, and then halted for the midday lunch. After a rest of three-quarters of an hour, the troops resumed the march. Our march has been through a very level country, mostly covered with pine forest.

I have noticed for the first time the evidence on the pine forests of the manufacture of turpentine. The trees have a cup-like cavity cut in them near the root—above this a scar is made, thus [here Dr. Smith drew a crude sketch of several Vs one above the other], extending only through the bark and outer sap. About four inches are thus removed immediately above the cup at each tapping. The trees are many of them thus scarred for 20 feet & upwards. I have noticed several new evergreens today; and large numbers of robins were occasionally to be seen. They arc generally in flocks, as in the north, during the early fall.

The country appears very desolate and poor. The houses—I ought to say the hovels, exhibit the appearance of the most squalid poverty. We reached the place selected for our camp for the night about dark. Camped in a large field which afforded a fine opportunity for defense in case of an attack—we are now 15 miles from New Bern. At this late hour (11:00 P.M.), the baggage has not come up, so we sit shivering over our bivouac fires, for the night has become intensely chill & cold.

Friday December 12. Drumbeat called us up at 4:00 A.M. from a broken & disturbed sleep of two hours. It was 2:00 o'clock before we got baggage to make ourselves halfway comfortable—our breakfast was hurried and scanty. At day-break, the 85th fell into line & moved out toward the main road. A short distance beyond our camp, the enemy had blockaded the road by felling a great number of trees into it.

But the pioneers had been at work during the night and removed them, so that we were not delayed. The New Jersey Ninth had crept through the blockade early last evening & camped a mile in advance of our Brigade. Five miles out from our night camp & 20 from New Bern, our advance encountered several hundred of the enemy. An impetuous charge of the Third NY cavalry scattered them like chaff before the wind. They left several dead & wounded on the ground; & several prisoners were taken. The wounded were yet on the ground when we came up—ghastly victims of the dread carnage of war. Our road today has been for the most part through a country covered with pine forests—mostly second growth.[2,3]

December 13. Our march was late in the evening last night. Camped on a bleak field, with little promise of any superior accommodations in the sleeping line. Managed, however, to get some dry grass together & upon this spread our blankets beneath a cold lowering sky. We were in the immediate vicinity of the enemy, and also understood it. Our pickets were thrown out, and all were soon fast asleep. It could not have been midnight when the report of a musket on the picket line awoke me, another & another quickly succeeded. The report of the third gun had not sounded when almost every man of the thousands that lay stretched on the broad field was on his feet. I think I never put my "traps" so quick before. But word soon came from the front that it was a false alarm, and [we] were soon again stowed snugly away under our blankets.

Our line was formed by daybreak, and the whole column in motion early, as the first rays of the morning sun. About noon, the head of the column halted after passing half a mile beyond the road which turned off to "Deep Creek," then retraced its steps & took the road to Kinston via the last-mentioned road.[4]

At 2:00 P.M., the sound of our advance battery gave notice that we had found the enemy. As the regiments of our Brigade came into line, other batteries opened. The resistance was the bridge across Deep Creek, where the enemy had planted two guns & thrown across the road a small earthwork. But the battery was quickly silenced. The Ninth New Jersey, 85th PA, followed by the 85th NY, took a bypath at the foot of a large swamp, which was the reservoir of the creek; & along which had been

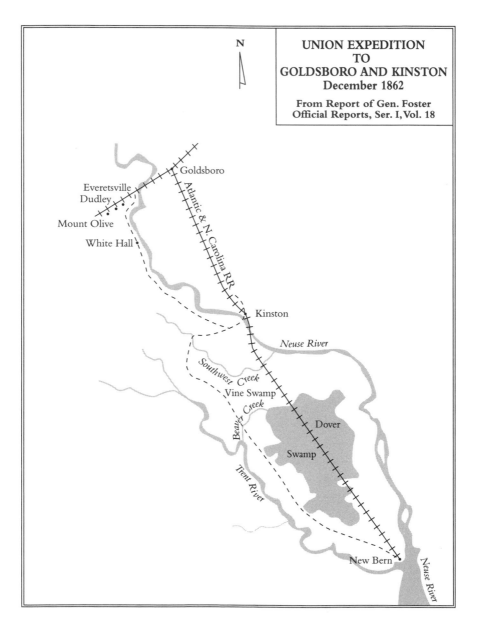

N

**UNION EXPEDITION
TO
GOLDSBORO AND KINSTON
December 1862**

**From Report of Gen. Foster
Official Reports, Ser. I, Vol. 18**

Goldsboro

Everetsville
Dudley

Mount Olive

White Hall

Atlantic & N. Carolina RR

Kinston

Neuse River

Southwest Creek

Vine Swamp

Beaver Creek

Dover

Swamp

Trent River

New Bern

Neuse River

constructed a dyke, which afforded passageway for two men abreast—had this been defended, the difficulty of effecting a crossing would have been much greater. Once through the woods & swamp and the flank of the enemy was turned—they now lost no time, but fled at a double quick, hotly pursued by the Ninth NJ & 85th PA. The two guns of the enemy, planted at the bridge, were taken, several of their dead & wounded left along the road by which they retreated. Several prisoners were also taken.[5]

We camped for the night in a pine forest, three miles from Kinston. The Ninth NJ camped in advance, & the regiments of Wessell's brigade next, in line of battle. Our battery, that led the advance, engaged the enemy again just at sunset. But the gathering darkness put a stop to hostilities for the night. Coffee was hastily made & our supper speedily disposed of, when the order to put out all fires was complied with. No enemy would then have supposed that thousands of armed men, ready at a moments notice to spring forward to a life & death struggle, lay beneath the dark shadows of that wood. The day has been very pleasant & warm—at midday, it was as warm as summertime.[6]

December 14. Sunday morning! The blessed Sabbath dawned bright as ever did a summer day, and was warm and sunny all the day. We were ordered to be under arms at daybreak. It is evident, to my mind, that we must fight a severe battle today. The remark of Colonel Wellman this morning as he emerged from the blanket beside me, to wit—"I do wish we may not fight today"—it was the reflection of my own feelings. We have fought so many battles in the course of the war on the Sabbath.

The sun was just visible above the horizon when the column began to move. Our march was very slow—the advance was evidently moving very cautiously. We had not proceeded more than two miles before the sound of artillery announced the presence of the enemy in our front. On moving up to the front, I found Morrison's battery engaged, supported by the Ninth N Jersey. The artillery had not been long engaged when the rattle of musketry announced the opening of the ball on the part of the infantry. The 103 PA moved up through the dense wood & swamp which separated the Rebel position from the main body of our troops and were soon briskly engaged. The 85th NY was then ordered forward to the support of the NJ Ninth and came into position on their right. The Ninth at this time was being hard pressed. I was standing beside General Wessell's about this time, and saw an officer hurrying from the front, & he exclaimed, "General, the Ninth is falling back, and one of the other regiments near it is firing wildly." Just at this moment, a cheer went up clear & strong from the midst of the wood, where the rattle of musketry was loudest—"There is a charge by the enemy," exclaimed the officer—my heart sank—I feared a moment for the result. But there was no occasion for fear—the cheers came from the gallant Ninth NJ, when the 85th NY took position at their right, & partly in front of them, thus relieving them.

The 92nd NY had been ordered up to the support of the 85th NY & the 96th soon after came in. The battle now raged with great severity.

Two batteries of our artillery were engaged, and the volleys of musketry were incessant along the whole line occupied by the 103 PA, Ninth NJ, 10th Connecticut, 92, 96 & 80th NY regiments. I accompanied the 85th until they reached the position occupied by the enemy, when the wounded from the regiments occupying the center of our line were so numerous as to require all the surgical force in the field.

While standing near the position of the 85th, I was more than usually impressed by the unpleasant advent of a solid shot; probably a ten-pound ball. One of my hospital attendants, Delos Barber, stood near a rail fence and well at the end of one of the lengths; I stood at the other end when the cannon ball referred to crashed through the top rail near its middle. Several of my hospital attendants stood immediately behind the fence & directly in range of the shot; how they managed to fall quick enough to have the ball pass harmlessly over I cannot tell—but they did. As for myself, I do not think I stirred an inch—in fact, it does not seem to me as if I could have done so, so rapidly was the flight of the missile. It was but a few moments, and another cannon ball plunged among us—it does seem a wonder that it should have passed directly through & among our group of eight or ten persons, & not injure anyone. I have heard all kinds of missiles, shells, solid shot, musket balls & Minie bullets hiss & scream around me, but I confess I have never seen the time when I was indifferent to their danger. I am not a coward. I can face danger that any man can, but the battlefield has never been & I believe never will be a place I shall covet. Those who declare that they are indifferent, and care not for the danger of such fields of blood when the lurid flash of the cannon leaps out from the cloudy canopy & the rattle of thousands of muskets whose leaden messengers, like hot irons when plunged in the water, hiss with lightning speed past the ear, is a liar & the truth is not in him. For a brave soldier, give me the man who feels & knows every moment his danger, and yet dare face it.

I was very busily engaged for the remainder of the time until the firing ceased in front in dressing the wounded. In the meantime, the 85th had engaged the flank of the enemy; as it approached, Companies B & F were thrown off on the right as skirmishers—three companies on the left were wheeled to the right. As soon as the skirmishers had uncovered the enemy, & his numbers & position ascertained, the word was given & the main body of the regiment delivered a volley, and pushed forward to the charge, cheering loudly—the left of the enemy broke in confusion & fled toward the bridge across the Neuse. At the same time, the 103 PA forced the enemy from their position in the center, though with heavy loss. It was now a race for the bridge. Had the center of the enemy's position not been so vigorously pressed, until the sweep of the attack upon the rebel left was completely successful, the victory could not have failed to be much more disastrous to the enemy. I have no doubt a thousand more prisoners would have been taken had the attack on the left been earlier & vigorous.

At the bridge, the enemy threw away hundreds of stands of arms, abandoned all their artillery & made effort to burn the bridge. Cotton & pitch were distributed at different places on the bridge and fired—several poor wretches fell, by the bullets of the victorious pursuers, into the fires they had kindled, presenting when I passed the bridge, the most frightful sight that could be presented. They were literally roasted, all their clothes burned off, and the flesh a complete crisp. The flames of the burning bridge were with difficulty distinguished.

The NY 85th [Smith's own regiment] was the second regiment that crossed the bridge—the Ninth N Jersey being the first.

The battle commenced at 9 A.M. and closed about 2 1/2 P.M. Before 3 P.M., we were across the bridge & in possession of Kinston. The enemy burned the cotton & corn stored in town. We passed through the town & camped a mile beyond it on the road to Goldsborough—our camp for the night was in a cornfield. Fires were allowed to make coffee, and then extinguished.[7]

December 15. We were in readiness to move at daybreak. The troops all returned through the town, across the bridge, and took the road to Goldsborough, on the south side of the Neuse. Colonel Ledlie of the artillery was left in charge—at Kinston, to destroy all Confederate property & burn the bridge across the Neuse—this he done effectually. We have marched about ten miles today, and camped about 7 P.M. in a dense second growth of pine woods. The day has been very pleasant & warm and this evening, though the wind blows a gale from the south, it is warm. The signs tell of rain. The sky is clouded, yet here & there stars peep out from behind the swiftly moving clouds.

Tuesday December 16. Fell into line shortly after daylight. Two brigades are in advance, which makes our start somewhat later than usual, as they must stretch out on the road before the head of our own brigade moves. It was about noon when the boom of artillery in the front told us that the enemy were disposed to dispute our further advance. Our batteries were briskly at work at Whitehall when I came up. Several regiments of infantry were engaged with the enemy, who fought from behind works thrown up on the opposite bank of the Neuse, which is here very narrow. The engagement lasted about two hours before the enemy was entirely silenced. Our loss in killed & wounded was about 130. The troops moved on six or eight miles beyond Whitehall and camped for the night. The soft Spring air of yesterday has changed to a chilling wintry wind. The evening is very cold—it will be hard to keep warm lying on the ground and in the open air.[8]

Wednesday December 17. I crawled out of my blankets at 4:00 o'clock. Slept in my clothes, as usual & with the addition of my overcoat & thus managed to keep comfortable.

All was ready for the march at daylight—fell in soon after. About 12 N. the heavy cannonade in the advance told us that the work which was the real object of the expedition had commenced. Our brigade drew up in line of battle on a little plateau overlooking the ground occupied by the batteries. The view from this position was one of the finest I have seen. The troops were drawn up in two lines in the field below, our own brigade forming the third & evidently intended for a reserve. In the first line, two batteries were at work with their supporting regiments stationed at proper intervals. In the second line, batteries and infantry alternated & was much stronger than the first. The batteries were directing their fire upon the bridge of the Wilmington & Goldsborough Railroad, which here crossed the Neuse, under cover of which a force advanced to fire the bridge. The rattle of musketry about 2 P.M. announced the approach of the infantry to the bridge. The bridge was defended by a strong force of the enemy and several pieces of artillery at the opposite end of the bridge. But the fire of our artillery was too severe for them; under it, the NJ 9th and Mass. [illegible] approached, receiving a galling fire from the enemy's sharpshooters on the opposite bank of the river.[9]

It was not yet more than 3 P.M. when a dense black cloud of smoke rose from the bridge—it rapidly increased until the forked tongues of flame could be seen to leap out from the night-like cloud. There could no longer be a doubt—the bridge was on fire. The bridge was a wooden structure, covered, and, being built of the pitch pine of this country, burned with great rapidity. The fire on both sides closed. In 40 minutes after the cloud of smoke was first seen, a great crash was heard, a vast cloud of intensely black smoke rose to the sky, and our mission was accomplished. Cheer upon cheer rang out from the thousands of brave fellows on the field. The railroad for a long distance was destroyed—the rails torn up and ties burned.

And now the head of the column was turned toward New Bern. We had proceeded two miles on our way when orders were received to return. Artillery firing in our rear, in the direction of the bridge, had for the last half hour again become brisk.

We reached the field again at dusk & formed in line of battle. Morrison's battery was belching away in the direction of a bridge above the one destroyed—a road bridge. [This is probably the "county bridge" referred to in Confederate General Evans' report.] Soon after the main body of our force had withdrawn, a considerable force of infantry made its appearance having crossed at the bridge mentioned with the evident intention of making an attack on the rear & capturing the battery left to protect the rear. But Morrison gave the attacking force so warm a welcome with grape & canister that they broke & fled.

We remained on the field but a short time, and resumed our homeward march. Reached the ground we camped on last night about 8 P.M. and camped. I have not been so nearly used up since I left New Bern. I was not well this morning, and ate very little—even coffee did not relish. Ate a few cookies in the saddle at noon, and have finished up the day with a severe sick-headache. I have been chilled all day. The sky has been clouded, and the atmosphere freezing cold. The prospect for a comfortable sleep on the ground in this bleak, open field, is not promising.

Thursday December 18. We rose early this morning. The morning was severely cold—marched ten miles and halted for coffee and lunch—resumed our march and camped at eight in the evening. I have never seen the troops more weary. The whole army is camped in view, and the wagons parked within the lines for protection in case of an attack.

The ground on which the army is camped is rolling, and the scene surpasses anything of the kind I have ever seen. The thousands of campfires, the spectral forms, that seem so much in the distance around these fires, the hundreds of covered army wagons, long lines of artillery & cavalry, picketed in different parts of the vast field, presented a view such as is not often seen, even by an old campaigner. I chose a remote fence corner, in the lee of a wood, which in some measure broke off the chilling wind, and there spread my blankets. Col. Wellman does not share them tonight—he has taken an ambulance. Since the battle of Kinston, his head has troubled him severely. Any unusual excitement or over-fatigue induces symptoms of congestion of the brain or the membranes of it, in the immediate vicinity of the wound that he received at Fair Oaks.

Friday December 19. It has been an unlucky day for me. We resumed the march this morning at an early hour—I rode forward to the scene of the battle of the 14th instant [Kinston]. Reached the building used as a hospital for the wounded, situated near the end of the bridge which had been burned, about 10 A.M. Here, I fed my horse & assisted in dressing the wounds of the wounded & preparing them for being carried by ambulances to the landing four miles below this, to be put aboard a transport for New Bern. At one P.M., I mounted Kit & hurried on to overtake my regiment, which had passed while I was engaged.

I should mention the circumstance of meeting here the Confederate Surgeons Riley & Taylor of South Carolina. The former is Brigade Surgeon on General Evans' staff. They came over from Kinston under a flag of truce to receive the wounded Confederate prisoners, which after being paroled were turned over to them. Three miles from Kinston & on a more direct road to New Bern than that by which we approached it, the troops halted for dinner.[10]

Before the column was in motion again, at the earnest request of Col. Wellman, I started with him to secure a place for him on the transport which was receiving the wounded. We rode to the place of embarkation rapidly, a distance of three to four miles, and after I had seen the Col. safely on board, returned at a rapid pace, overtaking the regiment a short time before it camped for the night.

I had scarcely dismounted when I saw that "Kit" was sick—she hung her head as I had never seen her before. I sent for a farrier from Company B—3rd NY Artillery, & the man done all he could for her, but she grew rapidly worse and died before 11 P.M. the same evening. Poor Kit—dear Kit—good Kit, how much I shall miss you. She was the superior of any horse I ever owned, and the equal of any I have known in the service, where both man & beast are tried to the utmost limits of their endurance. With this tribute to thy worth & excellence, and lying between and near to, two rebels slain in their flight from the battlefield of the 14th instant— I leave thee forever—peace to thy ashes!

Saturday December 20th. Had a good nights rest last night. When we camped, I took possession of an old and dilapidated house, formerly used as negro quarters, so that I had a floor to lie on once more. The march was commenced in better season than usual this morning, so that we made about 15 miles before dinner. It has been the coldest day of the season thus far. We camped tonight ten miles from New Bern. The wagons parked near us, so that I had my tent for a screen from the biting frost—the first time I have enjoyed it in several nights. It is the sharpest & coldest night of the season. In my very heart, I do pity the poor fellows who lie on the frozen ground by the thousands on all sides of me, wrapped in their blankets only—no shelter tents, even. A keen, sharp north wind creeps into every crevice, and through their blankets, chilling them severely. I rode Colonel W's horse part of the distance today, but walked most of it.

Sunday December 21. We were early on the march—all were anxious to reach New Bern, and all were in excellent spirits. We reached the ground on which we camped before leaving New Bern, by 12:00 N.—my tent was soon up; went to the city as soon as I had taken a hasty dinner.

I found Col. Wellman at the Gaston House—not much improved. He must have quiet. Finding a steamer that was to leave for New York in five minutes, I wrote a hurried letter to my dear absent friend, and put it in the care of the clerk of the steamer to be mailed in New York.[11]

Took Colonel W. & called at Col. Ledlie's quarters—I met there my old acquaintance, Dr. Dimon of Auburn, Cayuga County, NY—he is now surgeon of the artillery brigade. Met also Lieut. Davis, Colonel L's Adjut. & a very pleasant gentleman he is; Lt. Prince, Col. Stuart and several others—accepted an invitation & dined with the officers above-named. Enjoyed an excellent dinner with the doctor & friends, and the dinner had the additional luxury of being served in good taste.[12]

The Col. & staff occupy a large and fine house & have all necessary comforts around them. Dr. D. tried to find private quarters for Colonel W. & myself, but did not succeed.

Dr. Theodore Dimon is a surgeon of large experience, a gentleman of cultivation & much excellence of heart. He once had a very good fortune, left him by his father. But I believe now is not possessed of very considerable property. As a physician & surgeon, he has few superiors in military or civil life. I left Colonel W. to be cared for by Dr. D. & returned to camp—found all abed—that bed the ground, of course.

The day has been a beautiful one. Indeed, we have had the most favorable weather that could have been hoped since we first left New Bern. In looking back on this expedition, and its results, I cannot see that it has effected results, or secured an object that would repay the government for the cost of life and treasure. Probably 15,000 troops took part in the expedition & it has cost is about 500 men in killed and wounded.

The great object intended, I imagine, was to effect a diversion, draw troops from the force before Burnside on the Rappahannock [at Fredericksburg], and in case he should be successful in pushing the rebel force under Lee back upon Richmond, prevent any reinforcement or communication from Charleston or any of the Gulf States via the Richmond & Charleston Railroad. News of the failure of Gen. Burnside to carry the Rebel works commanding Fredericksburgh [*sic*] reached us a few miles from New Bern—the pickets informed us. And this is very discouraging. How long, oh, Lord, how long?

NOTES: CHAPTER FIVE

1. Frederick A. Snelling of New York State joined Berdan's Sharpshooters as Assistant Surgeon in 1861 at the age of thirty. In 1862, he applied for the post of Brigade Surgeon and asked for an age waiver, being over the upper age limit. Gen. Abner Doubleday requested Snelling's services, but a political enemy tried to block the appointment, claiming that Snelling was a "homeopathic physician." Snelling stoutly denied this charge, but his record contains an ad for a book he wrote, called *Hull's Jahr—A New Manual of Homeopathic Practice*. In spite of this, Snelling received the desired appointment. In February 1864, he submitted his resignation, because he had been offered "a position [in New York City] of considerable pecuniary value and professional importance." (The private soldiers did not have the luxury of resigning when a business opportunity arose.) Snelling died in 1878.

    David G. Rush of the 101st Pennsylvania enrolled at age twenty-nine in December 1861 at Lancaster, Pennsylvania. In July 1863, he was appointed acting medical director at Plymouth, North Carolina, and that September, surgeon-in-chief at the same place. He held that post when captured by the Confederates in May 1864. After ten days as a prisoner, he was paroled and served the rest of the war at Fort Monroe. For his efficiency at the Battle of Kinston, General Wessells gave him the "highest commendation." Rush received additional commendations in 1862 and 1865. A possible explanation for the tension between Smith and Rush may be found in the following: Although Rush graduated from Philadelphia's Jefferson Medical College before the war, it seems that his father's poverty prevented Rush from obtaining a suitable undergraduate experience. He wrote, "My want of a liberal education which is deeply felt and stings me with humiliation." In June 1866, he was arrested for investing in a plantation near New Bern, but was cleared of wrongdoing. In 1891, he was president of the Chicago Alcohol Works.

2. The two opposing commanders in the coming fight were John G. Foster and Nathan G. Evans. Foster, the Union commander, graduated from West Point in 1846 and was brevetted twice in the Mexican War. A well-trained engineer and an authority on underwater demolition, he emphasized thoughtful use of the terrain in warfare, rather than the bloody frontal assaults so common with other leaders.

   Evans, the Confederate commander, completed West Point two years after Foster and had long experience with cavalry on the frontier. In his Confederate service he held many responsible posts and distinguished himself at First Manassas and Ball's Bluff. However, in the last two years of the war, he was court-martialed twice, once for drunkenness and once for disobeying orders; although he was acquitted, he was considered incompetent by General Beauregard and removed from command. After the war, Evans claimed to have undergone a moral reformation. A much more sympathetic view of Evans may be found in "Shanks . . . Portrait of a General," by Jason H. Silverman, Samuel N. Thomas, Jr., and Beverly D. Evans IV, *North & South,* Vol. 3, No. 3, March 2000, pages 33–45.

3. The pioneers included officers from each regiment, two men from each company, and three hundred African-Americans.

4. General Foster reported that on December 12, upon reaching the Vine Swamp Road, he sent a diversionary force as a feint up the main road to Kinston, while he sent his main column up a road "to the left." *OR,* Ser. I, Vol. 18, Ser. No. 26.

5. Foster's report for December 13 describes the fight at the crossing of Southwest Creek. The Confederates had destroyed the bridge and opposed the crossing with four hundred men and three cannons. Ibid. Dr. Smith's description adds details to the history of the battle.

6. Defending Kinston were Evans's Brigade, the 61st NC, Mallett's Infantry Battalion, and Bunting and Starr's Batteries. Evans estimated the Union forces at twenty thousand men; the actual figure was closer to ten thousand. The Confederates had roughly two thousand men. Ibid.

7. Smith's description of the battle, although limited to what he could see personally, accords well with the commanders' after-action reports.

8. After the war, the name of the town was changed from White Hall to Seven Springs. The present town is on the south bank of the Neuse, two miles downstream from Cliffs of the Neuse State Park.

9. This was the goal of the expedition: cutting the Wilmington and Weldon Railroad. Confederate major general G. W. Smith noted that the masonry pier and abutment remained intact after the fire, and predicted early repair. (Trains were running across the Neuse, on a temporary bridge, within three weeks after the raid.) Smith concluded, "I regret that this grand army of invasion did not remain in the interior long enough for us to get at them." Confederate losses were 71 killed, 268 wounded, and 400 missing or captured.

10. Taylor is almost certainly Benjamin W. Taylor (1834–1905), a graduate of the Medical College of the State of South Carolina, at Charleston. Dr. "Riley" is probably Elbert F. S. Rowley. (Ruth Ann Coski, of the Museum of the Confederacy, points out that "Rowley," pronounced the South Carolina way, would sound like "Riley" to Yankee ears.) Rowley was born at Greenville, South Carolina, in 1844, served with the 2nd South Carolina Cavalry, and obtained an M.D. at the University of Pennsylvania after the war. F. Terry Hambrecht, M.D., personal communication, 1999.

11. The Gaston House, one of New Bern's two leading hotels, opened for business a few years before the war. It was reserved for officers during the Union occupation. The location was the south side of South Front Street, between Craven and Middle Streets.

12. James H. Ledlie commanded the 3rd New York Light Artillery. He was a civil engineer, designing railroads before the war. His military career came to an end at the Battle of the Crater, near Petersburg, where he huddled in a bombproof, far from the action, while his troops were massacred from lack of planning and the absence of ladders. Theodore Dimon was a surgeon with the 19th New York in 1861 and with Ledlie's artillery regiment in 1862. In January 1863, he was appointed surgeon-in-chief of artillery at New Bern. An unusual letter in his file, addressed to Maj. Gen. Henry W. Halleck, salutes Halleck as "Dear Nephew" and requests that Halleck use his influence to obtain a hospital post for Dimon.

CHAPTER SIX

Between Battles

New Bern was a pleasant place when the war was at a distance. The climate was generally mild, the inhabitants tolerated their occupiers with reasonable good grace, and the officers, at least, could find homes in which to stay. Steamers arrived and departed several times a day, carrying supplies and mail. Would the absence of external stress bring tranquility to the often-restless spirit of our diarist?

Monday December 22. Found quarters this P.M. at Mrs. Allen's on Broad Street. Colonel W. shares them with me, and we pay the moderate (?) sum of $8.00 per week—for this house, table, board, a large & pleasant room, lights, fires and two well-furnished beds—these last a luxury to me. I guess I can appreciate these conveniences now.

How surprisingly fine the weather is. The sky is as clear, and the sun shines as warm at midday, as it averages in summer in our northern climate. There has been not even a drop of rain for the past three weeks, or a flake of snow. The birds sing and the roads are dusty, or would be if this sand, which is so characteristic of the South, could float. This pleasant weather is very favorable to our soldiers, and a blessing which they, in their shelterless condition cannot but appreciate.

Wednesday December 24. I got up this morning pretty early, considering how enticing my luxurious bed invited me to remain—went to camp and had surgeon's call—found very few sick & none seriously so. Called at Dr. Dimon's hospital & at Academy Green Hospital at the request of Surgeon Edmeston of the 92nd New York.[1]

I have spent all my leisure in writing letters to go out in steamer, which sails for NY this day at 4:00 P.M. After this was done, time hung heavy on my hands, and commenced Godolphin—by Bulwer. Its reading drew out a discussion between Colonel W. & myself on the influence of woman on the character of man; and in the course of the evening, on the probable presence & influence of Spirit friends.[2]

I find he is earnestly desirous of religious enjoyment—believes he has earnestly sought, but never found it, though he once yielded to friends and joined the church. His feeling of protection in the hour of danger—as in battle, is decided & firm, and attributes it to the ministrations of a sainted father. He mistakes a little—a merciful Heavenly Father may permit the spirit of his father to be a ministering angel.

Thursday December 25. Christmas, once more; and a more bright, warm, sunny day the summertime need not boast. I shall in future know what is meant by the "sunny south"—to wit: a long day of sunshine & gentle breezes, extending from March to January.

I find my hostess & her fair daughter are intensely "secesh" [secessionist]—they set a good table, however, and are courteous and kind. And they have today demonstrated their ability to get a good Christmas Dinner. Turkey & its "fixins"—wined cream, cakes, oranges, raisins, nuts et cetera, made up the dessert.

I strolled about town after dinner—came across the cemetery. It is enclosed by a wall of rocks composed of marine shells & carbonaceous deposits of that class—a fit setting for the remains of our common humanity which are interred within the enclosure. The cemetery shows few evidences of taste; there is no regularity in its arrangement and little display upon the stones and monuments which mark the last resting place of the dead. A flock of robins chirped & twittered merrily in the numerous cedars which add a darksome feeling of solemnity to those who linger amid the grounds of the Cemetery.

For two successive Christmas days, I have been absent from the home circle. The social of this day have been enjoyed without me. Where shall I be another Christmas? He who knows all things only knows; and it is not for me to know the future—why should I wish to; perhaps I should shrink back in dread and alarm at what it would reveal. Yet I fain would look. I often feel that there is an aching void within me—a deep inexpressible longing for some thing or condition which I do not possess. Circumstances have tossed me too & fro—indeed, I have [been a] creature of circumstances, instead of making circumstances minister to some great & noble purpose, which I ought to have had constantly before my mind. I am conscious of powers undeveloped—of a hidden & giant might within, which, properly directed, may enable me to do more good in the little world in which I shall move, than I have ever done. Never was the strength of my mind greater—never was the physical man stronger, and never did my soul so thirsting for a larger liberty, and a more elevated sphere of action than now. I will, then, henceforth, live for some purpose more useful & noble—away, then, for the future, every idle act, word & thought!

Friday December 26. It is more like early fall in our northern climate than mid-winter. I can hardly realize that we have passed the winter solstice and are again approaching the long days of summer. I anxiously wait for the decision—whether we remain here, or return to Suffolk. Scarce an officer or soldier in our brigade but hopes to return. The climate here is most delightful for a winter residence, and the conveniences for comfortable living are better & cheaper than at Suffolk.

But the discipline & administration of this department is bad. Such discipline as I find here, cannot fail to demoralize good soldiers and certainly cannot make good soldiers of raw & inexperienced ones. No event of importance has occurred today—visited the Stanley General Hospital.

Saturday December 27. Mr. Schroeder put his head into my room soon after breakfast, and announced the return of General Foster last evening at 11:00 P.M. (He had been to Washington) with the news that this department (North Carolina) constitutes the 18th Corps de Arme. Well, this decides it—we are to remain in North Carolina, for if this command be raised to the dignity of a Corps, then the force here will be increased, rather than diminished.

Before 10:00 A.M., I learned that a large addition to our force here is to be made from the troops at Suffolk. From the same source comes the news that Colonel Hunt is made a Brigadier General, Colonel Ledlie, Colonel Heckman, Colonel Stevenson & Colonel Potter of North Carolina ditto. These are promotions cheaply earned, it seems to me. But in the case of Colonel Heckman of the Ninth New York, well deserved. He is a most gallant officer.[3]

Before the dinner hour [I] had orders to report to General Wessells, at 1:00 P.M. for the purpose of receiving orders to proceed to Suffolk & arrange & bring the baggage and the rest of the men of the 85th NY Vols. to New Bern. Surgeon Rush of the 101st PA, and the quartermaster of each regiment goes for the same purpose.

At 2:00 P.M., we were on board the steamer & at 2:00 o'clock and ten minutes, were fully underway down the river. Just at dusk, when twilight was deepening into night, we passed into the chocolate-covered waters of Pamlico Sound. A drizzling rain commenced falling shortly after we left New Bern, and has continued until a late hour this evening (10:00 P.M.).

Sunday December 28. All night long, the rain has dripped and poured from the upper deck of the steamer upon the bulwarks of the main deck— lying on the floor of my cabin, my sleep was not sound—outside impressions and the hard planks beneath me, combined to keep me wakeful.

With the earliest dawn, I was on deck—the waves of the Sound were tossing high. The clouds were sweeping swiftly by, here and there broken, & countercurrents of air swiftly moving other clouds in a contrary direction—this proclaimed the spirit of the storm broken. By noon, the clouds had cleared away, and the sun shone bright and clear. The remaining portion of the day was clear but cool.

Sunset found us in the waters of the "North River." A more beautiful sunset I have rarely seen. Soon after twilight had deepened into darkness, we entered the "Carolina Cut" of the "Burnside Canal," then crossed "Currituck" Sound, passed through the "Black Water" into the "Virginia Cut" of the canal and thence into the "Elizabeth River" or the South Branch of it.[4]

Monday December 29. I had a hard bed last night, out on the deck of the little steamer "Emily." The night was cold. A white frost covered the decks—passed three schooners last night in Currituck Sound—they were suspicious-looking craft—doubtless were engaged in smuggling salt or other articles. Reached Norfolk about 8:00 A.M.—took a train for Suffolk before 9:00 A.M. & reached Suffolk at 10:00 A.M.

All the baggage of the regiment had been sent to Norfolk, enroute for New Bern. My accumulated bundle of letters I got at Norfolk, happening to meet there Williams, the regimental P.M. [probably postmaster], just as he was going on board the steamer with the mail, bound for New Bern.

Sat down & enjoyed some of my letters while Louisa prepared me a warm breakfast. And first of all, strange to say, I selected from my letters as the sweetest morsels, the letters of a dearly loved friend—and next in order those of my dear boy. After dinner, visited the camp of the 130th NY Vols.

Occupied quarters for the night with Captain Kinney. Major Scott called in the evening. Visited my hospital late in the evening. Dr. [John M]. Palmer called on me at the quarters of Captain K. early this evening. He is appointed second assistant surgeon of the 85th NY Vols. The doctor is a very clever man, and has considerable ability in the treatment of disease. I apprehend, however, he is too much inclined to be "all things to all men," and cannot keep the counsel & confidence committed to him by friends who trust him. It is late—I have sat up to write letters.[5]

Tuesday December 30. Wrote some letters early this morning—then visited the hospital of the 130 NY Vols.—found Phillips of Belfast, Allegany County, dead—Leach of Pike nearly dead and Spencer of Pike hopelessly sick unless he gets home—Isaac Van Nostrand is here, and yet poorly. Called at Dr. Gall's to get Dr. Palmer relieved from his duty—did not succeed. Orders came at 11:00 A.M. to go aboard the cars for Norfolk—then I sent to the hospital for the convalescent patients.[6]

While I was at the sutler's getting a lunch, the train moved off & left me. After waiting an hour or two, I got off on another train. Reached Norfolk nearly night. The day has been cloudy—rained a little soon after noon—threatened rain all day. The men had arrived safe & were comfortably quartered in a building near the wharf. I put up at the National Hotel. The early part of the evening I spent with Captains Kinney and Cochue. Their room—the latter part of it in writing a long letter to a Dear Absent Friend in Pike. I have invited my excellent young friend Comstock to share my bed with me, and he has long since gone to dreamland—a nice, sweet-looking bed awaits me and I will "fall in."[7]

Wednesday December 31. It is the last day of December—how swiftly it has gone—and the year, too, has gone. One of the most eventful in the history of civilization. To me, it has been one of the hardest, most perilous and diversified with the most extraordinary experiences of my life. It made its record in my intellect, and my physical powers, which will never be effaced. It is scarcely possible that the coming year will bring to me so many & varied and wonderful experiences as the year that is closing. Most of the morning, I spent in my room writing—dined at Barnard's—a most excellent eating saloon. The day has been fine.

January 1st, 1863. A new year has dawned bright as ever did a spring morning. The air is bracingly cool. Made my bed on the cabin floor of the [steamer] "Emily" about 1:00 o'clock this A.M.

I have had as strange an experience last evening as I have ever had in any evening of my life. Accompanied by Lieutenants Fay and Bradley, we called at several homes [houses of prostitution] on Church Street [apparently in Norfolk, Virginia]. I have never before indulged even my curiosity enough to visit such a place as these. The temptation to err, or to wrong the trusting and faithful far away, was never less than while beholding the sensuous and depraved beauties last evening.

My soul loathed, while it beheld the degradation of those frail fair women. Never before have I been able to see so plainly the vast gulf that separates these pariahs from the virtuous & good woman. And never have I appreciated & so loved the good & faithful one that waits to bless me with a virtuous love, as since my experience of last night.

I left the men to be cared for by the surgeons of the other regiments and took passage in the little steamer "Halifax" for New Bern. I was induced to do this because I had no assistant surgeon with the regiment, the regiment having been supplied with medical attendants during my absence by Dr. [W. Q.] Mansfield of the 92nd New York.[8]

The journey today has been pleasant—the air is chill, but the sun shines bright. I have been much interested, today, in a sweet girl of 11 summers who is on her way to Beaufort to visit her father—the child's stepmother accompanies. The similarity of her fortune to that of my own dear boy, has contributed to increase my interest in her. We reached the waters of Albemarle Sound soon after dark, and expect to find our little craft at Roanoke Island in the morning.

Friday, January the 2nd. I reached my boarding house after the colonel had retired, about 9:00 P.M. I found Colonel W. well, as usual; had a pleasant chat with him, notwithstanding the lateness of the hour.

Saturday January 3rd. The camp of the 85th has been moved across the Trent [River]—two miles from the town. It is situated on the highest ground in the vicinity or, indeed, anywhere about the city & a good drill ground surrounds it; but it is bleak and sandy.

Sunday January 4. I have much writing to attend to; for this reason, I have concluded to board in town a few days longer. Mrs. Allen, with whom I board, is an elderly lady with very motherly ways, except when her Rebel proclivities are displayed. She has a very pretty daughter of some 20 years, "Miss Susie," who is very charming, so long as the "secesh" in her is not roused. She has one or two brothers in the service of the Rebellion.

It has been difficult for me to realize that it is the Sabbath. The sound of the "church-going bells" first apprised me that it was a day set apart for rest & the service of the Most High. Ah, how little rest there is for the soldier today; and how little service or devotion to the God who had in mercy preserved me thus far. The sun is so warm, the sun shines so bright, that it is difficult to imagine it is mid-winter.

Saturday January 10. I have taken up my quarters in camp today—the weather is still propitious, and to a life-long sojourner in a northern clime, surprisingly warm and pleasant.

Sunday January 11. Convalescents that I left at Norfolk came into camp this evening. All well, except George Masters, who is very sick with typhoid pneumonia. Colonel Wellman came to camp to stay today. The colonel is very little better—I fear he will not be able to continue in command. Dr. Palmer came with the men, and will hereafter act as second assistant surgeon of this regiment. A letter from Assistant Surgeon JD Lewis received a few days since (he that <u>was</u> assistant surgeon) informing me that he was on duty at the Finley Hospital encourages me to believe that he is reinstated. The health of the regiment is most excellent—never better.

Thursday January 15. This evening, I have received a very surprising letter from Mrs. Daggett [the woman caring for Dr. Smith's children]. She announces the very humiliating fact that an officer or man pretending to be such came to the house the seventh instant, searched it, examined a box I sent home from Washington last summer & took away certain articles under pretense of sending them to the Provost Marshall at Washington. For the benefit of those who may be interested in my future, and who will be affected by my good or bad reputation, I will briefly give a history of the circumstances connected with this matter.[9]

In March 1862, when about to leave Washington for the Peninsula, I gave Assistant Surgeon JD Lewis of this 85th New York directions to pack my effects such as my rubber overcoat, a few pair of sheets, perhaps two or three, and other articles which I cannot now call to mind, in a box, with the effects of Colonel JS Belknap; this direction was given by permission of Colonel Belknap, to have them so packed. Dr. Lewis did so pack them or cause others to do so. I do not remember to have seen the box after the articles began to be packed in it. This box was marked with the name and address of the colonel—to wit, Colonel JS Belknap, Olean, Cataraugus County, New York. I think the box or its contents was not afterwards mentioned by me, or by the doctor, until the events to be mentioned caused it to be.

In the month of June 1862, ill health compelled me to leave my post and go for a respite, Dr. Lewis then being, and having been for near six weeks, absent on detached service. Before leaving, I obtained an order from Colonel Belknap to get the box above referred to from the government storehouse in Washington with the understanding that I should send it to my home in Granger and if convenient [to] send the colonel's effects from their to his residence in Olean, or to let them remain at my home and he would get them at some future convenient opportunity. When I left for the north, it was my intention to have gone direct to Washington and have the box forwarded before I left for home. But feeling too ill when I reached Baltimore, I went directly homeward via Philadelphia and New York . . .

[There follows here an eight hundred-word description of who had possession of the box of articles, at what location, and at what date. The sum of this is that Dr. Smith has been accused of stealing government linens, an act which he stoutly denies. He feels humiliated and embarrassed.]

This is all the credit I get for saving with the greatest care and economy every comfort that comes within my reach, for the use of the sick and wounded of my regiment. The brave men for whom I have labored and provided with a brother's care will be my sure and willing witnesses in all the far-off coming future. But I have never been more disheartened than I am this evening. Not because I am disposed to yield for one moment in the contest with my enemies, but because I am so situated that I cannot defend my interest or my character—I am almost an exile and bondsman here; and I feel as a man may be supposed to, who is bound hand and foot while his enemy's dagger is at his heart. Those who have engaged in this crusade against me are able to employ their leisure amid the comforts of home, and the enjoyments of those social pleasures which I have long been denied.

Saturday January 17. Lieutenant Colonel Wellman is anxious to resign. I have succeeded in persuading him to get a leave of absence for 60 days instead. I gave him a "certificate of disability," and before noon, his leave was granted. He sails tomorrow in the "Dudley Buck."

I part with the colonel with much regret. One of the few inducements to remain in the service is gone with him. He has been, and is, my most trusted & valued friend. We have shared the same quarters on the "tented fields," and the same blankets beside our bivouac fires for months. And there has been many feelings and interests in common. His temperament is sanguine, and this leads him towards the indulgence of almost his only fault—exaggeration. This is by no means greatly indulged, or a serious fault; its tendency is rather to lead him to highly color his fancy pictures, rather than to misrepresent them. His habits are unexceptionable; he neither chews, smokes, drinks or degrades himself with fair but frail women, or takes the name of God in vain. Brave, possessed of the most sterling integrity, a pleasing and manly carriage with fine social powers, he is at one and the same time equally the soldier and the gentleman. His intellectual qualities are not of a high order; indeed, his education was not thorough, though his intelligence is very superior and his business capacity superior.

He returns with the hope of finding some opening for business connections in the lumbering localities of northern Pennsylvania. In which, I am to join him, at an early day this spring or summer coming. But there are many improbabilities of these plans being realized; but if they should be, I can foresee the probability that the whole sphere of my future will be wholly changed. I have dreams based on this event which will, if realized, give to me a new and larger field of action for years to come.

It is possible that Colonel W. may resign before he returns. In this event, Captain Clark will be promoted to his place. Adjutant Aldrich will succeed Captain Clark & my hospital steward, John O. Goodrich, will be strongly urged for the position of adjutant. Major King is a rascal beyond a doubt, and disgraces the position he occupies. Since Assistant Surgeon JD Lewis wrote me from Washington that Major King was the man who reported him to the War Department and recommended his dismissal from service, I have not been able to treat him with the respect due to a man, much less an officer.[10]

January 18. Colonel Wellman left this morning—bade him good-bye at the boat—I have not often parted with a friend whom I shall miss so much. The worry I have felt for the last day or two in relationship to the matter of the box and its contents, before alluded to, contributes much to increase my depression and down-heartedness. The colonel will make the effort to secure me the justice which is my due & this content me until his success is known to me.

Last evening, (the 17th) I received a letter from Miss Lyon under date of the fourth instant. The letter is marked by evidences of an increasing devotion to the pleasures and allurement of social life. It worries me greatly. I fear I shall never be able to realize my hopes of her intellectual improvement & see her possessed of those accomplishments which I have so much desired she should acquire. And if I am disappointed, it would be better if we had never met. For two weeks previous to the date of this last letter, she seems to have been so much absorbed by society as not to find time to write a word to one who has devoted to her every leisure moment, when it could contribute to her pleasure & happiness.

L.H. Kinney, Captain, Company D, was also discharged from service (resigned) the 17th. He is an estimable man and his loss to the regiment as a good man is to be regretted. As a soldier and officer, he has not been efficient or very useful. In June last, he received news of the death of his wife—the captain was then with the regiment at White Oak Swamp. He went home soon after, was appointed a recruiting officer for the 85th & did not return to the regiment until the 12th instant, though he got back to Suffolk some four weeks earlier. Before he reached New Bern, I secured him a very pleasant situation as Captain of the Ambulance Corps in this army corps. He entered on its duties with but half a heart, I imagine, being determined to resign. Family interests, his motherless children et cetera, constituted his great reason, though disability from hemorrhoids was the ostensible one and a difficulty from which I have no doubt he suffered. The wind blows cool today, but it is warm and sunny.

Tuesday January 20. The day has been exceedingly dull. I went to town to get the monthlies [monthly magazines], but found them sold out—got "Les Misérables" and bought "Rob Roy" for Frank. Rained smartly before I reached camp—continues at this hour, 9:00 P.M.[11]

Wednesday January 21st. Captain Kinney left for the north this A.M. I have been very busy today, writing. It rained until late last evening; and the day has been lowering & gloomy throughout, continuing to rain by spells all the evening.

Friday January 23rd. No event of importance has occurred in our quiet camp today, except the advent of Assistant Surgeon J.D. Lewis. He has been restored to the service by order of the President & sent back to his regiment. There is every reason to believe that his dismissal was secured by Major R.V. King, who advised him to the step he took in going to visit his dying sister, and gave him a pass or leave of absence for four days (which he had no right to do, to go beyond the limits of his own authority) and before that pass had expired, reported him [Lewis] to the Department and recommended his dismissal from the service. And I learned today for the first time that this rascal [King] endeavored to convince Dr. L. before he left for Washington in December last, that I was the man who had reported him to the government and secured his dismission.

And from what I can learn [he] was very industrious in trying to make this belief general among the officers of the regiment. Although I was untiring in my efforts to procure the restoration of the doctor, I am led to believe that a few really believed until today that I was the instrument of his discharge. The evidence of the major's effort to screen himself by throwing it on me, exists in a letter written by him to Colonel J.S. Belknap, in which he charges me as the man who procured Dr. Lewis' dismissal. The evidence of his own complicity rests at present on the assertion of Reverend Charles L. Bacon, of Trumansburgh NY, and Reverend Mr. [Frederick] Knapp of the Sanitary Commission, who found the letter of Major King reporting Dr. Lewis as absent without leave and recommending his dismissal therefore.

I cannot better record my own action in this matter than by introducing an extract from a letter from Dr. L. from Washington, under date of January 8/63, [in which] he says: "It was through yours and Colonel Belknap's influence that I was again put on duty. My heart is full of gratitude to <u>you;</u> more than I can express; and may the God of Battles shield and protect you in the hour of peril."

The letter above referred written by Major King to Colonel B. was given by Colonel B. to Dr. Lewis and has been the means of convincing even the few friends of Major King of his duplicity & meanness.

The officers of the 85th, or about 15 or 18 of them, went to the quarters of General Hunt, who is commanding this brigade, in a body this evening, and respectfully requested him, in consideration of the extraordinary course of Major King with Dr. Lewis, that while the regiment should remain under charge of the major, to receive with circumspection any & all matters emanating from him [King], which in any wise affected the interest of any officer of the regiment.

Sunday January 25th. Major King resorts to the expedient of denying the authorship of the communication on file in the Adjutant General's office, which reports Dr. L. & recommends his dismissal—declares it is a "vile forgery;" swears by his Maker that he has written no such letter, et cetera, et cetera, and announced his determination to procure a "leave of absence" and go to Washington & clear the matter up. It would be cleared up by a deeper villainy, I imagine, if this plan should be carried out. To head this off, rather than from any expectation of its being granted, I have caused a petition to be signed by every officer in camp asking that a <u>disinterested</u> officer be sent to Washington to investigate the matter.

I rode to the city today, Dr. P. accompanying. Called at General Foster's headquarters to prevent Major getting his "leave of absence" through, in case it should have passed the offices of the generals of brigade & division before the reception of the petition above mentioned.

The day is fine—the weather is remarkably good. I cannot realize that my friends at home are in the midst of storms of snow; while here there is more sunshine than September there usually supplies. The day has nearly gone, & I have seen nothing to apprise me that it is a day of rest. Oh, I long for the Christianizing, humanizing, influence of the Sabbath, once more. God only knows how hard I try to live daily a life of obedience to His will. A thousand dangers stand along my way to tempt me from the path of right—I am nothing of myself—He only can give me strength through Grace & Grace can give me victory over temptations.[12]

Thursday January 29th. I received a letter today from Miss F.A. Lyon. It gave me the heartache. She speaks of the summer to which I have alluded in my record of the 15th instant, and says; "I cannot believe you guilty, though it looks dark now." These words went straight to my heart! My face burned for hours—not with shame; for I have nothing to be ashamed of; but with indignation not unmingled with grief that one so near my heart should for one moment believe it possible that I could be guilty of a mean act. And she said much more, which told me that she was greatly afflicted at what my enemies were saying. Oh, she little knows how much I had suffered in silence, knowing of this slanderous & wicked attack on me & feeling myself so powerless to resist & defend myself on account of my absence & the distance which separates me from my interests. If she had known, she would not have given my already-aching heart this additional pain. There is doubt in those words of hers—and that consciousness has blistered & burned into my heart. True, she tells me that her love is undiminished—that she will not forsake, though "all others do." And I bless her for those words, even while her doubts make this heart ache so. I cannot answer the letter now—I will convince her that a single doubt has done me wrong, before I can write.[13]

I have prepared and sent to Mr. F. Lyon, this evening, a statement by Dr. J. D. Lewis & myself, that ought to convince even an enemy of my entire innocence of the charges that have been made. But in this is my real humiliation—that I must explain to my friends to save myself from the condemnation which enemies hasten to make. In this hour, when I look over the long list of my friends, I can see one whom I know will not fail me—whose heart would not entertain a moment's doubt—it is my dear, gentle, loving mother. She would have soon wrong her own soul as believe that I could dishonor her. And there is one other whose name shall be unnamed, who has sent me words of cheer and of abiding faith, and sent them through the pen of a husband—God bless thee, my fair friend; the tribute of a grateful heart shall ever be yours.

January 30. High winds & storms have prevailed for a week past—so much as to prevent the expedition which has been preparing here for several weeks past from going to sea. They succeeded in making a start from Beaufort [he doesn't say which one] (where the whole fleet had rendezvoused) yesterday, or the 28th. It was determined that the troops composing this division should be a part of the expedition; to my great regret, at the last moment, it was determined that this division should remain, to defend the city in the case of an attack. Recent information seems to have convinced General Foster that the [enemy] is in great force in the neighborhood of Kinston & Goldsborough, with the design of attacking when the troops that are taken for the expedition shall have sufficiently weakened the force here. I imagine the expedition which has sailed is intended for Wilmington or Charleston.

Three divisions have embarked—namely, [Henry] Naglee's, [Orris] Ferry's & several ironclads [he omits the third division] have been lingering in the harbor of Beaufort, which looks as if the wall were to be battered—they went down to Port Royal [South Carolina] some days before the fleet sailed & will probably wait for the fleet there.

Sunday February 1st. We have passed the two longest months of winter and not one flake of snow. It continues to be very warm during the day & scarcely more than a severe frost at night. Nothing of interest today. Have remained close in my quarters until toward evening. I took a long walk—to the ground on which the battle for the possession of New Bern took place.

Tuesday February 3rd. Snow whitened all the ground this morning and continued to fall until middle forenoon. I have seen few severer storms at the north, while it lasted. Before noon, it cleared away & the sun shone out now & then but the wind is wintry chill.

This P.M. went gunning—poor luck. Saw only a few plover, wakeups, larks and robins—I have tried to kill time today, because it hung heavy on my hands. I am restless as mortal can well be. Surely, there is enough to make me so, conscious as I am, that though I may discharge my duty ever so faithfully—labor ever so hard, suffer ever so much of hardships and danger, I am still pursued by the slanders of enemies, whom I can neither silence or defend myself from, as I am now situated. And my greatest unhappiness is because some of my friends may be induced to believe what enemies report.

Wednesday February 4. Last night was by far the coldest of the winter. This morning seemed like a taste of Allegany winter. The paymaster, Major Staples, paid the regiment today for four months—30 June to 31 of October—so this mythical being is no longer a myth. There is great neglect somewhere—for the troops composing this brigade [have] seven months pay due them this morning.

It has been a sour, chill day, all day—wind blowing sharply from the north. Had the pleasure (?) of riding to the city to call on Major Staples this evening [he] having made a mistake in paying the money to the major committed to my care for transmission in draft to Charles Dautremont, which leaves me $100.00 out of pocket. Found Major Staples very willing to correct any mistake.

Thursday February 5th. The regiment moved into barracks on the banks of the Neuse. The day has been one of the most unpleasant possible—commenced raining around 9:00 A.M. & continued until a late hour this evening without a moment's interruption.

I received a letter from Honorable J.W. Sherman today—he tells me of the wildly false reports that are in circulation in relation to my personal effects sent home in July last from Washington; or rather, the false reports that the box contained much clothing, sheets, blankets, et cetera, belonging to the government. My soul is vexed at this almost beyond endurance. I try to possess my soul very patiently, being hopeful of justice from the public in the course of time.[14]

Yet, it may never be accorded me. I feign would have my friends believe me incapable of a mean act. But I am conscious that there are some who have almost feared that I have done this thing—one in particular in whom I should have believed would have been the last, except my loving mother, to have had one doubt.

Friday February 6. 12:00 noon. It rained all night—was sour & gloomy this morning, though not cold. At 9:00 A.M., the rain began to fall again & it continues to patter on my canvas cover with as much industry & zeal as when it began.

My quarters are anything but pleasant—the ground is soaked full of water beneath my feet; fir boards for floor are out of the question—I am pretty well soaked myself, and the rude apology extemporized for a fireplace yesterday amid the rain, smokes as if determined as if to be revenged for its bad looks. On the whole, I am quite out of sorts & decidedly blue. I think I am looking away in imagination to the snow-covered hills of my native & loved north, too much to be happy today. Oh, for a brief glimpse of the reality—for a loving embrace of my dear little ones.

11:00 o'clock P.M. Have indulged this evening for the first time in my life in playing billiards. Never knew the game before, and this is the chief reason of my playing. But I confess not a little of the temptation arose from the desire to kill time. It passes very slowly; I count each day and thank God it is one of the number less—one of the less before what?—perhaps, gladness. My life has thus far been one of more sorrow and clouds than pleasure and sunshine. Oh, for a mansion of peace, far removed from the strife & vexations of this weary world, where I can enjoy the society of my loved ones. The day has been lowering during the P.M., but the rain ceased shortly after noon.[15]

Saturday February 7th. The sunny south is itself again today. It has been bright and spring-like. Last evening, at a late hour, I heard bad news from the squadron blockading Charleston Harbor—two Rebel rams came out of the harbor and captured one of the [Union] vessels & sank another. My hopes almost die within me when I see that our heavy task of subduing these Rebels is not yet half done, and disasters very frequently attend our efforts. The only mitigation to this news is news of the capture of the PRINCESS ROYAL, a vessel that attempted to run the blockade into Charleston. She had on board an Englishman with a new projectile, which he was to penetrate our ironclads with. I imagine his experiment will be some time delayed.[16]

Sunday February 8th. Cloudy but warm today. Attended church at the Presbyterian Church. One of the regimental chaplains preached an excellent sermon—text: "Cast thy burden on the Lord."

Visited the Foster and Stanley General Hospitals to call on the three or four sick of the 85th in them. In the P.M., visited Lieutenant [Theodor] Rynder of the 58th PA, who is sick at the Gaston House. Finished Victor Hugo's "Les Miserables" this evening—it is an elaborately finished romance, in which the vices & passions of French society are portrayed

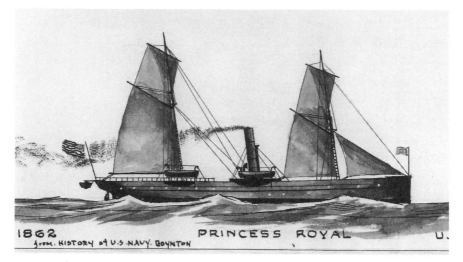

Dr. Smith was quite excited by the capture of the British blockade runner Princess Royal, *noting accurately in his diary that she carried advanced technology dangerous to the Union cause.* U.S. NAVAL HISTORICAL CENTER PHOTOGRAPH NH63848

with a masterly vigor, & at times with the most intensely exciting interest. This is the last work of this kind that I shall indulge in for a long time.[17]

The hours & the days hang like burdens on me, but they must be improved. With this evening, I shall commence a more thorough & industrious course of study—every one of my leisure moments must be improved in study & improvement of my mind. God willing, I have much yet to accomplish before I go to my rest. At least, I can prepare myself for a greater usefulness and new fields of conquest in the vast universe of knowledge until the message comes that shall bid me rest from my toil.

I have never been so much determined & almost, it seems to me, inspired, to struggle forward and upward as for a few days past. I owe this in some degree to the enemies who, taking advantage of my absence, have for a few months pursued & persecuted me with slanders, in hopes of destroying my social & political standing. A kind Providence has given me the imperious will that will not allow me to stop anything short of a complete triumph over every obstacle which enemies can put in my way. Yet, let me here confess that my courage & determination which tonight so strengthens my soul, arises from my dependence on the strong arm of my Heavenly Father. In every step, I humbly ask that He will preserve me from the evil with which I am surrounded, & be my guide & guardian. Oh, how earnestly I have prayed that He would direct all my ways—He only knows how anxious I am to be subject to His will. My heart is very often full of sorrow—so heavy that it would seem a relief to lay it down in the quiet of the grave; but then I soon realize that these troubles and trials bring me a sense of my dependence upon God, and so I try to realize that they are for my good.

Monday February 9. I have seen few days in May more warm and springlike than this has been. After the morning duties were discharged, "Surgeon's call" and "Inspection of camp," I walked down to the city—just for exercise. I find study scarcely suffices to keep my spirit light and buoyant. I cannot shake off this heaviness which oppresses me so much. I try to do so, but it comes back

Capt. William Starkweather paid Dr. Smith a social call during one of Dr. Smith's periodic depressions. Smith found the friendly conversation wearisome. U.S. ARMY MILITARY HISTORY INSTITUTE

again so quickly—I am not able to conceal from myself, by an unflinching will and determined courage to press on, despite the obstacles that enemies put in my way, that their efforts have the effect in such an hour as this of making me weary of life. I do not think I would care to live, but for my dear children. If these are spared me, I shall have something to love, & be loved, though all the rest of the world is cold, & turns from me.

Lieutenant Starkweather has kept me engaged by his call all the early part of evening & Adjutant Aldrich helped me finish it—they didn't know how much I desired the luxury of being alone this evening or they would have made shorter calls. It is 11:00 P.M. & I must retire.[18]

Received this [a clipping from the January 27, 1863 Angelica (New York) *Reporter,* which was not attached to the original manuscript of the diary] and I fear it is not judicious or timely. I would have preferred that nothing had been said until an authoritative denial could be published, supported by proofs which would not admit the chance for argument on the part of my enemies.

Wednesday February 11. The weather continues to be very fine. It is more sunny and pleasant & has been for the whole winter thus far, than it averages in May at the North. I was surprised today by the advent of Dr. R. Stebbens of Friendship. He comes ostensibly to visit a nephew sick in the Foster General Hospital. He is a most excellent man, and I bid him a most hearty welcome to my humble fare.[19]

I was greatly disappointed in not receiving letters from Colonel Wellman. News of him shows that he has been in Washington, & was in Albany the 5th instant—this being the case, I can't see why he has not written me.

A long letter also from Miss F.A. Lyon—she writes words of cheer, hope & love—but those bitter words in her last letter ring in my ear—"I cannot believe you guilty, but it looks dark now," oh, why should <u>she</u> believe for a moment, or doubt for a moment, my innocence. I cannot—I will not allow a single attention on my own part to make her blush. I will be silent until I am vindicated, & she learns that she has wronged me by her doubts.

Medical Inspector Mussey, and Acting Medical Inspector M. visited the 85th today—I think they found everything very satisfactory.[20]

Thursday February 12. It has been a fine day. The daily routine of duties—called this A.M. at Acting Medical Director's to see him and Dr. Mussey—then visited Foster General Hospital. Called on Mr. Albright, Clerk of Commissary of Division to get an arrangement about my hospital fund, which accumulated during the months of January & February 1862.

Saturday February 14. Saint Valentine Day. Finished the February number of the Atlantic Monthly this eve and enclosed it to Miss L. with a budding flower, the [illegible] gathered from the parent shrub yesterday, growing in the open air. Also sent the January number today to the same person. The February number of the Atlantic [magazine] is not equal to the January number.

Second Assistant [Surgeon] Palmer is detailed to take charge of the sick of the 24th Mass. & Dr. Lewis received orders today to attend to the sick of the 132nd NY Volunteers. This leaves me to manage alone again. Attended "Surgeon's Call," inspected barracks & then went down to the Court Martial now in session, as witness in the case of Carman Underhill, who is arraigned for "disobedience of orders" & "cowardice on the field of battle." I was not called on—couldn't have done him any good if I had been—poor fellow, he is naturally a coward; and is also so greatly inclined to think that his fellow soldiers have no sympathy with him when he is deserving of it.[21]

Sunday February 15. The weather is warm and summer-like—the frogs croak & "peepers" peep, with all the spirit they do in warm, murky evenings in the midsummer at the North.

Surgeon's call & inspection of quarters being over about noon, mounted and rode over to the battlefield about four miles below the city, where Burnside engaged & drove the Rebels who were posted for the defense of New Bern. Drs. Palmer & Stebbens accompanied. The position occupied by the Rebels was a very strong one. To have approached it in front would have cost General Burnside many more men, & very probably resulted in his repulse. But he stormed their line of rifle pits on their right, near the railroad. At this point, the enemy had no artillery, and the rifle pits were taken with a dash. The right of the enemy being taken, or turned, the center & left were quickly seen falling back toward New Bern. The sun has been clouded & rain occasionally fell in spurts, driven by furious wind from the South.

February 16. The wind blew a hurricane last night—thought my canvas house would surely fly away. This morning, the wind was sobered down. The clouds fly across the sky in hurried masses, and the wind is somewhat chill.

At this 3:00 P.M. I have finished all the routine duties of camp, besides having prepared several sets of discharge papers for soldiers of the regiment, and walked down to the Foster General Hospital & to the post office. Now that I sit down with nothing to do, this heavy heart of mine aches with an increased pain. I cannot well understand why my soul is being so tried. If it is to teach me dependence on the God Who Rules and Reigns—if it is to draw me nearer to Him, and teach me patience and resignation to the inflictions of enemies—if this heart-heaviness is given me in mercy, & not in judgment, or to separate me from the fond desire to live, & prepare my soul and desires for the land where sorrows do not come; then, Amen! "Let thy will be done." Help me, oh thou Omnipotent Judge, to sink into thy will. If it please thee that I should walk in a fiery furnace, let shining ones walk at my side.

Tuesday February 17th. The day has been cloudy & a drizzling rain has been falling a part of the day—the copy of an uncomfortable fall day at the north.

Purchased a gold watch today—one of the Waltham make, No. 10395. Eighteen carat fine, also chain & key, for which I paid $125.00. This may be an unwise expenditure—but it is the first liberal indulgement in so expensive an article of my life, if it is so. I have long been destitute of a good watch, waiting until circumstances should enable me to get a superior article. It is not vanity or desire for vain show that induced me to make this purchase.

I have felt today as if the clouds in <u>my</u> sky were not as heavy & dark as they have long seemed—it seems as if there were more light coming from source; I cannot see where from. It is a sort of feeling like that with which the traveler looks for, & sees, or imagines he sees, the first faint light of the morning's dawn. This may be merely imaginary—only the result of exhilaration of spirits. I have tried sometimes to believe there was a mysterious communion of the soul with the future; which, escaping our grosser senses, diffused almost imperceptibly & dimly its knowledge and influence upon our spirits.[22]

The chaplain of the 103rd PA Volunteers passed me hurriedly this P.M., saying, "Farewell, Doctor." He has resigned & goes home in the Steamer which leaves NB today. A twinge of pain seized my heart at the thought of his pleasure, & my own inability to enjoy the same.[23]

Wednesday February 18th. Clouds and rain has ruled the day. In the afternoon, the clouds hung less heavy and threatening. The rains ceased, and the atmosphere was as warm as after an April shower. After "Surgeon's Call," & visiting patients in quarters, I sat down to my reading—am now reading up the publications of the Sanitary Commission, and "Erickson's Surgery." I design to make a rapid service of professional studies, and at an early day go to Washington & avail myself of the Order of the Secretary of War, sent me last June, to be examined by the Examining Board of USA Surgeons. The order was sent me while the law creating Brigade Surgeons was in force. Shortly after the reception of this, the office of Brigade Surgeon was abolished by act of Congress, & the inducement to go before the Board was consequently gone.

In the determination to avail myself of this now, I am governed by two reasons or purposes. First, the desire to get to Washington to present my vouchers & settle with the Government, so that all my deal with it may be covered by a receipt in full, expressing the entire satisfaction of the government. Second, to secure a position in charge of a hospital, which can only be done through a successful examination. I have been in the field nearly 18 months and am weary of the routine of camp life—am sorry to say that my evening has been mis-spent—in playing whist with Dr. Stebbens, Dr. Palmer & "John." It is not often that I thus waste my time & opportunities. Tried to make amend by reading until a late hour—half past 11:00 P.M., but these eyes have so nearly rebelled at the tax I have put on them for a while that I have found it a punishment instead of pleasure.

Thursday February 19. Clouds prevailed in the forenoon & sunshine in the afternoon. The sunset gives promise of a fine day tomorrow. I visited Colonel Classon [*sic*] of the 132nd NY this A.M.—case: simple abscess of the leg. Then called on Major Staples & at the Foster General Hospital. In the afternoon, employed myself earnestly with my book. Early in the evening, feeling the need of

Col. Peter J. Claasen of the 132nd New York Infantry had a large abscess on his leg, which Dr. Smith drained. Claasen's saucy reply to a nagging inspector general resulted in a dismissal from the army, but Maj. Gen. Ben Butler returned Claasen to duty.

MASSACHUSETTS COMMANDERY, MILITARY ORDER OF THE LOYAL LEGION AND THE U.S. ARMY MILITARY HISTORY INSTITUTE

exercise, I walked down to the office of the Sanitary Commission and called on Dr. Page—the doctor is very much of a gentleman. He has lived several years in this state & practiced medicine here.[24]

Another day is well nigh gone, and I thank God that there is one less between me & <u>change</u>—that it be for the better, I anxiously hope and if it be for worse, if my heart must be more sad and heavy than it is now, then the sooner it comes the quicker I shall have passed through the fiery furnace. There is consolation in the thought that there is rest for the weary heart by and by—where pain and sorrow <u>cannot</u> come—in the quiet grave!

Friday February 20th. High winds most of the day, which tossed the dry sand hither & yon, & filled the eyes of all who were out. But the temperature was very springlike, & the sun shone bright. The evening is glorious; the stars never displayed themselves more beautifully, the moon hangs its crescent love [*sic*] in the western sky, and early in the evening, Venus blazed amid the departing glories of the setting sun. I have star-gazed a long time this evening—my soul was in a fit mood to commune with anything beyond this world. There are a few, a very few, in this world whom I should be so happy to commune with, that I could cheerfully give some of my days, for the privilege of a few brief hours with them.

The usual routine of "Surgeon's Call" & inspection of camp over, I sat down to my books. Dr. Frick, Surgeon of the 103 PA, called on me this P.M.—walked into the city at twilight for exercise. No news from the north for some days past. The impression seems to prevail that the troops sent from here have disembarked at Port Royal—delay and disaster seems to wait on all our movements by sea and land.[25]

Sunday February 22nd. Washington's birthday! As stormy and dark as the times are, at 12:00 N., the cannon began its thunder in every direction around the city—a salute of 100 guns was being fired in honor of the illustrious dead. The rain fell in torrents & the wind blew a gale, giving to the scene a closer imitation of a terrible thunderstorm than I have ever witnessed. Immediately after the salute was fired, the bells in the city rang a merry peal.

Pity, thought I, & most appropriate, that they do not now toll a dirge because there is no Washington to save what a Washington secured.

This evening, called at Mrs. Allen's—took tea and by request of Miss S. Allen, accompanied her to visit a sick relative—Mrs. Mathews—found her friend very ill—there is scarcely a possibility of her recovery; tuberculosis is doing its work. Have employed the day for the most part in visiting & reading Erickson.

I should have noticed the fact that yesterday Mr. McAllister, engineer of the steam transport "Hussar," called on me—I found that he had lost a pair of high-top boots from his stateroom, which was occupied by Major R.V. King during the passage of the regiment from the Chowan River to this city. His loss & all the circumstances convince me that the statement of Lieutenant Butts is entirely correct, to wit—that Major King stole the boots. He is a disgrace to the regiment.

Monday February 23rd. A chill, raw day—freezes considerably this evening. I have been engaged on a report of the sanitary condition of the regiment—or, rather, a history of the regiment & its movements since its organization, with particular reference to its sanitary condition. I hear this evening that the "Dudley Buck" has arrived with the mail from New York.[26]

Wednesday February 25th. It has been a delightful day, bright and sunny & the atmosphere bracing, yet & not too cool. This is the most cheerful winter of my life—it would be the most happy, if my loved ones were with me, and all my anxieties and care for the home I have loved so well were at rest.

There has been a grand review today—a review of the 18th Corps. I finished my report of the regiment, referred to in my record of the 23rd, it covers some 30 [handwritten] pages. Called on Mrs. Mathews this P.M. I am faithless of being able to do her any considerable good—to soothe & make her comfortable is the best I can do. The Destroyer has set his mark on her.

Thursday February 26. It has rained by spells all day. It is very warm, seems like summer after a shower. I have received two letters from Colonel Wellman today—one dated February the 1st, and the other February the 12th, from his home. The first letter was mailed at Philadelphia and its delay may have been of great injury to me. It contained an order, or permission, from the Secretary of War, to be examined by the Board of Army Surgeons in session at Washington, and for an endorsement by the President of the Board naming February 23rd as the day for the examination. This is past, but I must try and go; the colonel thinks it vitally necessary that I should see Colonel Baker in relation to that "box."[27]

It does seem to me that I have suffered enough on account of that affair—I will be patient, oh, Lord! Only let it be manifest to my mind that this affliction is sent in mercy—for my good, and not in judgment—not in punishment of my many shortcomings in duty to Thee.

[I] presented my application for leave of absence at General Foster's headquarters—am promised that I can probably have it in time to go to New York by the "Dudley Buck," which sails the 28th at 12:00 N. On the strength of this, I have engaged a berth on that steamer. Yet I have fears that I shall not be allowed to go.

Friday, February 27th. The day has been warm but cloudy—I have succeeded in getting a leave of absence for 20 days to go to Washington, and I go tomorrow. I have spent most of the evening in preparation. 9:00 P.M. returned, but too weary to study. The sound of singers in an adjoining tent, singing "Oft in the Stilly Night" strikes my ear, & imagination carries me back to days when I first heard it—long years ago, when the hopes of early youth bid high, and all the future was colored with rainbow hues. Oh, God, give me to feel those happy hours again, sanctified and made real, by the calm, sweet joys that flow from <u>Thee</u>.

Saturday 28th February. The day has been cloudy & threatening storm. Called on Dr. Mussey at 9:00 A.M. by appointment. Received a very flattering letter of introduction to Dr. M. Clymer, President of the Board of Examining Surgeons, also letters to his wife.[28]

Was mustered at 10:00 A.M. Went aboard the "Dudley Buck" at about 1:00 P.M. Fifteen minutes past 1:00, the steamer left her dock & stood down the river. About 10:00 P.M., we shall be in sight of Cape Hatteras Light & the steamer will anchor for the night, owing to the difficulty of getting over the "swash" at night.[29]

NOTES: CHAPTER SIX

1. Alexander Edmeston served with the 92nd New York nearly the entire war, with the exception of a brief stay on the hospital ship *Thomas Collyer* in July 1863 and a month off duty with severe conjunctivitis in September 1864. When his regiment was mustered out, he stayed on as "acting staff surgeon."

2. Edward George Bulwer-Lytton (1803–73) was well-known for his popular historical novels, particularly *The Last Days of Pompeii*. His was the high Victorian style, with nearly endless, convoluted sentences. The opening phrase, "It was a dark and stormy night," may be his most enduring legacy.

3. Lewis C. Hunt ranked near the bottom of his West Point class of 1847. He commanded the American detachment during the "Pig Wars" in Washington's San Juan Islands, near Seattle. On the Goldsboro expedition, he commanded a brigade of Wessell's division. Hunt died in 1886 at Fort Union, New Mexico. Colonel Ledlie has been described earlier.

   Charles A. Heckman was a sergeant in the Mexican War and a train conductor between the wars. In his 1863–65 service with Army of the James, both Edward Ord and Ulysses S. Grant were dissatisfied with Heckman's performance, and he was passed over for promotion. Thomas G. Stevenson recruited the 24th Massachusetts and was its colonel. General Foster recommended Stevenson for promotion to brigadier. He was killed by a Confederate sharpshooter at Richmond in 1864.

Edward E. Potter served ten months as a commissary in Foster's brigade at Roanoke Island, and in May 1862 was authorized to recruit the 1st (Union) North Carolina Infantry and be its colonel. The recruits were white citizens unsympathetic to the Confederacy. Potter's later assignments were administrative. He never married and died alone in a boardinghouse in 1889.

4. This same route is now the Virginia–North Carolina portion of the Intracoastal Waterway.

5. Levi H. Kinney commanded Company D of the 85th New York. He was age forty-two when mustered in 1861. By June 1862, he was too sick for field service and was sent to Allegany County on recruiting duty, where he spent $400 ($16,000 in today's money) out of his own pocket. In January 1863, he returned to New Bern, where he served briefly in charge of the ambulance corps and was allowed to resign on the basis of severe hemorrhoids.

John M. Palmer, Assistant Surgeon of the 85th New York, enrolled September 1862 at age twenty-eight. He reported for duty at New Bern in January 1863, and in April went on General Spinola's expedition to Washington, North Carolina. In July 1864 he was sick with "remittent fever"; in December 1864, he was sued by the estate of Capt. John B. Loomis, 11th Pennsylvania Cavalry, to whom he owed $175. Palmer died in 1871 at Corry, New York.

6. The records do not reveal the source of Smith's antipathy toward Palmer.

7. Comstock's identity is unknown.

8. The exact location and sequence of his journeys on the steamers *Emily* and *Halifax* are unclear. Sylvanus Fay of the 85th New York joined in December 1861. A year later, he asked for leave, stating that his partner in the *Olean Times,* back home, was cheating him. Dr. Hand also certified that Fay was sick. Pvt. Alfred Bradley was promoted to lieutenant in January 1863. In April 1864, Dr. Palmer recommended a medical discharge for Bradley, citing hemorrhoids, prostate disease, and a "morbid mental condition which will soon compromise his life." Before this recommendation could be acted upon, Bradley was captured by the Confederates and spent the rest of the war as a prisoner.

The theme of strongly moralistic men and their fascination with prostitutes is an ancient one in life and literature. Dr. Samuel Johnson, the great writer so assiduously studied by James Boswell in the 1700s,

was one such. So was the brilliant Victorian politician William Glad-
stone. Fiction, too, abounds with examples. Somerset Maugham's *Rain*
gave us Sadie Thompson and her would-be savior; their duet of piety
and lust has been the basis for at least three movies. Sinclair Lewis's *Elmer
Gantry* was another parson torn by a mixture of attraction and repulsion
when confronted with temptation in the form of a female body.

9. Here commences a convoluted story of Smith's alleged theft of some
Army bedsheets, a tale concocted by his political enemies at home.

10. Reuben V. King began his Army career with the 85th New York as
captain of Company A. He was promoted to major in February 1862.
He was in trouble seven months later, while in charge of the post at
Newport News. The commanding general visited, and King could not
be found. The general wrote, "Where is King?" King's excuse was that
he had gone to visit a wounded brother at Norfolk. Dr. Smith's suspicions are, in this case, apparently well founded. It would seem that the
"brother" was, in fact, a scarlet woman. In April 1863, when King was
forced to resign, Col. Belknap wrote, "I am well-satisfied that the good
of the service will be promoted . . . by accepting this resignation."

11. *Les Misérables* is the work of the great Victor Hugo (1802–85), whose
other contributions include *The Hunchback of Notre Dame* and the
memorable thought, "Without France, the world would be alone." *Rob
Roy* is another of Sir Walter Scott's Scottish border romances.

12. Smith's "temptations" remain unnamed.

13. Here, I confess to a sense of concern for Dr. Smith. His need for reas-
surance seems boundless. He seems to manifest a deficiency in Christian charity, being so quick to assume mischief on the part of his
beloved, when the record, at least, gives no evidence of such.

14. Judson W. Sherman (1808–81), a native of Angelica, was a Republican
congressman from 1859 to 1861 and served briefly as a commissary of
subsistence.

15. Our diarist clearly equates billiards with sin; judging by the diaries and
letters of other Civil War participants, Dr. Smith is certainly at the con-
servative end of the spectrum.

16. On January 31, 1863, the Confederate iron-clad rams *Chicora* and *Palmetto State* emerged from Charleston Harbor and attacked the Union
blockaders. The *Keystone State* and the *Mercedita* were both badly damaged, and dozens of Union sailors were burned to death by escaping

steam. On January 29, 1863, the British blockade runner *Princess Royal* was captured off Charleston by the USS *Unadilla*. Dr. Smith was well informed about the importance of the seizure. The ship carried two complete steam engines of "great power," a number of Whitworth rifled guns, and a skilled mechanic, John Chalender, who was sent to teach the Confederates how to manufacture "steel-pointed projectiles." *Navy Official Records,* Ser. I, Vol. 13, page 551.

17. Novels, like billiards, are also seen to be a sign of moral weakness.

18. William L. Starkweather enlisted as a private in September 1861 at age twenty-eight. He was soon promoted to sergeant and by January 1862 was a second lieutenant. He endured a year as a prisoner of war after his capture at Plymouth and was discharged as a captain in April 1865.

19. A George B. Stebbens reported for duty at Lincoln General Hospital in Washington, D.C., in June 1864. Beyond this, the medical officer files have no other Stebbens information. R. Stebbens was probably a civilian.

20. W. II. Mussey was described to the surgeon general of the army as "head and shoulders above anybody else in Cincinnati in the Surgical Department." As a lieutenant colonel and medical inspector, he served in the Department of North Carolina from June 1862 to June 1863.

    Even today, tetanus is usually fatal. Mussey published cure of a case, using Extract of Cannabis Indica, 5 grains every ten minutes for four hours, with a gradual reduction of the dose over the next few days. After an equestrian accident, he requested a brief medical leave, giving the cause of his injuries as "a sudden transition from my saddle to the ground." Although his head was injured, he recovered rapidly, report-ing, "A thick skull is not to be despised!"

21. Jessee Carman Underhill, Company E, 85th NY, enlisted at Angelica at age twenty-seven. He was five feet, 8 inches tall, with blue eyes and black hair. He was sick in the hospital most of the time from Decem-ber 1861 to September 1862. He was returned to duty just before the expedition to Goldsboro. On his return to New Bern, he was charged with cowardice, having hidden during the actions at Kinston, White Hall, and Goldsboro. (National Archives, RG153, NN133.) He was convicted and sentenced to have half his head shaved, be paraded through the streets of New Bern with a placard on his chest reading, "Coward," and then spend the rest of his enlistment in a military prison

with a twenty-four-pound iron ball attached to his left ankle. General Foster remitted the sentence and returned him to duty. Underhill was captured and spent the rest of the war in the prison at Andersonville.

22. In religious terminology, scrupulosity is a minor sin, a condition of unwarranted and excessive doubting, which inhibits a full spiritual life. In psychiatric terminology, scrupulosity may be an obsessional disorder, while the wide and unexplained mood swings might fit the definition of cyclothymia.

23. This was mostly likely Chaplain F. M. Bird.

24. Col. Peter J. Claasen did not suffer fools gladly. He was court-martialed in September 1864 for insubordination. An acting assistant inspector general had demanded a detailed inventory of "surplus ordnance." Claasen replied that he was using the ordnance that he had, that he had no "surplus," and closed by suggesting that inspectors seemed to have more leisure time than colonels. Claasen was convicted and sentenced to be dismissed in disgrace. Maj. Gen. Ben Butler returned Claasen to duty. (National Archives, RG153, NN3174). The major was James W. Staples of the 78th New York. Dr. Page has not been identified.

25. Abraham Frick, age twenty-six, joined the 101st Pennsylvania as assistant surgeon, at Lancaster in September 1861. Fourteen months later, he was promoted to surgeon and transferred to the 103rd Pennsylvania at New Bern. His records show him contracting malaria during the Peninsular Campaign. In 1891, he was still in the Army, serving in several forts in New Mexico.

26. Appendix E contains Smith's report.

27. This would be Lafayette C. Baker, head of the Federal secret service and one of the most controversial characters in the war. Before the war, he had been a vigilante in San Francisco. During the war, he ferreted out crooked contractors and shut down dozens of saloons, gambling joints, and whorehouses in Washington, D.C.

28. In Smith's medical officer file is a note by Dr. Clymer, in which he quotes Dr. Mussey's letter, which describes Smith as "the very best medical officer in that Army Corps."

29. A swash is a channel of water through or behind a sand bank. This swash is probably Hatteras Inlet, one of the few channels through the barrier islands of North Carolina's famous Outer Banks.

CHAPTER SEVEN

The Doctor Is Examined

There is a tradition that surgeons in the era of the Civil War were ignorant drunks, whose only skill was that of sawing off arms and legs, callously tossing the amputated limbs out the nearest window. While it is true that they knew nothing of bacteria, antibiotics, and x-rays—knowledge held by no one on the entire earth in 1861—there was a considerable body of medical knowledge, in particular, anatomy as it related to surgery. In addition, there was widespread understanding of at least six other crucial medical verities: the use of quinine in the prevention and treatment of malaria; vaccination as a preventive of smallpox; fresh fruits and vegetables as preventives of scurvy; opium and its derivatives in the treatment of pain and diarrhea; mercury in the treatment of syphilis; and the use of general anesthetics, such as chloroform, for relieving the pain of surgery. As Dr. Smith traveled north toward this examination, his mind was, once again, troubled by worry about his fiancée's faithfulness and his children's health. In addition, he had tired of Army life and feared not only the disgrace of failing the examination, but also the unwelcome prospect of further service if he passed the examination. His fretting and ruminations were further compounded by the allegations that he had stolen some government bedsheets; though this may seem trivial to us today, in Dr. Smith's mind the accusations loomed large, indeed. A pall of black smoke from the *Dudley Buck*'s smokestack hung over the craft, and an invisible dark cloud hung over the doctor's brooding mind. As the steamer's paddles drove the craft north into Pamlico Sound, his protracted conversation with his diary continued.

Sunday March the 1st. Weighed anchor soon after daylight. The morning looks dark and weather threatens. An hour's run & we were over the "swash" & abreast of the fort. Here, we discharged some cargo—

provisions for the soldiers, and stood out for sea. The sea was running high among the breakers, but we passed the inlet in safety—the channel among the breakers is scarcely more than 80 feet wide. Before noon, the weather cleared up, and the ocean became much more calm and smooth. At sunset, the long line of coast was dimly seen to the west—the broad bosom of the Atlantic spread away on all other sides. I have been miserably "sea sick" all the morning—threw my breakfast to Old Neptune & went without dinner or supper.

Monday March the 2nd. 2:00 P.M. It is one of the most beautiful days imaginable. The sun came up as bright & glorious as it ever rose from the bosom of Old Ocean. The sea is like molten lead—no ripples on its broad face, but a vast undulating movement, as if beneath the glassy surface it was full of elastic life. Have been studying most of the day; but it is not agreeable work—the unsteady movement of the steamer gives me a feeling of nausea. By 5:00 P.M., we shall be off the Delaware Capes, & from thence it is but 100 miles to New York—speed on, good steamer—I am anxious to know the worst.

Tuesday March 3rd. When I went on deck this morning, we were opposite the Highlands and Sandy Hook just ahead. The morning was a gloomy one—a cold, drizzling rain falling and the fog so thick that the shore could be but indistinctly seen. At 9:00 A.M., we were inside The Narrows, feeling our way up the bay, through a fog so dense that a ship could not been seen three lengths ahead. Fifteen minutes before 10:00 A.M., the steamer was going into dock; feeling that a few moments might be very material to me, I climbed over the taffrail, valise in hand, & hurried to the deck of an adjacent ship & made for the Philadelphia Depot— got there just in time to hear the word, "All aboard," and get aboard. Reached Philadelphia 15 minutes before 2:00 P.M. Left at 2:00 P.M. for Baltimore—reached Baltimore at 7:00 P.M.—left for Washington half past 7:00 P.M. and reached Washington one-half past 9:00 P.M. Left my valise at the Ebbett House & went to 465 - 12th Street, to find my friend Richardson—never was more glad to find or meet a friend than I was to grasp his warm hand. Stayed with him—talked until 12:00 M.

Wednesday March the 4th. A chill, cold day today—but not cold enough to freeze. The streets are a sea of mud, as of old—when I was here a year ago.

Called on Colonel Baker, Provost Marshal, this A.M. with my friend Richardson. He [Baker] referred the consideration of the matter to Judge

L.C. Turner, Judge Advocate. Called on him & found him very kind and courteous. Made out a report, which entirely exonerates me from blame or complicity in any fraud & gave an order to have the articles taken from my premises restored—I am happier tonight than I have been for a long time. I thank the good God for his kindness in thus rescuing me from the hands of my enemies.[1]

I find the Hon. Augustus Frank is the man who informed the government that I had appropriated 160 hospital sheets & 40 woolen blankets—this he has done to please some of my personal & political enemies in Allegany & gratify his own malice which he has entertained against me since I led the Congressional delegates from Allegany out of the convention at Warsaw in 1858—the convention which first nominated him for congress. In the P.M., called at Dr. Lindsay's to call on Mrs. Mussey, wife of Medical Inspector General Mussey, by Dr. M's request. Reported at Surgeon General's Office this P.M. and left Dr. Mussey's report there. I have arranged to take my meals at the Ebbett House and room with Major Richardson. Early in the evening, called on Major Williams P.N. USA at his house. He has an interesting family—spent an hour with them very pleasantly. Later in the evening, was at Willard's Hotel & met a number of old friends—Durfee of Hornellsville, Thompson of Corning and Cutler of Almond, et cetera, et cetera.[2]

Thursday March the 5th. Have been busy all day, but it don't seem to have amounted to much. Called again at Major A. Williams—came back to my room and tried to study, but my eyes are very heavy tonight, for I have not slept much for a few nights past. My friend is out tonight to hear Mason Jones lecture on Dean Swift—and my eyes are so heavy that I can't set up for him. I ought to have noticed that I called today at the military commission in behalf of Lieutenant Spencer Martin [85th New York], who is dismissed [from] the service for not reporting to the Provost Marshal as ordered by the Officer of the Patrol Guard when he was in Washington the 19th of January last, and on his way to the 85th. He is quite sick—but for this, I do not pity him. He has got a venereal disease and is only reaping the reward due all who degrade themselves.[3]

Friday March 6th. The day has been quite pleasant. Called on Dr. Clymer, President of Army Medical Board about 12:00 N. Was kindly received and referred to Surgeon General to get a new order for examination. Called on Assistant Surgeon General and got the order, which was then referred to Dr. Clymer to name the day for my examination. He kindly named the 23rd day of March, so that I could have time to visit my home and friends before it expired—that is, my leave of absence.

Met several friends and acquaintances in the afternoon. My good friend, Major Richardson, went to the Provost Marshal's Office and gave order from the War Department for the delivery of my box. The marshal gave an order for the box to be delivered and sent to Adams Express. Yesterday, I gave my friend Richardson $10.00 to be put at interest until his daughter is 18 years of age—then to purchase with it such an article as shall be a memorial to her of her father's grateful friend.

Saturday March 7. A drizzling rainy day all day today. My friend Richardson went to the Provost Marshal's Office and found the "box" had been sent to the express office. He then wrote the following on a card, which was put on the box, the direction, or my address being on the box in point—"Erroneously taken by a government agent on January 7th and returned by order of the War Department to Surgeon Smith." Then came the consideration of getting a leave of absence to go to Allegany to visit my friends in the interval between this date and the one appointed for my examination. Accompanied by my faithful friend, I went to the War Department and was referred to General [of the Army] Halleck— here, I had no difficulty and the desired permission was quickly granted.

I purchased a ring today for a friend. At fifteen minutes to 6:00 o'clock P.M., I started for the cars to go home. I got to the depot five minutes too late—I suppose it is for the best, but I need faith to "see it." In company with Major R., I went to see Laura Keene play—she acts well—is not a first-class actress, but is far above the average.[4]

Sunday March 8th. The blessed Sabbath, once more. I took breakfast at the Ebbett House, and then sat down in the pleasant rooms of my friend to the enjoyment of a quiet lunch, as I have not realized for a long time. What a luxury it is—and how much I enjoy it. Major R. wants me to attend church with him, but I prefer this quiet. Not that I feel averse to the influence of God's ordinances or the precepts which are inculcated through and from the pulpit—oh, no! For my heart is full of gratitude to Him Who Rules and Reigns in Heaven and Earth.

Early in the P.M., I took dinner with Mr. Shaffer and lady, by invitation. Shortly after dinner, Mr. Cornelius Underwood came in and nearly spoiled the P.M. I should have been glad to see him, at many another time, when I was not so much in love with the quiet of the day. Mr. Underwood was journal clerk when I was in the Assembly and now is a clerk in the State Department. He is a good clerk, well posted in the political movements of the day, and a cordial friend of William Seward and Theodore Pomeroy, but is impulsive and talks too much to be a politician on his own account—in other words, without someone of superior mind and talent for a balance wheel. His home is in Auburn. I bade my excellent friend good-bye at 5:00 P.M., and took a "bus" to the Harrisburg Depot at once—here, I found I could get no further than Harrisburg until 2:30 tomorrow.[5]

Monday March 9th. 1:00 o'clock P.M. I took a berth on the sleeping car from Baltimore and had a refreshing night's rest. This sleeping car was the most elegant I have ever seen. I arrived in Harrisburg about 1:00 A.M., but kept my berth until 6:00 A.M.

I took breakfast at the "City Hotel" & then strolled out into the city—I visited the capitol and public grounds. I was disappointed in the capitol—it is not a fair representative or worthy the great state of which it is the capital. [Harrisburg is the capital of Pennsylvania.] The same may be said of the appointments in and about the Senate Chamber and House of Representatives. I made some purchases and returned to my hotel and sat down to my books, for I have brought with me Erickson, Towne, Willson, et cetera. The far-off hills, crowned with their snowy mantle, are looking grandly magnificent. I feel almost like falling down and worshiping these, the hills of my native north. At 2:00 P.M., I was on the way home. I reached Elmira at 11:00 and a half at night.

10th of March. I was aboard the express train from New York and speeding homeward—the train was three hours late. I reached Belvedere about noon, and found my friend Wellman waiting for me—with him, I rode to Angelica—I had a hasty consultation with my friend in relation to the publication of my vindication in the next issue of the Reporter. I procured a horse and cutter of Mr. Fisk and left for home about 3:00 P.M. I called at Cox's and took tea—I was much gratified to find William Franklin, Esq., and lady, George Fisk and lady, and other friends there. I reached home about 5:00 P.M. My dear babe knew me well, and seemed greatly delighted. My heart is full of gratitude that I am permitted, once more, to clasp this dear memorial of the lost loved one.

March 11th, Wednesday. Soon after breakfast, I drove over to father's. Here, I met my beloved Frank—his surprise at the meeting was great, and he wept freely, tears of joy—my prayers are answered, that I might be permitted to embrace my dear boys once more. All were well—father, mother and brother.

After dinner, I rode over to Pike and on my way, called on Dr. Mabie. On my reaching Mr. Lyon's, found my dear friend Miss L. out—her mother went for her, but she returned unsuspecting the advent of one who waited with impatient love to clasp her to his heart. Her surprise was a most interesting incident—and the greeting she gave me was the most conclusive declaration that her love was unchanged. I could not remember the doubting words she wrote me in the hour of my trial, when so much affection was evinced in this reunion. My visit has been a most happy one—the happiest ever enjoyed by her side.

March 12 Thursday. I left for home about 10:00 A.M. Miss L. accompanied me to her uncle's L_____ V_____ [probably Luron Van Nostrand]. I enjoyed the ride greatly. Arrangements for our future chiefly engaged our minds. In the P.M., I went to Angelica to meet friends, by agreement. Frank followed me with Cub and a rig to take me back to Granger. I left Angelica for home between 9:00 and 10:00 P.M. It is arranged that Colonel Wellman will meet me on the train at Belvedere next Wednesday—11:40 A.M., and we will go on to Washington together. I reached home near 12:00 at night.

Friday March 13. Many friends called on me. Late in the P.M., I went over to Luron Van Nostrand, where Sarah and my babe had preceded me early in the P.M. I took tea and had a pleasant visit—I returned home about 8:00 P.M.—Frank kept house in the absence.

Saturday March 14. As per agreement, I went after Miss Lyon—she spent the day with us—a pleasant visit it has been, but would have been more so if I had less callers and visitors. In the evening, Luron and his daughter, Emma, came and took tea—spent the evening, and Miss Lyon returned with them.

Sunday March 15. Many friends have visited me today. After dinner (and I had the company of my excellent and worthy friend, William Van Nostrand at dinner), I rode down the street and called on his family, also on Mr. Isaac Van Nostrand & the widow of Aaron Von Nostrand—poor widow. My heart deeply sympathizes with her; she has lost her eldest child since the death of her husband. The remaining part of the P.M. and evening, I spent at Luron's—had a pleasant visit, for the society of my much-loved friend contributed to it. I returned home before 9:00 P.M.

March 16. No business of importance today. About 11:00 A.M., I rode over to L.V.'s and took Miss L. to Pike. The day is fine, but a chill wind blows from the northwest. The sleighing has been very fine since I returned, and I have enjoyed and improved it much. The ride of today was particularly pleasant—it is the last to be enjoyed by her side for a long time, and the consciousness has contributed not a little to heighten the pleasure. I reached Pike about 4:00 P.M.

This evening has afforded me one of the most delightful visits of my life—no dimming veil has been between my heart and hers. The interviews with this dear friend since my return have greatly contributed to increase my affection for her—I cannot but believe the same is true on her part. She has fixed the day, by my own solicitation, for the important event to transpire, if God so wills that it shall be—that event, our marriage—the day of 16 July next! Will it be the happy day my heart and hers now hope and expect it will? Many dangers lie between me and it. I know full well—a long distance will separate us before that time, but I humbly trust, and pray, and believe, that the kind Providence that has preserved me through so many dangers will restore me to her, that I may comfort and bless her with the great love which her own affection has created in my heart for her.

Tuesday March 17th. At 9:00 A.M., I bade my dear friend good-bye, with emotions of pain such as I trust I will never need experience again, should we meet once more. That last sweet kiss, and love embrace, will be the point of interest on which through the long, weary days of absence I shall look with feelings of mingled pain and pleasure. Let my heart be hopeful and staid on thee, my Heavenly Father, through the long days and months of separation. I drove to father's from Pike, took a hasty dinner with them, and bade them once more good-bye. I made some calls on my way home, and reached there at 3:00 P.M. The remainder of the time I am determined to spend with my beloved children. Many friends called in the course of the P.M. and evening.

Wednesday March 18. At 7:00 A.M., I clasped my dear babe to my heart in a last embrace—oh, no! Let me not say a "last embrace"—I have faith that this sweet little one will be spared to welcome me again. But he is unwell, and my heart has forebodings, and will have, until I hear that he is quite well.

Frank went with me to Belvedere to take my horse and cutter back. I called on friends in Angelica—Sherman, Horton, Judge Grover, et cetera. Judge G. is a man whom I greatly respect and is my cordial friend, but he is a timid and suspicious one. I am surprised to find Sherman so earnestly faithful.

The article in today's Reporter I have inserted as a part of the records and evidence of the circumstances I have before spoken of. I bade my dear Frank good-bye a few moments before 12:00 N. The choking voice and quivering lips of the dear boy told me of a struggle that tore his young heart. God grant that I may not be very long separated from you, my beloved son. About 4:00 P.M., I reached Elmira—I called at the Daguerrean artist's and had Adaline's photograph finished, for Colonel Wellman to take on his return.

March 19. I reached Washington about 10:00 A.M. this morning. I went to the Ebbett House and breakfasted, and Colonel Wellman took a room there—then I called on Major Richardson. After 12:00 N., Major R. and Colonel W. and myself went to the office of Dr. Clymer. The colonel proposes to be discharged on a certificate of disability. I commenced boarding this P.M. at Major R.'s place of boarding. I sat down to my books this evening. I shall go before the Army Medical Examining Board next Monday. I have no ambition to pass the board, as the rank conferred will only be that of Assistant Surgeon in the regular army, and more than this, I am tired of the service. Nevertheless, I am "booked for the ride." It was the only plan by which I could get away from New Bern or attend to my personal interests here and at home.

Friday March 20. The colonel did not get his papers through today— I have been very busy with my books—I have been all alone today. Major R. has left me in possession of his rooms, and I do so much enjoy it. I wrote several letters—to friends, prominent among them my dear friend, Miss L.

Saturday March 21. I have been alone during the day. Major R. is still away. Colonel W. was my bedfellow last night. His papers are through and he is free. I wish I was as honorably relieved of my duties as Surgeon of the 85th NY Volunteers.

Sunday March 22. I have spent all day in my room, or with Colonel Wellman. I stayed with him last night. The colonel leaves tomorrow.

Monday March 23. I was engaged four hours at the rooms of the Army Board. The examination today was on hygiene and anatomy. The examination is conducted very strict and close. The queries are often more abstract than practical. Colonel Wellman left at 6:00 P.M. for home—I am very homesick. I have very little ambition to return to North Carolina. There has been enough in the last four months to make me sick of the service.

Tuesday March 24. The examination today was on Practice. The queries were imminently practical. I am much fatigued in mind and body. To sit four hours in succession and tax the mind, as this examination does, is very severe. I spent all my leisure with my books.

Wednesday March 25. The examination today has been on surgery—four hours steady thinking and writing. The subjects today were as follows—fractures of the acromion and their [differential] diagnosis from luxations of the humerus into the axilla. The second subject was luxations of the inferior maxillary and their treatment. The third subject was hydrocoele, its varieties and treatments. Fourthly, what are the conditions on which secondary hemorrhages after amputation depend, and what are the best modes of treating them.

I never undertook a voluntary task in my life that seems so much like a penance as does this examination. If I should pass, I shall feel much as the fellow did when he raffled for and won an elephant—I shall not know what to do with it. I cannot accept the post of Assistant Surgeon in the regular service. The short time I intend to remain in service, I prefer the position and emoluments of Surgeon of the 85th New York Volunteers. Indeed, I had rather fail than vacate my position for one less in rank, though it may be an honorable one.

Thursday March 26. One more day is nearly gone, and there is one more less between me and those I love. Another day and the fourth day of this tedious examination is past. The examination today was on literature and science. The subjects on which written responses were today demanded were as follows—First, "What were the causes of the last war with Great Britain; in what year did it commence; in what year was the treaty of peace signed, and who were the commissioners who signed the treaty?" Second subject was, "What were the conditions on which the House of Hanover succeeded to the English throne. Name those who have ascended the throne belonging to that house." Third, "Describe one species in each class of the vertebrated animals." Fourth, "Name the different roots and grains from which alcoholic beverages are distilled in different parts of the world."

Tomorrow, the examination will be oral—indeed, a portion of the candidates were so examined today. I have some mind to withdraw from the examination tomorrow. I have no ambition in it, or desire to receive the appointment which a successful examination will give. I have looked with much expectation and disappointment for letters from home and from Miss L. I am worried lest they are some of the sick. I am sure my dear friend in Pike would not have neglected to write me if she was well.

Friday March 27th. A bright spring day has gone and, oh, how wearily and tardily it has passed. I am exceedingly disheartened tonight. I had determined to withdraw from the examination this morning, but it was not allowed. So, I am booked for a through passage. But it is an awful bore, feeling as I do—with the little ambition I have to enjoy any profit or honor that may come of it under the most flattering results. But I am so disappointed in not hearing from my dear friend in Pike or from home. I cannot imagine what the difficulty is—perhaps she is sick, but in that case, her friends would surely write. It cannot be she is neglectful so soon of my often-repeated injunction—oh, no, I will not believe it—but I sometimes fear she is not energetic and efficient enough. Perhaps I should not feel and say this, if I was not feeling so disappointed this evening that I have had no word from her—for this reason, it may be and probably is an error in my judgment. It would relieve my heart very much to get one word of love from her, or an assurance from home that all was well there.

Saturday March 28th. 6:00 o'clock P.M. A dark, rainy and gloomy day is closing. It is not more dark and gloomy without, than it is in my heart. No word yet from my loved ones—it is indeed a misfortune to have loved ones, when the soul is so harrowed by anxiety for them. I have been engaged today at the Douglass Hospital, operating—and have not made a satisfactory job of it—at least, to myself. Well, this examination is closed. Now I would I were in New Bern—or if I could honorably return home, I would hail the opportunity with pleasure. If I am permitted to resign at once, after my return to the regiment, I am resolved to do so.

Sunday March 29. 11:00 o'clock A.M. A bright, sunny day without invites me to a more cheerful and hopeful feeling, but my poor heart is very heavy and anxious. I was in some degree an hour since, by receiving a letter from Frank and Mrs. D., saying that my dear babe had quite recovered and they were all well. I hear nothing from Miss L. I cannot understand her silence, unless it be on account of illness. My thoughts this morning turn to Him who sees the sparrow's fall. Oh, for grace to stay my heart on Him. I desire no earthly goods so much as I do a free and full communion with the throne of Divine Grace. It is my most anxious desire to gather round me once more my little family and lead them by my own examples in the path of duty, and up to Him whose "ways are the ways of pleasantness and whose paths are paths of peace." God, my

Heavenly Father! Wilt thou not guide me in peace and safety to the realization of that desire. I think I could die in comparative satisfaction if I could feel that I had laid broad and deep the influences of a Christian example in the hearts of the loved ones of my home circle—or those who will compose it when I shall make it complete.

9:00 o'clock P.M. I believe I am getting nervous—my sleep is disturbed, and for sleeping or waking, I feel morbidly restless. I was reading today until I grew so weary that I lay down and fell asleep. I could not have slept long, when I was awakened by the consciousness of my name being whispered near me. The impression was so distinct, that I can scarcely believe I was mistaken. No one was in the room—I have, indeed, been alone all day. This was about 3:00 o'clock P.M. It could have been only the effect of my feverish imagination—anxiety and apprehension have so afflicted and agitated my mind that it is no wonder it should be disturbed by strange fancies. I have finished reading the April number of the Atlantic Monthly this evening, and enclosed it to Miss L. Her silence fills me with apprehension. But I will try and rest in the trust and faith that all is well.[6]

Monday March 30. The morning is bright and cloudless and a bracing atmosphere comes from the ice fields of the north. One year ago today, I embarked with my regiment at Alexandria for Fort Monroe. I did not leave the wharf, however, until early the morning of the 31st. An eventful year has passed since then. I would not pass through another such year, with all its cares, anxieties, responsibilities, hardships and perils to health and life for a mine of gold. If we must meet certain preordained circumstances and events—if a foreknowledge of them could not avert then, our ignorance of the future is a great blessing.

Now, our imagination colors the future with more or less of gladness and hope; and this hopefulness constitutes the greatest measure of our happiness in this life. With the certainty of disappointment, of failure, of grief and sorrow before us, life would be a burden. The few pleasures that dawn on us here are sufficient to attach us full enough to the world; it is therefore, doubtless His good pleasure, that sorrows and disappointments should come to take our hearts from earth and attach them to the fadeless glories of an immortal life. Oh, that my own afflictions and sorrows may have this good result—let Thy afflictions and sorrows come in mercy, Lord, and not in judgment, and with Thy grace, I will humbly kiss the rod that smites me.

9:00 o'clock P.M. I called at the Surgeon General's Office at 2:00 P.M. and was informed that I had passed the Board and their report was favorable. I am surprised at this. I expected nothing less than an adverse report; I have been so much disconcerted and confused in my examination for the last two days. My heart has been ill at ease; indeed, I have been very anxious and unhappy. My heart is very grateful to the Great Giver of All Good for bringing me safely through this examination. If I had failed, it would have reflected upon me and my future very discreditably. And worse than that—it would have disgraced me, as failure, or rejection by the Board would have involved loss of commission, according to a decision of the Surgeon General. Three other candidates with whom I commenced the examination all failed. I have been writing letters to home friends this evening—I shall leave for New Bern tomorrow via Fort Monroe and Norfolk. I had a social chat with Mr. Schaffer's family this evening.

Tuesday March 31st. It is the last day of March, and one of the sourest and most disagreeable of the month. There has about two inches of snow fallen during the night, and now and then a spurt of snow continues to fall.

Norfolk April 1st. I left Washington yesterday at 3:00 P.M. amid a storm of snow and rain. Soon after 8:00 A.M. yesterday, it began to snow steadily and several inches must have fallen. But it melted rapidly. In leaving the hospital quarters of my friend Major Richardson, I must pause to pay him the tribute of my heartfelt thanks for many, very many attentions and kindnesses shown me. This is one of the noblest and warmest hearts it has ever been my fortune to meet. The milk of human kindness is ever gushing out of his generous soul. God bless thee, and thine, my good and noble-hearted friend. I reached Baltimore about 1:00 P.M. and went to the Maultby House and took dinner. At 5:00 P.M., I was aboard the steamer for Fort Monroe.

Just one year ago, the day I left Washington, I left Alexandria with the 85th New York Volunteers for the same destination. Fort Monroe. It had snowed considerably on the 29th of March 1862, so that the conditions of things underfoot and overhead was much the same as last year, when I embarked for the Peninsula. Most earnestly do I hope the ensuing campaign will not bring to me such an accumulation of hardships and privations as the last.

I reached the fortress this morning at 7:00 A.M. I went immediately to the Office of the Adjutant General of this department (Seventh Army Corps, General Dix commanding), to find the original letter of Major R.V. King, reporting the absence of Dr. J.D. Lewis and on which report the doctor was dismissed from the service. Major King denies ever having reported him and has had the impudence and cool audacity to charge me with being the author or cause of his dismissal, at a letter to Colonel Belknap. I was fortunate in finding the original, in which he [King] used the following language—"Assistant Surgeon J.D. Lewis left the regiment September 18th. It is supposed he had a furlough of 15 days, but it has never been seen at these headquarters—he is now reported absent without leave." The signature to the report is unmistakably that of Major King. I took the boat for Norfolk at 10:00 o'clock A.M. I find I must wait here until Friday morning, the 3rd of April. It will be a long and tedious detention to me, impatiently anxious as I now am, to get to my regiment. I am stopping at Bircher's Hotel—and a fine illustration it is of the whole city—empty and desolate; the type of ruin which seems to wait on all there is in the city.

Thursday April 2nd. A cloudless but windy day—the dust flies in clouds along the streets and crinoline is tossed high. The afternoon is warm, but is unpleasant to perambulate the streets. I have wandered round and round and about the city, restless and discontented. I am too anxious to get back to New Bern to be very patient of this delay. I returned to Bircher's Hotel early in the evening, and to my room, where with "Bruce the Hero King" in hand I whiled away an hour or two and find myself in mood for sleep.[7]

Friday April 3rd. It has been a chill and cloudy day—it seems today very little like spring at the "sunny south"—but very much like the varying mood of early spring at the north. I have formed several new acquaintances today, and renewed several old ones. Among the first, I name Robert Russell of this city, employed now by R.B. Smith and Company and for near a year in the Rebel army. He seems most glad to get free of the service and is at heart a sound Union and loyal man. He is also a most estimable and worthy young gentleman in his personal and moral relations.

Walter Hough is another gentleman of today's acquaintance, and in many respects differing wildly from the one last described. Mr. Hough has seen much of the world, has mingled with the most favored classes of society, and though possessed of much that is generous and good, has become stained by some of the worst vices. His Amours with the "fair and frail" have evidently been very numerous—his use of profane language is very reckless and in some respects he appears to me to be wanting in principle. He is engaged in business here with Mr. Stuart of New York.

In the evening, the time hung so heavy on my hands that I was persuaded by a friend to attend the theatre. I met Captain [Peter] Regan of the 7th New York Battery here—also saw Lt. Col. Thorp and lady (wife). A friend whom I met today (James Cook of Granger) who has just returned from Suffolk & is now on his way home with a sick friend of the 130th NYV tells me that Thorp continues to indulge very freely in strong drink—that on one occasion while he was there, he was so intoxicated that he could not get from the town (Suffolk) to his camp, his horse came into camp without him, and he returned the next morning, though his wife was waiting [for] him at the camp. Ah, the heart of that wife is destined to many a heartache—if they both live, not many years will pass before his degradation will drag all that cling to him, down where none can save but God!

Saturday April 4. The air has been chill and the sky clouded all day. About 3:00 o'clock P.M., it commenced snowing, and the wind, which during the whole day had been blowing a gale from the northeast, drove the snow in blinding clouds along the streets. During the afternoon and evening, some six inches of snow fell. I have rarely seen at the north a more wintry day than this P.M. and evening have been. There is no possibility of leaving here, and no indication that a boat will be sent through the canal for some days to come. I can only imagine what the cause of the detention of the boats is. I have sometimes thought it was from apprehension of an attack on them by guerillas. The wind has blown so furiously that at high tide today (12:00 noon), the water came up into the lower streets of the city. I retired early to my room at Bircher's.

Sunday April the 5th. The morning gave promise of the beautiful day it has been—before noon, the snow had nearly disappeared and the sidewalks were again quite comfortable for pedestrians. I have lounged away most of the day at R.B. Smith and Company's store, by times trying to kill time in reading W.M. Reynolds' "Robert Bruce," a most wretchedly-written affair—much inferior to some of his "Romances."

Late in the afternoon, I took a stroll with W. Hough to the town or city point. The aristocratic part of town. There are many fine residences in this part of the city. The walk was continued until after dark, and I returned to the room of my friend at the National, where I spent the evening.

The history of my friend Hough is not unworthy of a note, insofar it bears upon his present course of life as a libertine and "man of pleasure." Somewhat more than eight years ago, he was deeply attached to an interesting girl in Clyde, Wayne County, New York, by the name of Graves, and was engaged to be married. He was then engaged in a thriving mercantile business with his brother. His familiarity in the family of his affianced wife was, of course, without reserve. He was there almost every day, and he usually walked in without the usual ceremony of announcing himself or ringing.

One evening, he left the store earlier than usual to call on the woman, as he declares, to whom his heart was most passionately devoted. Passing into the parlor without announcing his arrival, and not finding her there, he playfully thought to surprise her and sought her from room to room until he found her in the embrace of a man then in the employ of her father. There was no actual criminality evinced in the position of the parties, but she sat in the submissive enjoyment of his embrace, with her head resting quietly on his shoulder. The outraged Hough turned instantly on his heel and strode from the room. It was in vain that the false girl rushed after him—he never entered the house or spoke to her again. He tells me that up to that time he never drank, swore, chewed or smoked, and had fondly hoped to lead an exemplary and happy life beside the woman whom he had learned to love with the most devoted tenderness.

Now, I think he is skeptical, and can hardly be made to believe that there is a faithful and virtuous woman. He is one of the finest-looking men, is in good circumstances and his family connections are unexceptionable. I have known many such instances as the one just narrated, that I am suspicious of the most exemplary of women when even rumor associates their names with the false and bad. I have often thought I would not trust an Angel when such temptations assail a woman. There is a world of goodness and sweetness in the soul of a pure and loving woman; and with it she may, if she chooses, lead the man who truly loves her, a heavenward course—she may be his guardian angel, the very light of his eyes, and cynosure of all of his earthly hopes. And if false—if she wrongs the love of a noble & affectionate heart by betraying the trust and affection with infidelity, the wreck she makes is dreadful to contemplate. It may never be known to the world what he who is betrayed suffers, or what has caused the change in him, which makes him reckless of self and determined on the wreck and ruin of the fair ones who can be bent to his purposes. Some of the most determined libertines I have ever known, I am compelled to believe, owe their characteristics to the fickleness and faithfulness of one whom they once devotedly loved.[8]

At 10:00 P.M., I returned to Bircher's Hotel. Late this P.M., I met the captain of the small side wheel steamer "Undine," who assured me he should leave for New Bern tomorrow at 12:00 noon. I am hopeful, therefore, of getting off.

NOTES: CHAPTER SEVEN

1. Levi C. Turner was judge advocate of volunteers for the Union army.
2. Augustus Frank (1826–95) served three times as a Republican congressman from New York. He was a delegate to the Republican National Convention of 1856. Ebbett's Grill and the Willard Hotel are still among the capital's favored establishments. Major Williams has not been identified.
3. Mason Jones has not been identified. In the case of Lieutenant Martin, Dr. Smith sounds more like a moralist than a medical man.
4. Laura Keene was on the stage at Ford's Theatre the night Lincoln was shot.
5. William Seward was Lincoln's Secretary of State.
6. This episode fits the description of an agitated depression with a mild bout of hallucinations. Since Dr. Smith remained productive another forty years, this was clearly not a serious mental illness, but may have derived from a persistent tendency to mood swings and obsessional thinking.
7. Crinoline usually referred not just to the fabric, but also to the lightweight hoop that held out the vast skirts, *de rigueur* in 1863 fashions. A high wind could turn the skirt inside out, revealing the wearer from the waist down, while concealing her from the waist up. More ominously, if the wearer stood too close to the hearth, the large volume of air under the highly flammable skirt acted as a chimney flue; this resulted in thousands of fatal burns and hideous scarrings every year.
8. The psychology here is of interest to more than just feminist sociologists. Dr. Smith clearly believes that a single bad experience with a woman entitles a man to a lifetime of vengeful and destructive behavior, a strange abdication from his usual stance of self-responsibility and self-improvement.

CHAPTER EIGHT

With Muffled Oars—
The Siege of Washington

Afer the *sturm und drang* of administrative and emotional conflicts, our diarist was suddenly thrust into the more gripping terrors of actual combat. In the spring of 1863, the Army of Northern Virginia was once again short of supplies. Maj. Gen. James Longstreet eyed the rich stores of ham, bacon, preserved fish, corn, and flour that filled the barns and smokehouses of the fertile watersheds of the Blackwater, Chowan, and Tar Rivers. He launched an attack designed to bottle up the Yankee occupiers in their defenses long enough for Confederate foraging teams to load their wagons and head north. Maj. Gen. D. H. Hill was given the task of besieging the Union forces at Washington, North Carolina; by March 30, 1863, the twelve hundred Union defenders were surrounded. Although Hill outnumbered the Union forces ten to one, he had no intention of sustaining the losses likely in a frontal assault; artillery bombardment and frequent shows of force were quite sufficient to keep the Yankees where they were supposed to be—immobile—while the Confederates made off with the provisions stored at hundreds of farms and plantations. Of course, the Union defenders at Washington had no idea that they were merely being penned up, and fully anticipated a major attack. It was at this point that Dr. Smith returned to New Bern.[1]

Monday April 6th. At 12:00 N., I was at the dock of the steamer Undine and found that the order for her departure had been countermanded. I resolved to have an interview with General Viele and ascertain the cause of the detention of the steamer and if it was possible that I should be compelled to remain much longer. I found the general very pleasantly disposed, and willing to remove all restrictions to the departure of the boat. An order was immediately given that the steamer should leave. I am satisfied that the trips of the boats through the canal have been suspended for some days past for fear of guerillas on the route. I had barely time to reach the landing, when the lines were cast off and our little steamer headed up Elizabeth River.[2]

I have several times passed the Gosport Navy Yard since its destruction, but never before so fully comprehended the extent and value of the structures and machinery destroyed. The evacuation of this yard and its partial destruction (for it took both Federals and Rebels to completely destroy it) was one of the most stupid errors and fatal mistakes of the Federal government. It has committed many blunders—none more unfortunate than this. The frigates then in the yard in fighting condition could have been so placed as to have commanded the navy yard and Norfolk in spite of any force which could, for a long time, have been brought against it by the Rebels. The immediate consequence of the partial destruction and entire abandonment of the yard was the possession of more than 2,000 pieces of cannon, and a large amount of materiel of war. At 4:00 P.M., we were in the immediate vicinity of the entrance to the Virginia Cut of the canal and hard aground.

The steamer Sylvan Shore lay within musket shot ahead, also aground—she is bound for Norfolk and had Commodore [Alexander?] Murray, several army officers and a hundred contrabands on board. We got off about 6:00 P.M., steamed through the Virginia Cut, into the Blackwater [River] and anchored about half past 10:00 P.M., after getting aground several times. The darkness of the night made it impossible to move further before daylight.[3]

Tuesday April 7. As soon as it was light, we got underway and reached the waters of Currituck Sound about 9:00 A.M.—passing through this, the North Carolina Cut of the canal was passed before noon, and we entered North River, thence into Albemarle Sound was but two hours voyage. At 4:00 o'clock P.M., we were off Roanoke Island and made the landing at the Island to receive orders and coal up, if it be determined that this steamer shall go through to New Bern.

I have made some queer acquaintances during the journey. One of whom, known throughout this country as the "Widow Camel," is a somewhat of an eccentric woman and a hard case. She is a woman of 35 years of age, short, thick-set, ruddy complexion, talkative, full of animation and vigorous energy and not ill-favored in countenance. But from all I can hear of her, I judge her to be a bad woman. She cannot be better illustrated,

perhaps, than by repeating a story which a gentleman sitting near me and a
neighbor of the widow asserts to be a fact. When her husband (or the man
said to be her husband) died, a neighbor took her in his buggy to the place
where he was to be buried. After he was buried, and she left the grave, she
turned and looked back at the grave and exclaimed—"There, G_____d
d_____n you, you won't watch me any more."

She lives near the swing bridge on the Carolina Cut of the canal, and
is reputed to have made considerable money since the war began, by getting goods at New Bern & Roanoke Island, taking them home and selling
them across the lines.

Another is a woman by the name of Arnsbey, wife of a captain of that
name [Anson Arnsbey], in the 171st PA Vols. She is going to New Bern
to see her husband. She is the daughter of Dr. Barney of Independence,
Allegany County, NY. She had two brothers in the 86th NY, one now
dead and the other discharged. She is talkative, ill favored, 35 years of age
and not remarkably smart, though she thinks she is. But I ought not to
discuss the demerits too freely of one so little entitled to notice.[4]

Wednesday April 8. We were near the middle of Pamlico Sound
when I turned out this morning. The water is smooth and the morning
fine. P.M. We have had a beautiful day. We reached New Bern about
dark—on going to General Foster's headquarters, I found that the 85th
had marched about 2:00 P.M. today across the country in the direction of
Washington, North Carolina. Fourteen regiments of infantry, three batteries of artillery (16 guns), and three or four companies of cavalry compose
the expedition under command of General Spinola.[5]

They go to relieve and reinforce General Foster, who is at Washington with but 1,500 to 2,000 men, and surrounded by the enemy. The
river on which Washington is situated (Tar) is blockaded by the batteries
of the Rebels. I at once made preparation to follow the regiment tomorrow morning. At 11:00 P.M., I received an order to proceed to Washington, NC, in the steamer Thomas Collyer, which is to leave tomorrow
morning. I found a number of letters awaiting at my quarters, where John
O. Goodrich, Dr. Palmer and 60 to 100 remained at camp. I was surprised
and no less happy for the surprise to find three of my letters from my
Dear Frances, all written since I last parted with her. They were properly
directed, but wrongly sent on to New Bern. And I have wronged her in
my reflections on a preceding page—she has been faithful to her promise,
and her letters breathe the spirit of a pure love. But I should be so much

happier if I could see that the rumors of enemies concerning me do not influence her and make her unhappy.

Thursday April 9. I arose this morning much the worse for wear. I sat up until 2:00 A.M. to finish letters before I leave—wrote a long one to my dear friend Miss L. I hadn't the time this morning to greet but a few of my friends in the regiment, who have remained in camp. I went to General Headquarters, heard the dispatches to General Foster read, and went aboard the steamer a few minutes before 8:00 A.M. Patterson, of Company E, accompanied me, having my things in charge. The steamer has Lieutenant Colonel [Joseph M.] McChesney and two officers of the Signal Corps on board. The colonel has dispatches for General Foster—the signal officers are accompanied by some six soldiers of the Signal Corps. The

Col. Joseph M. McChesney commanded an unusual unit: an all-white Union regiment of Southern troops, the 1st Regiment of North Carolina Volunteer Infantry. At the siege of Washington, North Carolina, he traveled up the river at night with Dr. Smith, gliding silently past the waiting rebel guns.

design is, in some way, to get information to General Foster of the troops that are advancing to his succor. I have very little confidence in the leader of the expedition—General Spinola.

The attempt to take the dispatches through, past the blockade on the river below Washington, or to attempt to pass in a small boat, through the picket boats stationed on the river at night, is full of peril. My orders direct me to report to the commanding officer at Washington, NC, and I must be one of those who try the chances of Rebel bullets. I fain would live for the sake of dear loved ones far away. And in the hands of a Kind Providence, I put my trust, and commit to His Almighty arm the care and protection of those fondly loved ones for whom I cherish an affection as strong and enduring as my life.

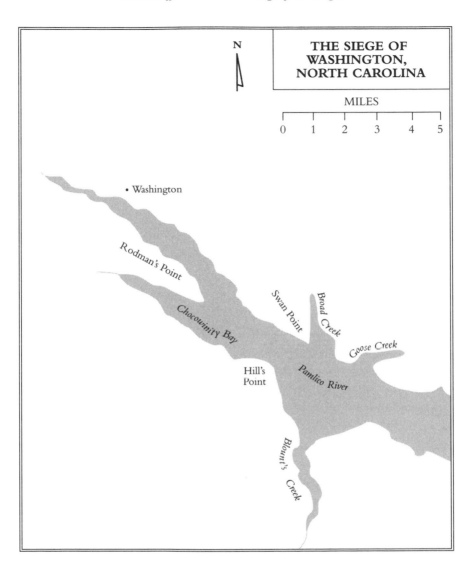

THE SIEGE OF WASHINGTON, NORTH CAROLINA

N

MILES

0 1 2 3 4 5

• Washington

Rodman's Point

Chocowinity Bay

Swan Point

Broad Creek

Goose Creek

Hill's Point

Pamlico River

Blount's Creek

Twenty-five minutes before 3:00 P.M.—we are near the mouth of the Tar River. In less than an hour, we shall be in the vicinity of the Rebel batteries. The tremendous motion of the vessel, caused by the working of the engine, makes it a difficult task to write.

As soon as twilight had fairly settled down on the waters of the broad river, we pulled out from the Collyer in a cutter, and went aboard a small river schooner, which was loaded with ammunition for the beleaguered force at Washington. Our little craft [the schooner] bore a stout name— The Champion. Two other schooners of like size and with a like cargo, lay alongside, destined to try with us the feat of running the blockade. Soon, it was quite dark; the steam transport Phoenix took the schooners in tow and moved up the river. By 9:00 P.M., we reached the anchorage of the gunboats, which at nightfall move up six miles closer to the enemy batteries than the position they occupy during the day, and were at this time as close to the position of the batteries as was deemed safe.

Here, the schooners were cast off [from the *Phoenix*], sails were hoisted, the light breeze blowing up the river filled the canvas, and the rippling of the water beneath the bows of the schooners told us that we were making good progress. Never did I watch and hope so anxiously for the westing winds than now. And as if in answer to our hopes, the wind gradually increased until we were moving through the water at a rate that left nothing to be desired. An hour passed, and all eyes had long been in search of the Rebel picket boats and any moment for nearly that time we had expected to be saluted by musketry from the banks, and perhaps artillery; for this had been the universal experience of those who had tried to pass up or down the river for the last ten days. Eight or ten marines snugly stowed between bales of hay on the deck, and the revolvers of the trio of officers, it was determined to make warm work for any of the picket boats which it was known the enemy stationed on the river at night, who might attempt to board our craft; and if any should stand across the bows, to run them down was fully determined on. While in this state of momentary expectation, and full of resolutions to go through or face worse, a steamer was seen directly ahead. What could it be? Surely, none of our own had gone up as far as we then supposed we were, and the Rebels certainly had none in the river. "Schooner ahoy!" was the challenge from the deck of the steamer—"Aye aye," responded the master of the Champion. "What schooner is that," demanded the sentinel on the steamer. "Steamer Champion" was the reply.

"What steamer is that?" inquired the commander of our little craft. [illegible], replied the same voice. The same we had passed an hour before. The truth was, the pilot, a "contraband" who pretended to know well the river, had turned completely around in the river and was going down the river when we were hailed by the gunboat. The sky was clear overhead and attention to the stars should have prevented such a mistake. A dark, hazy condition of the atmosphere near the surface of the water, without its being a fog, rendered the coastline so indistinct that by taking that for a guide, it is easy to see how such a mistake might occur. It was

Our diarist watched as the Commodore Hull *traded shots with Confederate artillery. The Hull was hit ninety-eight times. This illustration shows the ship in a later engagement, at Plymouth, North Carolina.*
U.S. NAVAL HISTORICAL CENTER PHOTOGRAPH NH61859

resolved to man the cutter of the steamer Commodore Hull with armed oarsmen and <u>row</u> up the river to the besieged town. Accordingly, Lt. Col. McChesney, bearer of dispatches, with his dispatches attached to a piece of lead, so as to sink them if likely to fall into the hands of the enemy, Capt. Taylor of the Signal Corps, Lieut. [illegible] of the navy, myself, two privates of the Signal Corps and the eight marines mentioned, shoved off from the steamer Commodore Hull, with oars muffled and amid the profoundest silence. Onward we swept, the dip of the oars so dexterously managed as to not make any noise that might be heard a few rods distant—"Steady, men—careful, there," was the frequent whispered command of the naval officer in charge.

In 30 minutes, we were abreast the Rebel batteries. Their campfires were plainly to be distinguished. Each moment, we expected a salute from the infantry pickets on shore, or from the boats of the enemy. The stars in Ursa Major were the guide of the helmsman, for a deep haze rendered the outlines of the shore only visible; and this probably greatly contributed to our not being observed. The lower batteries were passed. The battery at Rodman's Point and the "Marsh battery" had yet to be passed, and these are situated at the narrowest part of the river, and completely command it. The battery at Rodman's Point has Whitworth guns, whose ranges are from five to seven miles. The picket boats of the enemy were safely passed by what good fortune I cannot discover, as every attempt to run the blockade hitherto has resulted in a collision with them. The moon was now rising, and would soon make our boat a conspicuous mark. The men at the oars were ordered to "Give way, there"—"Give way strongly" was repeated in an earnest whispered command, and now the cutter flew through the water like a thing of life.

We approached the battery at Rodman's Point and felt certain of receiving its compliments. Not 15 minutes before we were in range, a mist rose from the river and so entirely enveloped us that it was impossible for the enemy to have discovered us. The same fog continued to serve as our screen until the Marsh battery passed, and now we were safe. A watchful and kind Providence interfered to preserve us. In a few moments, we were hailed from the shore by our own pickets.

The brave fellows who manned the oars evidently breathed freer. It had been two hours of unpleasant suspense, to say the least.

On touching the dock, we found the same good fortune had brought the two schooners, our companions in the beginning of the adventure, safe through. There was quite a crowd on the dock, waiting in anxious suspense for our arrival; being so much behind the schooners, there was much apprehension lest we had fallen into the hands of the enemy. It was between 2:00 and 3:00 o'clock in the morning when we set foot on shore. Lieut. Springer of the 44th Mass. and quartermaster of the post, kindly gave me a bed at his quarters—I was greatly fatigued and in need of sleep, not having slept but two hours Wednesday night. I soon found refuge in the sleep I was so much in need of, but in a short time, was aroused by the arrival of Col. McChesney, who came to share my bed.[6]

Friday April 10. I arose a little after 6:00 this morning, feeling much jaded and worn. I walked down to the Lafayette Hotel, a dilapidated concern, with Col. McChesney and got some breakfast—and a very good one it was, to what I had expected to get. I have rarely in my life enjoyed a morning more than this, although feeling very unwell and suffering from a severe headache. The morning is bright and glorious and the air is full of music from thousands of feathered songsters, congregated in the spreading elms, which line and embower the streets as far as the eye could see. The finely-shaded streets are a marked and charming feature of this beautiful little town.

There is no business, and few evidences of thrift and commercial prosperity in times past. But the fine residences of the wealthy inhabitants have an appearance of taste and comfort which I have scarcely seen equaled in any southern town. While on my way to the main fort where Gen. Foster has his headquarters, and which is situated south of the town, a gun from one of the batteries of the enemy opposite of the fort opened on the fort, quickly another and another followed.

Dr. Robert Ware of the 44th Massachusetts Infantry. This son of Boston Brahmins, during his Sanitary Commission work, was loved and admired by the female nurses. Dr. Smith embalmed him at Washington, North Carolina.
MASSACHUSETTS COMMANDERY, MILITARY ORDER OF THE LOYAL LEGION AND THE U.S. ARMY MILITARY HISTORY INSTITUTE

The guns from the fort soon replied; and for half an hour, the firing on both sides was very rapid. The guns of the Rebels were served with much skill, eleven shells and solid shot struck within the fort, one of these nearly cut away the flagstaff, and another tore through one of the corners of the magazine. The direction of their guns was well calculated to enfilade the left of our works, and would have told with terrible severity but for the trenches which had been thrown up to protect the men from just such a fire as the enemy now treated us to. Throughout the day, occasional shots were fired from the different batteries on both sides. Not a casualty occurred among our men during the day.

I called this morning, by request of Dr. Hubon, Surgeon of the 27th Mass., on Dr. Ware, Surgeon of the 44th Mass. I found him in almost a dying condition. He died about 12:00 M. [meridian] today. His disease is unquestionably congestive pneumonia. He was ill but five days. I am told that he was a surgeon of fine ability, and a general favorite in his regiment.

He is a son of Dr. John Ware of Boston. In the midst of life and health, he is taken from a field of usefulness and one in which he will be greatly missed. I am suffering very severely from sick headache today—so that I am scarce able to keep up. I am directed by Medical Director Snelling to take charge of the "left wing" of the defenses; this includes the 44th Mass. I only wait an official order from headquarters to report to Col. Lee of the 44th, who has command of the left.[7]

Saturday April 11th. 7:00 P.M. I sit by my open window as the day-light fades away, the soft, warm breezes of the sunny south fanning me as I write. It is a most beautiful evening—the thunder of the heavy guns in the fortifications around the town has ceased, and the voices of happy and gleeful children alone disturb the quiet of the scene.

I awoke this morning much refreshed and feel like myself again. Soon after breakfast, I embalmed Dr. Ware. The brief services for the deceased were performed at 3:00 o'clock this P.M. Maj. Gen. Foster, Brig. Gen. Posten, Medical Director Snelling, and some 30 officers were in attendance. Passages of scripture were read by the chaplain of the 27th Mass.—a eulogy on the deceased, a few words of exhortation, and prayer closed the services. All remained standing during the services, and when it was closed, each officer returned to his post, the emergency of our situation not permitting the poor tribute of following the remains to the vault, where for the present, they are deposited.[8]

I have all day been hoping to hear the guns of our troops advancing to our relief from New Bern. And I am not without apprehension of their failure to reach us. The general who leads them (Spinola) is entirely incompetent for the task before him, so far, at least, as military experience or education is concerned. The day has been very pleasant and quite warm. Today, as well as yesterday, I visited the wounded and many of the sick in the general hospital, under the charge of Dr. Hubon of the 27th Mass.

April 12. This has been anything but a day of rest—for a long time this forenoon, the gunboats were at work at the Rebel batteries at Hill's Point—the lowest on the river, of their batteries. About the same time, the gunboats "Eagle" and "Commodore Hull," lying in the river before the town, opened on a new battery erected by the enemy and evidently protected by cotton bales—in an hour, they knocked it to pieces and set the cotton on fire. The Rebels in charge of the batteries on this side of the river & east of the town seemed to get spunky at this, and opened on the fort with great fury. Our own batteries were not slow in responding, and some of the finest shots were made by our 32-pounder that I have ever witnessed.

The batteries of the enemy are about 1200 yards distant from our lines, and are numbered by us as No. 1, No. 2, No. 3, et cetera. Three shots in succession from one of our 32-pounders tore through the embrasure of No. 1, dismounting their guns and two of these three shells burst directly after passing the embrasure. The Rebels were seen to carry dead or wounded from this battery. In the meantime, and for most of the day, the gunboat "Louisiana" kept up an occasional fire on the "Cotton Battery" to prevent the enemy repairing damages. Toward noon, cannon were distinctly heard in the direction our reinforcements are expected. It was kept up some

Col. Francis L. Lee of the 44th Massachusetts. Dr. Smith thought Lee to be a good host, but observed that the colonel was "too little considerate of the feelings of others, and in the habit of using harsh language in the denunciation of others for trivial faults."

U.S. ARMY MILITARY HISTORY INSTITUTE

time, and must have been 15 to 20 miles distant. This was our forces, undoubtedly at or near "Blount Creek," where it is understood the enemy would dispute the passage with the advancing troops.

I am now messing with the field and staff officers of the 44th Mass.— Col. Wilson, commanding. It is a very pleasant mess. I have the blues severely tonight—various circumstances combine to give them to me so severely that I can't shake them off—thoughts of far distant loved ones contributed in no small degree to this. There is <u>one</u> who tests my truth and fealty greatly by the expression of doubts and fears in her letters. She does not seem to be able to learn that the surest way to make me feel the necessity of trying to forget her is to express doubts, fears and regrets. When I last parted with her, I thought the time for these changeful fears and regrets had forever passed. But hardly had I tasted the sweet illusion, when her letters dashed it away. Oh, why will she—I would have her cling to me as does the ivy to the oak, saying in all her acts and words that she desires nothing so much as to share with me not only my joys, but my trials and sorrows. But she chooses, rather, to comfort me by assurances that she "would give worlds if they were hers to give, if we had never met," if some reports circulated by enemies or retailed by gossipmongers are true.

I wish I could leave here a more satisfactory record. God only knows what will come of this. I pray that His hand and will may guide me through all and to the end. While I feel this assurance, I shall know that all will be for the best, whatever the event. The day has been warm and sunny, until late in the P.M., when a shower came up and refreshed all nature—it has been a cheering April shower.

Monday April 13th. A smart shower fell last night, and a drizzling rain continued to fall for a short time in the early morning. In the afternoon, it cleared away, and was quite cheery and warm—all nature seemed to be invigorated and rejoicing; and the birds seemed to be more full of song and sing more sweetly than usual.

In the afternoon, I assisted in the amputation of an arm immediately below the anatomical neck—operation circular. The arm of the limb had been amputated immediately above the elbow some 15 days since. Sloughing of the flaps took place, and two days since, erysipelas appeared and rapidly extended up the arm.[9]

The same cause (premature discharge of a cannon) caused an oblique fracture of the humerus at its middle, with considerable contusion of the soft parts. The result of the primary amputation has shown that the amputation should have been performed above the fracture of the humerus in the first instance. The amputation was made under a severe fire from a battery of the enemy then opened for the first time—the battery was located on the New Bern Road across the river. The fire was answered by the 9- & 11-inch guns of the [gunboat] Louisiana, in admirable style and soon silenced the new battery.

The batteries of the enemy east of the town refused to answer the challenge from the fort this morning, and have remained silent all day. Late this P.M., firing was heard in the direction our reinforcements are expected—Captain Renshaw of the navy reports the enemy drawn up in line of battle at Rodman's Point, and faced in the direction the Federal troops are expected. It is very surprising that the gunboats in the river below the enemy's batteries remain so inactive—there is either a want of courage or zeal on the part of naval officers in command there.[10]

The steamer Escort *ran the gauntlet of Confederate fire to bring troops and supplies to the besieged Union soldiers at Washington, North Carolina. The pilot of the* Escort *was shot in the head by a rebel sharpshooter and died at his post.*
COURTESY OF THE STEAMSHIP HISTORICAL SOCIETY OF AMERICA COLLECTION, LANGSDALE LIBRARY, UNIVERSITY OF BALTIMORE

Tuesday April 14. Breakfasted this morning at 6:00 A.M. The officers of the mess (44th Field & staff) wish to be at the fortifications early—the breakfast is therefore earlier and will be while the siege lasts. I was awakened last night about 12:00 o'clock by heavy firing in the direction of the enemy's batteries down the river—not very long after, I heard cheers in the same direction—they were unmistakably genuine Yankee cheers. I rose and hurriedly dressed and went down to the river—before I reached the wharf, I learned the cause of the guns and of the cheers.

The Escort, a large sidewheel steamer, had just arrived with the Rhode Island 5th Volunteers—and loaded with provisions and ammunition. The firing from all the Rebel batteries was rapid, but she passed without being once hit.

To Colonel [Henry] Sisson of the R.I. 5th belongs the credit of this achievement. General Palmer, who is with the fleet below the blockade, would give no order for the colonel to attempt the perilous feat; he obtained permission to go on his own responsibility, and came like the gallant, brave man he is. The arrival of the Escort is cheering and encouraging. But the news which she also brings, that the expedition under Spinola, for the relief of the forces here, has gone back to New Bern without any serious attempt to come through, is very discouraging.

At Blount's Creek, it is understood that the enemy had two pieces of artillery—which shows Spinola to be a dastardly coward or a base traitor.

The artillery in the enemy's batteries and in our own fortifications has been more than usually active today. The day has been cloudy and cool—towards evening, the sun came out and gave promise of a fine day tomorrow. The Escort is to try the chances of the blockade again tonight, and General Foster is understood to be going in her to New Bern.

I have the impression that some of the subordinate generals—like Spinola and Palmer, will have a bit of his opinion of their merits, if he succeeds in getting through. And it will not be long after he reaches New Bern before there will be a move which will decide our fate here, for he goes full of energy and terribly in earnest.

8:00 P.M. The evening has closed in with cloudy sky and it is therefore very dark. I have sent several letters on board the Escort to try the chance of getting them to New Bern to be mailed, one to my dear Frank—one to brother, Colonel Wellman and W. Moses.

Wednesday April 15. A drenching shower fell during the night, and with only occasional intervals, it has continued to rain most of the day. The ground is saturated, and the streets many of them afloat. The soldiers along the line of fortifications are well protected and sheltered. But the troops of the enemy must be in a pitiable condition, if without tents, as is currently reported. The Escort did not go down the river last night, owing to the extreme darkness—this morning, early, however, she passed down under a heavy fire from the Rebel batteries, but was without serious injury, as the signals from below indicated. If this feat of the Escort in broad daylight does not shame the cowardly naval officers below the blockade, then they are lost to all sense of shame and dishonor.

This evening, amputation of the thigh of a soldier of the 27th Mass. Vols.—he was struck by a piece of the leaden band of a shell from one of our own guns—another warning to avoid the fragments which usually fly from the band laterally—when the shell is but a few feet from the mouth of the gun.

The fragment penetrated at the anterior and lateral aspect of the upper third of the tibia, not entirely fracturing the tibia, sufficient to expose the medullary canal and wound the medullary artery, thence passing through and greatly lacerating the muscles of the calf. It passed out, and again entered at the inner and upper part of the poplitial space, and dissecting its way upward between the integuments and the fascia of the external layer of muscles. It was a case for amputation, but the shock of injury was such that to operate at once—that is, about 10:00 A.M., which was some hour or two after the injury, would have been fatal. The thigh was amputated about 8:00 P.M., reaction being very good. But the pulse became small and feeble during the operation—I have but little hopes of the patient's recovery. The case of amputation near the shoulder joint is doing remarkably well.[11]

The firing from the batteries of the enemy was very brisk this morning and was replied to with great spirit from our own guns. All the early part of the enemy's battery at the "Marsh" has been thundering away at the gunboats, but they have not deigned a reply.

Thursday April 16th. Early this morning, I was surprised by the news that five Rebel deserters came in this morning and reported that the enemy had evacuated their position in our front—east of the town. Scouts sent out to ascertain the truth soon returned & reported that the whole front was clear. Contrabands were set to work to level the batteries of the enemy. About 12:00 N. [noon], it was evident that the enemy's works on the other side of the river, at the Marsh battery, Rodman's and Hill's Point, had been or were being evacuated.

The small steamer "Ceres" was sent down to reconnoiter. After throwing several shells into Rodman's Point, she sent a boat crew of 12 men to the shore—when within 50 rods of the shore, a volley of musketry was fired at the boat by Rebels in ambuscade. The boat could be seen to drift helplessly down the river immediately after the volley was fired. This was evidently a ruse on the part of those who were not wounded to escape the fire of the Rebels. It was ascertained that one man was killed—the third engineer of the "Ceres"—one fatally wounded and one slightly wounded.

The Hunchback, White Head and Butterfield (gunboats) now moved up the river from their anchorage below the batteries. It is wonderful how these brave (?), hard officers should have dared to bring their vessels up, as it was yet barely possible the enemy's batteries might not be evacuated. At about the same time, the Eagle and Commodore Hull went down, to the Ceres, and all the vessels opened on Rodman's Point and the woods in their vicinity. The Louisiana, from her anchorage opposite the town, also opened her powerful batteries of 9-inch guns on the Jamestown Road. Throwing 15-second fuse (three miles range), this undoubtedly reaching the enemy if at the crossroads. Rodman's mansion, one of the finest

At the siege of Washington, North Carolina, Dr. Smith saw the Union gunboat Hunchback *hurling heavy shells at Confederate positions. Here is the crew gathered for a formal portrait. Nearly 25 percent of the crew is African-American.*
U.S. NAVAL HISTORICAL CENTER PHOTOGRAPH NH59430

residences in the country, took fire from the explosion of a shell and contributed in no small degree to the grand and magnificent panorama. Seven gunboats, throwing 8- and 9-inch shells were now at work, their sides enveloped in smoke, and from the dense clouds which surrounded them, a tongue of flame every moment leaped forth. On shore, in every direction, rose suddenly small dense clouds of smoke, which had scarce begun to break and roll away when the boom of the exploded shell came to the ear. It was one of the finest sights I had ever seen.

When our troops landed and took possession of Rodman's Point, the morning after its evacuation, the following note was found posted in a conspicuous place:

"Yankees!! We leave you not because we can't take you, but because it is not worth taking—and besides, the climate is not agreeable. A man should be amphibious to inhabit it. We leave you a few busted guns, some stray solid shot, and a man and a brother, on the wharf, who we rescued from the waves, to which some fray among his equals consigned him, but this tribute we pay you. You have acted with much gallantry during the siege. We salute the pilot of the Escort. Company K, 32nd Regiment North Carolina Volunteers."

This evening, I noticed two pickets sent up from the Rebel lines, on what I suppose to be their line of retreat—and a mile above the town, across the Neuse River, their signal lights are to be seen in the early evening. I had been to the bridge to ascertain the cause of several reports fired by our pickets and, while slowly sauntering back to my quarters on Second Street, I passed an officer whom I knew to be Dr. Hubon, First Assistant Surgeon of the 27th Mass. Volunteers. He was in the vicinity of a house I had heard was a resort for women of easy virtue—indeed, it was well understood to be such. His walk in that direction was sufficient to excite my suspicion—I passed, and saw him retrace his steps after passing the house a few rods, and go in. Returning to my quarters, which is in the same house, but the same room with the doctor's, I learned from his servant that he had just gone out, saying he was going to the hospital. I thought Dr. H. too much of a gentleman to stoop so low. Ah, well! It is but another evidence of the few good and true men in society. By and by, some warm and affectionate wife will nestle close to his heart, as happy and confiding as if he had never degraded himself by associations with a common prostitute—ah, woman! How little you ever learn to prize the nobility of that man's nature who preserves for his wife an honest and virtuous love. The day has been very pleasant—yet not uncomfortably warm.

Friday April 17. I have been greatly afflicted with ennui today—I am a little anxious to get back to New Bern to find any means of making the time pass swiftly when I am not engaged in professional duties.

After attending the morning call of the 44th Mass.—and there are but few sick now in the regiment, I visited the patients in the general hospital, by request of Dr. Hubon, who is unwell this morning; wonder if such a visit as he made last evening always had the effect to make him sick the next morning—ah, sir, you think less of yourself than I supposed you did.

Most of the gunboats slipped down the river this morning—the officers of the gunboats, or many of them, got together last evening and had "a good drunk." The excess to which officers in both the navy & army indulge reflects the deepest disgrace, and more greatly perils the interest of the service than any and all others combined. It is, indeed, sad and disheartening to see and know the extent of this vice in these branches of the public service.

From the best information that can be obtained since the retreat of the Rebels, it seems that the Rebels had about 5,000 men before our works on the east side of the river, under command of General Garnett, and 8- to 10,000 on the other, or west side of the river, under command of General D.H. Hill, Commander in Chief of this Department of the Rebel service.[12]

It is now known that when the Escort passed the enemy's batteries the morning of Wednesday, the 15th, she was struck 30 to 50 times by solid shot and shell; the brave pilot [a Captain Pedrick] who brought her in the night before unnecessarily exposed himself on this occasion, and was struck by a Minie ball in the head and instantly killed. The passage of the Escort in broad daylight, unprotected and unarmed as she was, completes the disgrace of the naval officers in charge below the batteries, who have feared to bring their gunboats in range of the enemy's guns. And it illustrates equally well the bravery and determination of General Foster, who was on board the Escort.

Saturday April 18th. Memorable as the birthday of my dear son Clarence. Four years ago this day, at 1:00 A.M., he was ushered into this "vale of tears." A sweet and beautiful boy, he has thus far grown to be, giving to my heart many bright promises and hopes of his future, if God spares him to man's estate—oh, for wisdom from on high to preserve him from the snares and wickedness of life, and guide [him] in the path of rectitude. My heart does not look with confident and trusting hopes for the enjoyment of any earthly pleasures in the future. The dear, gentle mother that bore him looked with fondest hopes on her little baby flower, and I thought to see her live many years to care for and be proud of it; but the Destroyer came, and just five short months from the day that she gave birth to her babe, angels ushered her into life everlasting.

The 43rd Mass. arrived today on the steamer Escort—they take up their position on the right of the center of the works. The news by steamer is that one brigade left New Bern the morning after General Foster reached New Bern, in the direction of Kinston, and about 5,000 men left the same day, taking the same direction that the expedition did, which left New Bern under General Spinola, the 8th instant.

Early this evening, an alarm was raised by a cavalry vidette, who was fired at twice by a body of men (about a company), three-fourths of a mile outside the works—one of the balls passed through his coat sleeve. The troops were very quickly at their posts, ready for any emergency—a couple of shells were thrown in the direction the enemy were seen. Everything and everybody settled down into their usual quiet and apparent indifference. Dr. [Theodore W.] Fisher, Assistant Surgeon of the 44th, arrived today from New Bern. I should now return to New Bern immediately, but for the possibility of the 85th [New York] would be heard from, or I could join it sooner here. This, of course, will depend on the directions give the troops when the retreat of the enemy from this place is known.

The day has been very warm—it is summer-like. The evening out of doors has been most charming. Early in the day, I wrote to my dear friend Miss L., also to Mrs. Daggett, and sent them to New Bern by the Phoenix, which left this P.M.

Sunday April 19. 10:00 A.M. It is a most beautiful morning. I spent a part of the early morning in listening to and observing the feathered songsters that fill the air with their songs. Most prominent among them is the Mocking Bird—not the thrush of our northern climate, but the southern Mocking Bird. The robin, the bluebird and the Rice Bunting are also prominent in the numerous choir of singers.

I have just heard that General Naglee and a part of General Foster's staff has arrived in town, being the advance of General Foster's force, that left New Bern the 16th instant, for the relief of this place. The main body is 12 miles from here. The troops have had only some 200 of the enemy to drive before them—a rear guard, left by General Hill, to retard the movement of our forces.

9:00 P.M. A cavalry company, forming part of the advance of the forces on the way here, came across the river about 3:00 P.M. They have the battle flag of the 7th Regiment, Confederate Cavalry, taken by them this morning. General Foster came to Hill's Point this morning, and from there, by steamer, to the town. The band of the 44th greeted him at his quarters with "Hail to the Chief." Well he deserves the tribute. General Hickman came in soon after General Foster, and in advance of the cavalry at 3:00 P.M. by the same road.

I had the pleasure of meeting Captain Cochran of the 85th New York, who came through with General Naglee and was one of the five companions of the general in his bold, rash act of riding into the town many miles in advance of his troops, and with the known probability that he must encounter at least pickets, and perhaps much larger bodies of the enemy. This, in fact, occurred when some 12 miles in advance of his own advance, a Rebel picket of five men was discovered. Nothing daunted, the plucky general remarked, "We are good for ten men," and instantly in a loud voice gave the word, "Charge, cavalry." On dashed the little band of five at the word, two of the number actually having no arms at all, and the others revolvers in hand. The dash and confidence of the charge had the intended effect—the pickets were taken by surprise and surrendered without firing a shot—the general was now in the condition of the boy when he raffled for the elephant and won it; he "didn't know what to do with it." It was more than rash to move on with prisoners whose numbers equaled their own, with almost a certainty of encountering the "retreat or support" of the pickets, and equally perilous to remain there, with the probability of having to encounter the "relief," which, at a certain hour would approach the station of the captured picket.[13]

An orderly was sent back with orders to bring up a detachment of cavalry. Fortunately, General Hickman had thrown out his cavalry videttes, five to six miles in advance, so that in an hour a squadron of cavalry arrived and took care of the prisoners. Captain Raines and several men came on in the ambulances, and were provided in the 44th Mass. and 27th Mass. hospitals. The 85th [New York] will camp within three miles of the town. The day has been warm and pleasant.

Monday April 20. The 85th NY and 96th NY, 101 & 103 PA came in this morning—had a most cordial greeting from officers and men. Have visited their camp twice today.

General Wessells dined with "our mess" (44th Field and staff). He is a most excellent old man—and never need a general want a more implicit confidence than the officers and men of his division repose in him. He is calm and cool always—brave in the hour of danger and thoughtful of the welfare of the soldiers under his command when on the march or in camp.

This P.M., an officer of the 85th New York (Captain Langworthy) informed me of the sentence of the court martial in the case of C. J. Underhill, of Company E, 85th New York, who was tried by court martial in February last for "disobedience of orders" and "cowardice." The sentence of the Court had not been promulgated when I left New Bern on February 28th, and from what I learned of the testimony of Underhill, I was led to believe the sentence of the Court would not be severe, if, indeed, they should inflict any sentence at all. But it is very severe, to wit—"his head to be half shaved, and drummed out of camp in presence of his own regiment—the day following a card to be affixed to his back on which is written Coward'; and he then marched through the streets of

New Bern by the Provost Guard during the day and then to be confined in Fort Totten, with ball and chain for the term of his service, with loss of all pay due or that become due him." This is terribly severe—I feel very sad, indeed, on account of his friends.

I do not think he [Underhill] has the keen sensibility to feel all the deep disgrace of his situation; but I cannot but feel how greatly his friends will feel it—I do feel and cannot but see that his officer, in preferring the charges and pushing forward his trial, has done it as he would have not done with and toward him, as he would if he had been one of the favored men from his own locality. I cannot overlook his action in this matter—it is not in the spirit I expected him to act when I contributed to give him a commission in the company. I expected to find him always the protector and adviser of his men; as well as

Lt. Col. Edward C. Cabot, Boston Brahmin and failed sheep farmer, was a self-taught architectural genius, whose commissions included the Johns Hopkins University hospital and the Boston Athenaeum. Dr. Smith noted, "His sketchbook certainly evinces much talent."

FROM RECORD OF THE SERVICE OF THE 44TH MASSACHUSETTS VOLUNTEER MILITIA IN NORTH CAROLINA 1862–1863, BOSTON, 1888, ANONYMOUS

their kind and considerate officer and commander. The day has been warm—toward evening, the wind came up, the sky clouded, and while I write, the rain patters against the windows.

Tuesday April 21. Morning. The threatened storm of last evening has passed—the wind still blows chill from the north coast. Visited the camp of 85th New York this A.M. to attend to the sick. Late in the evening. I have made arrangements to leave for New Bern in the morning, with the 44th Mass. There are more sick left in camp at New Bern than there are with the regiment. Dr. Lewis is with the 85th and will do all for them that will be necessary.

Wednesday April 22nd. Left Washington, North Carolina, soon after 6:00 A.M. on the steamer Thomas Collyer—Massachusetts 44th on board. The trip to New Bern was very pleasant—reached there about 11:00 P.M. The afternoon has been lowering, and in the evening, misted and rained a little.

In parting with the officers of the 44th Mass., with whom I have been associated for the past two weeks, I wish to leave here the expression of my grateful appreciation of their kindness. I have not often been associated with officers combining so much cultivation and gentlemanly bearing as does the field and staff of the 44th Mass. They are all from Boston, or its vicinity.

Colonel F. L. Lee has seen much of life and good society, but is less cultivated than the other officers of the field and staff. He is rigidly temperate in every respect but smoking—but he is in the habit of using profane language far too freely. His impulses are quick and the expressions of his opinion often made without latitude. He is too little considerate of the feelings of others, and is in the habit of using harsh language in the denunciation of others for trivial faults—particularly to his inferiors.

Dr. Smith much admired the military bearing of Lt. Wallace Hinckley, adjutant of the 44th Massachusetts— until the young man came to him for treatment of gonorrhea. The whorehouses of Washington, North Carolina, were some of the few businesses operating during the siege.

FROM RECORD OF THE SERVICE OF THE 44TH MASSACHUSETTS VOLUNTEER MILITIA IN NORTH CAROLINA 1862–1863, BOSTON, 1888, ANONYMOUS

Lt. Col. [Edward C.] Cabot is a very quiet, dignified officer and very much of a gentleman. I am told he is a superior architect & is much esteemed in Boston society. His sketchbook certainly evinces much talent.

Major [Charles W.] Dabney is one of the best-natured men in the world, if I may judge from his countenance, which is of itself a good recommendation; he seems open, frank & cheerful always; yet is very sensitive, and perhaps unnecessarily so for his own good, or the happiness of his friends. He has been in the mercantile business formerly, and engaged in the Calcutta trade [probably imports from British India].

Adjutant [Wallace] Hinckley is a young man of 22 or 23 years of age, and of prepossessing personal appearance. He has been educated at a military school, and has a decided taste for military life. At the first, he gave me a very favorable impression—manly and open in his address, he seemed one of the most gentlemanly and dignified of my acquaintances in the 44th. I was therefore not a little surprised when two days he came to me to be treated for a disease (Gonorrhea) that he must have contracted of some abandoned woman of the town.

NOTES: CHAPTER EIGHT

1. Foote, Shelby. 1963. *The Civil War,* Vol. 3. New York: Random House, page 257.
2. Egbert L. Viele, eminent engineer, topographer, and congressman, wrote a textbook for new officers, a work so splendid that it was adopted by both the Union and Confederate armies. Dr. Smith's access to the corridors of power (see his visit to Major General Halleck) is really quite remarkable. Smith clearly had a considerable degree of credibility; his staunch support of Lincoln before the war may be part of the explanation.
3. Contrabands were liberated black slaves, often hired by Union forces for construction, horse care, washing clothes, and similar activities.
4. Our diarist's derisive tone and eagerness to hear gossip are here seen again.
5. Francis B. Spinola was a lawyer, a Democratic politician, and a Brooklyn alderman. He was given a brigadier's rank as a reward for recruiting four regiments. In late 1863, he was removed from combat command and sent to run the recruiting station in New York City, where he was convicted of fraud. After the war, he was elected to Congress and served on the Committee on Military Affairs. Dr. Smith's opinion— that Spinola was a coward and an incompetent—seems well founded.
6. Springer has been not been identified. McChesney appears to be Col. Joseph M. McChesney of the 1st North Carolina Infantry (Union), white troops who opposed secession. McChesney began his career as a captain in the 9th New Jersey at age twenty-five. In February 1863, he

was commissioned lieutenant colonel in the 1st North Carolina by military governor Staby. He was wounded twice, once at New Bern and again at Washington. In May 1864, he appeared before a board of investigation, charged with pillage and arson at Washington, North Carolina, but no court-martial followed. In May 1865, he was discharged on disability secondary to his wounds.

7. Peter H. Hubon was an assistant surgeon with the 27th Massachusetts when he was assigned to be post surgeon at Washington, North Carolina. When he entered the Army, his professor of anatomy at Albany (New York) Medical College had written to the secretary of war that Hubon "will do honor to the Service." Hubon himself was less confident. In December 1862, he wrote to Gen. Foster, "It is within your power to do a poor friendless fellow a favor. I want the position of surgeon in the 1st N.C. Regt. [commanded by] Col. Potter . . . if you but say the word you can give me a good lift . . . the Surgeon Genl. Dale promised me early promotion, but seems to have neglected it." Hubon never received the post he sought; he died in 1879.

Dr. Robert Ware was age twenty-nine when he volunteered his services to the Sanitary Commission at White House, near Virginia's York River. There, he was loved and admired for his skill, compassion, stamina, and good humor. He joined the 44th Massachusetts and in late December 1862 was put in charge of North Carolina recruits at New Bern.

8. This was probably Chaplain C. L. Woodworth. General Posten is probably Edward E. Potter.

9. Erysipelas is a contagious infection of the skin and subcutaneous tissue, with pain, redness, and swelling, sometimes called St. Anthony's fire.

10. Acting Lieutenant Richard T. Renshaw commanded the gunboat *Louisiana*.

11. Here, at last, we have a chance to see Dr. Smith at work in his medical role. He appears competent and confident.

12. For a full description of the tactics and strategy of the siege of Washington, North Carolina, see Barrett's *The Civil War in North Carolina*, pages 156–62, as well as the *Official Records of the Navy*, Ser. I, Vol. 8, pages 656–70.

13. Cochran may be Capt. Frederick Cochen.

CHAPTER NINE

The Final Days

An enlisted man was mustered into the service for a predetermined period of time—nine months, one year, three years—and was required to complete that time. A commissioned officer could, under certain circumstances, resign and thus had far more flexibility in his commitment to the cause, when compared with the man in the ranks. The policies for furlough for officers and men were also different. There are thousands of court-martials of privates who went absent without leave after they were refused furlough for deaths in the family; even in cases where the soldier's wife had died, leaving no one to care for small children, the Army could be relentless. Yet, as we have seen with Dr. Smith, he had several furloughs home for what appeared to personal convenience. As his diary draws to a close, he arrives at Plymouth, North Carolina, and is thinking about resignation.

In these final weeks, his conflict with Maj. Reuben King reaches a crescendo, his mixture of fascination and repugnance regarding prostitutes is put to the test of Christian charity, and he has an upsetting revelation about his commanding officer.

Thursday April 23. On my arrival at my quarters last night, I found many letters awaiting me, but not one from my dear friend in Pike. I am greatly disappointed. A good letter from my dear Frank, however, greatly cheers me. I have been writing most of the day.

Saturday April 25th. The steamer Ellen S. Terry arrived from New York today. I received letters from several friends—two from the friend most prized—they tell me of love—aye, of devoted affection. The regiment reached New Bern from Washington, North Carolina, this morning—they came by steamers. This P.M., the paymaster, Major Staples,

Dr. George Derby of the 23rd Massachusetts joined Dr. Smith as a pall-bearer at the funeral of Dr. Robert Ware, New Bern, North Carolina.

U.S. ARMY MILITARY HISTORY INSTITUTE

paid the regiment up to the first of March. It is consequently a day of gladness and enjoyment among the men. The day has been fine.

Sunday April 26. I attended the removal of the remains of Robert Ware, Surgeon of the 44th Mass.—as one of the pall bearers. Drs. Coghill, USV—Morung, Surgeon Second Maryland—Derby, Surgeon of the 25th Mass.—Warren, Surgeon Fifth Rhode Island—Assistant Surgeon Fisher 44th Mass.—and myself constituted the pall bearers.[1]

The remains were taken to the Presbyterian Church, where Chaplain [Edward] Hall, 44th Mass., read appropriate portions of scripture, the regimental band performed sweetly several dirges; then after a prayer by Chaplain Hall, who was greatly overcome

Chaplain Edward Hall of the 44th Massachusetts was overcome with grief as he conducted the funeral of Dr. Robert Ware.

FROM RECORD OF THE SERVICE OF THE 44TH MASSACHUSETTS VOLUNTEER MILITIA IN NORTH CAROLINA 1862–1863, BOSTON, 1888, ANONYMOUS

while so engaged, the remains were attended from the church by a numerous escort, with arms reversed, to the New York steamer.

The day has been very warm and spring-like. The streets of the town now present a most beautiful appearance, embowered, as they are, by the trees which line the streets on either hand. The foliage is fully out—the streets seeming like a beautiful, green, arching bower stretching as far as the eye can reach.

Monday April 27th. Another day has nearly gone—there is one the less between me and home. How gladly I greet the evening shades—they were never more welcome. God forbid that I should be disappointed in my hopes of greeting loved ones far away, at the time appointed. The Reverend Mr. Stoddard of Angelica called on me today and remained to dinner. He came by the Spaulding to Beaufort from Fort Monroe. Late in the P.M., I rode out with him and called on the field and staff officers of the 44th Mass., and some of the officers of the Rhode Island Fifth. The

camp of the R.I. Fifth is one of the finest I have seen since I have been in
the service.

Tuesday April 28. I feel so unwell today that I have kept to my tent
pretty closely.[2]

Charges against Major R.V. King were formally signed by Captain
Nelson Chapin of Company K. First charge—conduct disrespectful to his
superior officer, in calling Lieutenant Colonel Wellman a blockhead &
scoundrel in a letter to Colonel J.L. Belknap. Second charge—conduct
unbecoming a gentleman and officer, in reporting that Surgeon W.M.
Smith had procured the dismissal of Assistant Surgeon J.D. Lewis from the
service, he (King) knowing the same to be untrue, and that he (King) was,
himself, the cause.

Second specification under charge second—conduct unbecoming an
officer and gentleman in "feloniously taking a pair of boots belonging to
the engineer of the steam transport Hussar, from the stateroom of said
engineer, which had, by courtesy, been given up to him during the voyage from the Chowan River to New Bern in December last, and appro-
priating the boots to his own use." Third specification under charge
second—"in rendering a false excuse to General Dix for his absence from
his command at Newport News, in saying that he was absent at Norfolk
in attendance on a brother sick in the hospital at that place." The truth
being that he was at Norfolk for the sole purpose of attendance upon the
pariahs of the town—for he has not a brother in the world.[3]

Charge third—conduct prejudicial to good order—"in absenting
himself from his command two days without proper leave, while in command of the regiment and post at Newport News VA."—this was the
absence above-referred to, in which General Dix requested him to
explain, and which he did by the falsehood referred to in the third specification of charge second.

The major is a bad man, and his presence in the regiment is very inju-
rious. There is true justice in the charges being made by Captain Chapin.
The captain knew him to be the rascal he is long before his associates in
the 85th New York knew him. In the fall of 1861, Major King (then captain) was engaged to be married to Captain Chapin's daughter. The day
was set for the marriage & the bride was dressed for the occasion. Instead
of receiving the bridegroom, the poor girl received a note from him dated
at Olean, New York, the residence of King, saying that he had received a
telegram from Elmira (where the 85th was then organizing) which com-

pelled him to leave for that place by the next train. And he did leave, but stopped at Corning that night—instead of occupying a bridal bed, he occupied a bed with a loose woman of the town. This is reported by Captain Seneca Allen of this regiment, who declares that he knows it to be true. I understand that Miss Chapin, who is a girl of good education and some accomplishments, has borne up well under the disappointment. She may congratulate herself on her escape from him, even as she did, for there are few men in the world more destitute of moral principle than the man she would have wedded.

Wednesday April 29th. Has been a very warm and summer-like day. I have been so much indisposed as to be able to leave my quarters but little today.

Major King forwarded a letter to Colonel Belknap this A.M. (for the major has some days past taken quarters at the Gaston House, having left the regiment in disgust because every officer but one voted for Captain Clark instead of himself for lieutenant colonel), in which letter he asks Colonel Belknap to "see Dr. Smith & Captain Chapin & have the charges against him withdrawn"—in which case, he promises to resign. This determination or expression of willingness to resign has been caused by his failure to get the leave of absence he wished, and which we succeeded in stopping at General Foster's headquarters. I understand Captain Chapin to have agreed to withhold them [the charges], if he (Major K) withdraws his application for leave of absence and immediately sends in his resignation.[4]

Thursday April 30. The regiment has been mustered for pay today—Colonel T.H. Lehman of the 103rd PA, the mustering officer. The colonel is very much of a soldier in his personal appearance, and bears himself in a very gentlemanly manner. But he is very unpopular with his regiment. He is often "half seas over" with liquor, and his courage is doubted by his regiment—both officers and men. Colonel Lehman is another illustration of the deceitfulness of a man's personal appearance, and the difficulty of knowing him by that alone. I received a note from Adjutant Hinckley of the 44th Mass., accompanied by a gold pen; a token of his appreciation of certain kindnesses & services [perhaps that of treating Hinckley's gonorrhea] rendered him. Received a letter today from Miss L., dated March 29th. It had wandered away to the 89th New York in search of me. This, in part, explains the long silence of which I complained on a previous page.

Friday May 1. It has been a beautiful day. I have never seen a spring that embodied so much of the beautiful as this. It has seemed all sunshine and flowers. The gardens are crowded with flowers, most conspicuous among them blossom, the rose—and far more rich, healthy and beautiful than its northern kindred are. Strawberries were in blossom three weeks since, & yet they say that vegetation is nearly a month late this year. We have orders this evening to embark tomorrow for Plymouth, North Carolina.

Saturday May 2nd. Embarked today about noon for Plymouth. At 2:00 P.M., the steamer Emily left her dock with half the regiment on board; the other part being on the Massasoit, which left her dock the same hour.

I am again deprived of both my assistants, and suffering as I have been for some time past, it becomes not only a hardship, but impossibility, for me to do justice to all my duties. There is reprehensible neglect on the part of those who have the control and direction of the Medical Department here.

In my present situation, I again find myself in contact with, and if I did but assert my rights, in conflict with, Surgeon Rush of the 101st PA Volunteers, who is not only my junior in rank, but an inefficient & unqualified surgeon, but happens to be an acquaintance of General Wessells. But for the brief period I shall remain in the service, I am not disposed to have any contest, if by the sacrifice of my own feelings, it can be avoided.[5]

Before leaving, this A.M., I learned that Major King's resignation has been accepted by all the generals—thus, passes away from the 85th New York one of the most malign influences and unprincipled men, that ever disgraced the regiment. "Go in peace and sin no more!"

Before leaving, I wrote several letters to friends at the north; Frank, my dear friend in Pike & others; then called at headquarters of the 44th Mass. & bid my friends there good-bye.

As the sun set, our noble steamer [the Emily] which, by the way, was [re]captured while attempting to run the blockade of Charleston Harbor some months since, reached the waters of Pamlico Sound.[6]

The gathering of officers this evening is a very happy one. Sergeant Withery with the violin & Corporal Howe with the guitar, accompanied by some of the fine voices of the officers, awakened some of the finest and happiest feelings of the soul with their melodies—the evening passed swiftly away. And I thought, while all seemed so genial and happy around me, if we were but bound for home, peace, and the honor and prosperity of our beloved country having been secured, how much happier all would be—almost too happy! I am feeling very worn and nearly sick—slept but little last night; I shall therefore take to my berth early.

[That same day, May 2, 1863, Dr. Smith wrote to his son. The relatively peaceful conditions at New Bern are reflected in Smith's possession of stationery with a letterhead, neatly set in Old English type, reading, "Head Quarters Medical Department, 85th Regiment, N.Y. Volunteers."] My Dear Frank, The 85th embarked today for Plymouth, in this state. We go down the Neuse River 40 miles through Pamlico Sound, past Roanoke Island, thence into Albemarle Sound to where the Roanoke River empties into that sound—near the mouth of the Roanoke Plymouth is situated—take your map and trace out our route. It is about [illegible] miles by water to Plymouth. I am able to be about and attend to my duties, but feeling more poorly than I have for some months past—I shall be all right, I guess, in a few days. The time flies slowly, I am so impatient to be with my dear boys again. But a kind Providence permitting, I shall see them again as soon as I promised you. I do not think there will be any more severe fighting in this Department for some time to come. They failed so entirely in their attacks on Newbern and Washington in this state, that they will hardly attempt anything of the kind again for some time to come. Most of the rebels that surrounded us at Washington have gone to reinforce the rebel General Lee in Virginia. I shall write you soon after I reach Plymouth. Be a very excellent boy, and attend to your studies & reading faithfully. Give Clarence a kiss for me. I remain your affectionate father, W. M. Smith."

Sunday May 3. The early morning found us off Roanoke Island—at 1:00 P.M., we were alongside the wharf at Plymouth. Immediately after landing, I called on the provost marshal of the town, Captain Sweet of the 27th Mass. Volunteers, and secured a small house for my sick. The 25th Mass. were ordered to return by the steamers which brought the 85th NY and 103 PA Vols. This afforded the opportunity, which was improved, of securing the quarters occupied by the colonel & staff occupied by the 25th Mass. So I am tonight very pleasantly quartered—the colonel, adjutant, quartermaster & my [hospital] steward occupy rooms in the same house.[7]

Plymouth has been a very pleasant village—now, it is a sad wreck of the "Glory of Bygone Days." Last December, the Rebels made a raid into it and burned the finest part of the town. It was then occupied by only one company of loyal North Carolina volunteers—they, of course, could make but a feeble resistance. This vandal practice of burning their own towns will be sadly realized by this mad people, when the strife is over, and they return to the ruins of their once-beautiful homes.[8]

The regiments quartered here were drawn up this P.M. along the line of works, to attend the ceremonies of raising the Stars & Stripes at the new fort. The sounds of martial music—the cheers of the regiments drawn up for the occasion—the roll of drums; the inspiriting strains of the regimental bands playing The Star Spangled Banner and the national salute fired by the artillery, affords me but little evidence of its being the Sabbath day. The throngs of gaily dressed wenches in the streets, is the only circumstance that would remind me of its being the Holy Sabbath. It has been a charming day today—pleasantly warm, with a gentle breeze blowing from the west.

Monday May 4. The evening, like the day, has been uncomfortably warm. At this hour, 9:00 P.M., my windows are all up to catch a little fresh, cool air, to refresh and relieve the sultry heat. Already I begin to realize the monotony of life we shall lead here—but God willing, I shall not many weeks suffer here from ennui.

May 11, 1863. During the week past, few incidents of any importance has taken place in the little world around me. I have moved my hospital to a large, fine house, recently occupied by a company of the 27th Mass.—it is the largest, finest building in the town. The 45th Mass. and all other soldiers except those belonging to our brigade have been removed to New Bern. The Reverend Mr. Stoddard left here the 7th instant, enroute for home.

News from the Rappahannock is discouraging—Hooker is reported by the Richmond papers as defeated, after having by a masterstroke of generalship successfully crossed the Rappahannock and advanced as far as Chancellorsville upon the flank & rear of the Rebel position at Fredericksburg—if the defeat of General Hooker is as complete as is claimed by the Rebel papers from Richmond of the 5th, 7th and 9th instant, the whole face of the campaign in Virginia is changed—some time must elapse before the Army of the Potomac will be in condition to again take the offensive.

I still have no fears but that the rebellion will be crushed, and the Federal arms be triumphant. But my faith arises more from my confidence in the triumph of the immutable principles of justice and right—from the belief that God will never permit the world to retrograde as it must if this wicked rebellion succeeds, than from confidence in the power of the north, its past successes or its future resources. The movements of the enemy in <u>our</u> front during the latter part of April, plainly indicates their preparation to meet General Hooker's advance. The forces of the enemy having almost entirely disappeared. Even the guerilla bands seem to have been withdrawn to swell the forces of the Confederate General Lee.

I was called this P.M. to visit a sick woman in a house occupied by some females of notoriously bad reputation—the house is in sight from a window of my room, and I have frequently seen ten or 12 sailors & soldiers of that low & debased class, that have no shame, waiting around the house for their turn to be served by the wretched females within.

The prompting of a common humanity decided me to visit the sick woman. I found only the sick woman in the house; her sister having gone out to procure some comfort or necessary. I left the door open wide when I entered; and it was well I did, for the stench quite turned my stomach, as it was. I have seen much squalid poverty & wretchedness and I have seen many filthy places occupied by human beings, but never in my experience one that equaled this—the poor creature was suffering from fever—sent Louisa with medicine an hour after calling. The weather for the past week has been surprisingly cool—clouds and chill winds have prevailed. But today summer seems to have come again.

Thursday May 14. Finished reading "Oliver Twist" today—the interest in the plot, or perhaps I should say characters, in this "epic," as Mr. Dickens chooses to call it, is better maintained than in some of his works; but the "pen and ink portrait" of his characters is not as well drawn as in some of his works. There is less of those facetious sketches and incidents. But the delineation of crime in London among the low and abandoned characters of that metropolis is drawn with a master's hand.

The steamer "Massasoit" arrived this morning, with mail from the north—had a good letter from my Dearest Friend, and one from Mrs. Daggett—they are all well, for which I am very thankful. I was not a little surprised this morning at a quarter to 4:00 o'clock to hear Colonel Belknap at the outer door asking admittance. His nephew, who sleeps with him, admitted him.

I have not given credence to the rumors, which several of the officers of the regiment seem to believe, that he is often in the company of abandoned women, and has one now in this town; but I can no longer disbelieve. He could have no legitimate business away from his quarters until that hour of the morning.

And this evening, my colored cook comes to me with a long story of Colonel Belknap's attempts upon her virtue—it seems he has importuned her, as the opportunity offered, for a long time. Indeed, if her story be true, and I have no reason to doubt it, for she has given many evidences of much integrity, truth & virtue, he commenced his advances soon after his return to the regiment. I am compelled to look upon him henceforth as a man of abandoned tastes, low-minded, and utterly destitute of moral principles; for he has a true and worthy wife at home. The day has been very warm.[9]

Friday May 15. Rose earlier than usual this morning to complete my correspondence in time for the steamer, which left at 8:00 A.M. The action of the officers of the regiment in selecting a major to fill the existing vacancy was embodied in a petition to the Governor and presented to me to sign yesterday. That action resulted in Captain Seneca Allen's receiving a majority of the votes of the officers present at the meeting; and the petition was in his behalf.

I may feel at liberty by and by to endorse the selection made; but I feel assured that the choice is not the one best calculated to serve the best interests of the regiment. And if he was not the ranking captain (except Captain Clark, who is recommended for the lieutenant colonelcy), he certainly would not have received the votes he did.

The captain [Allen] has some good qualities—he is open, warm & even generous-hearted to his friends and a brave man. But he frequently drinks too freely. Several times, I have known him to be so much intoxicated that he would have been utterly incompetent to command men in the hour of danger or of battle. And he is licentious—he seems not to attempt to restrain the indulgence of his passions for women—it is but yesterday that he came to me to be treated for venereal warts—sometimes called syphilitic vegetations. His disease is unmistakably the result of his connexions with abandoned women. His temper is often hasty, and in such moments, he is rash and inconsiderate in his judgment.

The morning was cool, so much that a fire was decidedly comfortable; but the afternoon has been uncomfortably warm out of doors.

I omitted to mention in its proper order that I received an order yesterday from headquarters at New Bern to take charge of the post hospital. The medical director must suppose that I have an unlimited amount of capacity and endurance, or else he is very inconsiderate to keep both my assistants at New Bern on detached duty, and put the care of my own regiment & regimental hospital and the Post hospital on my unassisted hands.

I was again, early this evening, summoned to visit the poor miserable pariah of which I have spoken before—the promptings of humanity induced me to go. Although one of my hospital nurses has been in daily attendance, more or less, since my first visit, the state of destitution & suffering in which I found her was truly such as to excite my sympathies. On a miserable apology for a bed, one dirty sheet covering a dilapidated remnant of what was once a feather bed, constituted all the bed or bedclothing. On this, the poor creature lay, without pillows, a dirty and worn out dress rolled up for a pillow and for a covering, one torn and much worn soldier's blanket was all the house afforded.

She was suffering greatly. For five days, she had taken no nourishment. The rations which the government allowed her, as it does all loyal & destitute persons, were not as such as she could use. [If the rations were hardtack, a sick person could not chew them.]

Plainly, and with all the feeling of my heart, I showed the wretched girls their terrible situation—the great danger that she that was sick was in—the little sympathy and relief the world would extend to such as they were, in their suffering and distress, and the peril to the reputation of those who should even come at the prompting of a common humanity to give them comfort and relief. With many promises, eagerly and earnestly they begged for assistance. I sent my cook to stay with them and do what she could to give them present relief; and from the hospital sent such comforts and medicines as they needed.

Saturday May 16. Dr. Palmer has returned to the regiment today— much to my relief. I called on the provost marshal today, and had him visit with me the wretchedly destitute girls referred to yesterday. He sent a very faithful colored woman to clean up the house and nurse the sick girl. I ordered a bed from the hospital, a clean pair of sheets and some underclothing to be taken to the house. When the poor creature was washed and dressed (for she has had no shirt or underclothing of any kind during her illness, and only a torn and much-worn calico gown—dirty and soiled with every manner of filth—to hide her nakedness) and laid in the clean, sweet bed, she seemed to realize for the first [time] how much more comfortable she could be than she had been. All that could be done for the poor creature under the circumstances shall be done, but there is little hope of her recovery. The mornings and evenings for some days have been refreshingly cool, and the midday abundantly warm for comfort.

Sunday May 17. The steamer North Shore came in this evening with the news that the steam packet Arrow, plying between Norfolk and Albemarle Sound, through the Chesapeake and Albemarle Canal, and the small mail steamer Emily, which generally waited near the junction of the canal with the waters of the Sound for the mail and passengers from the Arrow, were captured by the Rebels on Friday or Saturday last. The capture of the Emily was probably affected by first seizing the Arrow near Currituck Bridge, then placing a force in her cabin and ran out to the Emily before she had any suspicions of danger. One hundred and fifty men, with their days rations were at once sent aboard of two of the gunboats lying here and under the command of Captain Husser, left for the scene of the capture. Company C and a portion of Company G were detailed from the 85th New York to constitute a part of the force.[10]

Monday May 18. The sick girl referred to on several previous dates died this morning. The remaining sister is the most desolate-looking, frail, feeble, worn-faced child I have ever seen. She is truly but a child, being but 16 years of age. This afternoon, she came over through the quarters of my cook and wished to see me. She told me her history and pled for help to secure a place where she could be cared for and earn an "honest living." I gathered the following from her story.

Her father died while she was quite young, leaving an elder sister (the deceased), and an invalid mother, to be supported by her only brother, somewhat older than her sister. They were very poor, the brother working out by days. It is well known that the labor of the poor white man at the south is but poorly recompensed. When the rebellion compelled Union citizens at the south to take up arms against the Federal government or flee to someplace occupied by Union troops for protection, he came to this place (Plymouth). As soon as possible, he got his mother and sisters from their home, about four miles from Gatesville, North Carolina, and brought them to this place. Here they remained until December last. Early in the month, the Rebels made a dash upon the town, and under cover of darkness, succeeded in firing the town and laying the greater part of it in ashes. During the short time they occupied the town, they succeeded in securing many Negroes, and a number of the residents of the town who were suspected of Union sympathies, or were avowedly Union men. These were compelled to enter the Rebel army, or were sent to Sal-

isbury or some other inland prison. Among the number seized and taken
was the brother of this girl. The mother, already long since an invalid,
rapidly sank under the loss of her son and died the 25th of the same
month [Christmas Day].

Since that time, the daughters have had no home, or support, except
as they earned it themselves. That temptations should stand thick around
such, is no cause for wonder. And it would be rather cause for wonder if,
feeble, ignorant and destitute as they were, they had successfully resisted
the temptations that beset them.

My heart pitied the poor, forlorn, destitute creature, as with pale, wan
face, she pled that I would do something to find her a home—where she
could earn an honest living—"God knows," she said, "that's what I want."
And I promised her I would do all I could. But, what can I do? I would
gladly save her from a continued life of abandonment and prostitution; but
my efforts must, of necessity, be limited. I have arranged that she shall, for
the present, go home with the colored woman and the provost marshal
promises to supply her with rations at government expense.

A cool evening has succeeded the warm summer day. Richmond
papers of the 14th have been received today—the tone of the Rebels
seems much depressed; they seem to be greatly discouraged and disheartened, and acknowledge that there never was a time when they were as
hard pressed as now.

Wednesday May 20. The men who left here on Sunday evening on
the gunboats to re-take the Arrow and Emily, returned today. The steamers were captured in the way I have before suggested as probable, and
seem to have been taken up the Chowan [River], and probably its principle tributary, the Blackwater, to the vicinity of Franklin.

Another expedition goes in search of the Rebels tonight, consisting of
three gunboats, with an additional complement of 150 soldiers, 50 of
whom are from Companies B and E of the 85th New York. If they go in
the neighborhood of Franklin on the Blackwater, they will have a brush
with the enemy. It appears folly to me to attempt to follow the captured
vessels; they are both of much lighter draft than any gunboat here, and the
water is extremely shallow and the river very narrow in the neighborhood
of Franklin.

The officers of the 85th New York held a meeting this evening to
take action on the circular issued by the Governor of New York, asking
for information necessary to a complete history of the regiment since its

organization and biography of its officers. Surgeon W.M. Smith & Adjutant Aldrich were selected for that purpose. Had I been present, I should have entered an emphatic protest to my appointment—it will be a most unpleasant, ungrateful & laborious task, if faithfully, truly & carefully written.

The mail steamer Massasoit came in today, bringing many letters from home friends. My dear friend Miss L. is anxious and impatient for that reunion which, if God be willing, shall not be broken this side of the grave. My own heart is equally impatient of that blessed hour when I shall again clasp her to my heart. But I see many things to regret in leaving my post. Never were associations more pleasant & happy between a medical officer and all the officers and men of his regiment than mine have been. All the confidence in my professional skill that a man could ask or hope for has been bestowed upon me; and a larger degree of confidence in, and deference to my opinion in matters outside my department, than I am deserving of. And there are some minds with whom I hold companionship of a high order—with which I have enjoyed many, very many, hours of real pleasure.

My dear boy cheers me with intelligence that he is well and progressing rapidly with his studies. Indeed, the news from all my friends is such as to inspire my heart with thanks to God for His loving kindness and mercy to them. I shall not omit to mention as an important item in my news of today the fact of my brother being admitted to the bar on Wednesday, the 29th of April last.

Thursday May 21. The day has been one of the warmest yet—thermometer 80 in the shade at 1:00 P.M. I sent mail north this morning by the steam tug to Roanoke Island. It is exceedingly dull here—the health of the regiment is excellent, there being but [illegible] in the hospital and seven sick in quarters & none of these serious cases. The Post Hospital is yet, by courtesy, in charge of Dr. Flagg, so that my duties there are not burdensome. I have had strawberries in abundance for some days, by paying 25 cents per quart. Indeed, our fare is excellent and abundant at some $4.00 to $5.00 a week cost, however.[11]

Friday May 22. Thermometer 85 degrees in the shade today. The earth is getting thirsty. The steam tug with mail did not leave as I expected. She went at 7:00 o'clock A.M. today. Nothing of interest today—when that is the case, I think of home the more, and am impatient to be there.

Tuesday May 26. The change in the weather yesterday was very marked—thermometer 62 degrees. A dark, lowering sky with occasional drifts of fog. Today, the temperature has been the same as yesterday; and the sky has been of that darkly leaden hue, always so cheerless. No event of importance has occurred in the little world of which we are the center.

The expedition referred to on the 20th instant returned Sunday A.M. the 24th, having failed to reach the anchorage of the captured boats Emily and Arrow; the enemy had taken them up the Blackwater in the immediate vicinity of Franklin. The water was not sufficiently deep to allow the gunboats to approach within three miles of their anchorage. From this branch of the Chowan, the gunboats proceeded up another branch of the Chowan to Murfreesboro. After occupying the town a few hours, the expedition started homeward, making a descent on the Chowan upon a nest of smugglers and guerillas on the way back.

Wednesday May 27th, 1863 [the final entry in Dr. Smith's diary]. The cheerless sky of the past two days has given away to a bright and sunny sky today, though the morning was cool, the thermometer standing at 62 at 9:00 A.M. The afternoon has been quite warm.

I had almost forgotten to mention that Dr. Flagg left Sabbath afternoon, the 24th. The duties of the Post Hospital Surgeon, attended as they are by the additional ones of attendance on all the sick among the citizens and contrabands, and the care of the sick in my own hospital, are so numerous and pressing as to keep me incessantly occupied. Two companies of cavalry, Third New York and First North Carolina, the 24th Independent New York Battery, the two companies of the 96th New York doing guard duty in town, and the sick from the gunboats (generally four gunboats at this station), supply the wards of the hospital with its sick. The citizens and contrabands are not admitted to its wards. The citizens have no claim on the attention of the surgeon of the hospital, beyond that which humanity dictates.[12]

NOTES: CHAPTER NINE

1. Coghill is probably Mason F. Cogswell, an assistant surgeon of U.S. Volunteers. Edward P. Morong was born in 1833 in Alabama, took his M.D. at Harvard in 1854, studied a year in Europe, and opened his practice in Baltimore in 1855. On his application to be an army surgeon, he described with pride an operation that partially restored sight in a fifty-five-year-old man who had had severe eye infections that

destroyed the left eye and left most of the right cornea opaque. Morong removed the iris behind the clear section of the cornea. Despite this ingenuity, Morong seemed to be a magnet for controversy. He was accepted as surgeon for the 2nd Maryland Volunteers but was rejected by an examining board, who found his medical work "equivocal" and his status as an "advertising oculist" unprofessional. In June 1863, however, the medical director of the 18th Army Corps wrote to the surgeon general that "there has been some error" and stated that Morong had been on duty since April 1861 and was a competent and efficient surgeon. In October 1864, Morong was in Boston, claiming to be sick with malaria. Dr. D. W. Hand, in North Carolina, wrote, somewhat testily, "He was well when he left here! I have no use for him. He should be relieved from duty [fired]." In early 1866, Morong was stationed at Brownsville, Texas, where he was accused of eating the patients' food and stealing bedding. These charges came to naught, and six months later, he was brevetted lieutenant colonel for "meritorious service."

George Derby was surgeon of the 23rd Massachusetts and in 1865 was brevetted lieutenant colonel for "faithful and meritorious service." Ephraim Warren was surgeon of the 5th Rhode Island Heavy Artillery. He was in hospital July through September 1863 for an unnamed illness. In January 1864, he applied to take the examination for "surgeon of colored troops." In December 1864, he took the examination to be a surgeon in the new, elite Hancock Corps but failed and entered private practice. In 1892, the army billed him $48.25 for food eaten at New Bern in 1863. Theodore W. Fisher was age twenty-six when he was promoted to fill the vacancy created by the death of Dr. Ware.

2. In addition to diarrhea and episodic depression, it would appear that Dr. Smith also suffered from migraine headaches.

3. Perhaps Major King meant "brothel," not "brother."

4. This sort of endless squabbling was common in both the armies, North and South.

5. Smith's antagonism toward Rush, described in Chapter 4, has not diminished.

6. This note suggests that part of his diary may have been written retrospectively. The *Emily* and the *Arrow* were captured May 15, 1863 (some sources say May 16).

7. Captain Sweet may be Ripley P. Swift, 27th Massachusetts.

8. In 1865, the Confederates burned their own capital city, Richmond.

9. Smith was not alone in his sentiments regarding Belknap. Several men of the 85th New York considered Belknap a coward for having disappeared at the Battle of Fair Oaks. (Mahood, 1991.)

10. Husser is probably Lt. Cmdr. Charles W. Flusser, USN, who was killed May 19, 1864, fighting the Confederate iron-clad ram *Albemarle*. Rear Admiral Samuel P. Lee wrote, "He was generous, good and gallant, and his untimely death is a real and great loss to the public service."

11. Flagg was Dr. Samuel P. Flagg of the 25th Massachusetts.

12. Dr. Smith, as he closed his diary May 27, 1863, was at Plymouth, North Carolina. Eleven months later, Confederate forces captured the entire Union garrison at Plymouth, and Smith's comrades of the 85th New York spent the following year in Confederate prison camps.

CHAPTER TEN

The Next Thirty-Nine Years

D r. Smith submitted his resignation on June 13, 1863, stating "I respectfully tender my resignation as surgeon of the 85th Regiment of NY Vols. For reasons, please refer to the annexed Surgeon's Certificate of Disability. Hoping the above will meet with your favorable consideration." The attached report, signed by Abraham P. Frick, Surgeon of the 103rd Pennsylvania, read as follows.

> Surgeon W.M. Smith of the 85th Regiment of NY Vols. having applied for a certificate on which to ground his resignation, I do hereby certify that I have carefully examined this officer and find him suffering from chronic spinal meningitis, caused by injury to the spine by a fall received several months since; in consequence of which he has not been able to ride horseback for the last three months. Any considerable fatigue or exercise induced severe neuralgic pains in the muscles of the loins and hips. There is great tenderness on pressure upon the third and fourth lumbar vertebrae. For the last three weeks, he has suffered from tingling and numbness of the muscles of the thigh and lower extremities. In consequence of this disability, he is in my opinion, unfit for duty and I believe the period of his recovery to be remote and uncertain. I therefore recommend acceptance of his resignation. Plymouth, North Carolina, June 13, 1863.[1]

A fellow officer of the 85th New York, writing in the pages of the *Illustrated History of Allegany County,* represents Dr. Smith in the following manner:

Surgeon W.M. Smith resigned and returned home in June 1863. He was a great favorite with officers and men, because of his unvarying good nature and kindness of heart toward all. He was an indefatigable worker, and was especially tireless in his efforts to provide for the greater comfort of the sick and wounded, to alleviate their sufferings, or shield them from the exposures and inconveniences so common and almost unavoidable during the war. No regiment was better cared for than the 85th. The doctor was full of ingenious and thoughtful devices conducive to the greater care and comfort of his men, and was possessed of the rare foresight and ability to discern and secure such things as other surgeons and officers never thought or cared about until they were sorely needed, and generally could not be obtained. For these and other distinctive traits, Surgeon Smith was beloved and deeply respected by every man in the regiment. The morning he left us, the regiment was drawn up in line, at dress parade, and bade him good-bye with a sorrow and depth of feeling seldom felt, and still more rarely manifested by veteran soldiers. We all felt that we were losing a royally good man—one whose place it would be difficult to fill.[2]

Dr. Smith's resignation was accepted on June 17th, 1863. Less than a month later, July 16, 1863, William M. Smith and Frances A. Lyon were joined in marriage by the Reverend Daniel Russell at the Presbyterian Church in Pike, New York.

Later that year, Smith reopened his medical practice at Angelica, where he continued for nine years. In 1872, he was appointed Surgeon General of the State of New York by Governor John A. Dix, veteran of the war of 1812 and a Union major general during the Civil War. Smith served in this post until 1874, when Dix was defeated for reelection. Smith continued to be active in Republican politics and was a delegate to the 1876 National Convention, held in Cincinnati, Ohio.

During these years, his practice in Angelica was one of the most extensive in western New York. In 1880, he was nominated for the post of Health Officer of the Port of New York by Governor A. B. Cornell and remained in that position for twelve years, the longest term of service in the history of the office up to that time.

As a regimental surgeon during the war, he had been responsible for the health of one thousand men. By contrast, nearly half a million immigrants entered the Port of New York each year.

Smallpox, a disease few doctors today have ever seen, was a cause of major epidemics throughout most of history. This dreadful disease was usually fatal, always painful, and inevitably left the survivors scarred for life. Just as today, when the major source of tuberculosis is incoming immigrants, the major carriers of smallpox, typhus, and yellow fever were the immigrants of the 1880s.

On assuming office, Smith negotiated with the steamship lines a program in which immigrants were vaccinated before departing Europe or during the early part of the passage across the ocean. This measure was highly effective in protecting not only the incoming immigrants themselves, but all the citizens of the United States as well.

The lack of public confidence in the previous administration of the Port Quarantine Facilities was seen in 1857, when a mob of citizens, living near the health facility, burned it to the ground. Newer facilities, located on artificial islands in New York Harbor, had somewhat remedied this problem of proximity, but Dr. Smith still faced major hurdles, both political and economic.

Democrats in the State Legislature voted down appropriations for maintenance and repair of the new buildings, especially the smallpox and cholera hospitals, hoping that a public health disaster would discredit the Republican administration.

Another problem was with the steamship companies themselves. Immigrants held for quarantine observation in the port facilities were fed at the expense of the passenger line that had brought them to New York. Naturally, officials of the steamship companies besieged the health officer for early release of the suspected passengers, and politicians made alliances with the less scrupulous shipowners.

An example of the dangers lurking in every arrival is seen in the case of the *Polynesia,* which came into New York Harbor in June 1885 with eight hundred passengers in steerage. At the quarantine station, health officers found two children infected with smallpox. The ship's officers insisted that both children had been isolated as soon as their condition became visible. However, through the use of an interpreter, it was soon learned that one child had mingled with the other passengers for three days after the highly contagious skin eruptions had appeared.

Over the protests of the *Polynesia's* owners, every passenger was detained, and thirty-nine more cases of smallpox became apparent. If these highly contagious sufferers had been released into the overcrowded streets and tenements of New York City, a disaster of frightening proportions would have been inevitable.[3]

The fear and terror felt toward communicable diseases in the era before bacteriology and antibiotics may be seen in the following: Any immigrant showing signs of yellow fever or typhus was taken immediately to the quarantine hospital on Swinburne Island. Their clothes were removed and cast into a furnace. If the patient survived, he was kept on the island until considered entirely noncontagious. If he died, he was sealed in a coffin and buried deep in the quarantine cemetery on Seguine's Point. Friends and relatives of the sick and dying were neither permitted to visit nor allowed to remove the body elsewhere for burial.[4, 5]

As with any such office, subject to the scrutiny of politicians, newspapers, ship owners, and immigrant groups, there was criticism of the Smith administration of the Port Health Authority. The New York *Daily Tribune* called upon Gustav H. Schwab of Oelrich's and Co., agents for the North German Lloyd Steamship Company. Mr. Schwab's comments, published June 19, 1887, certainly cast a positive light upon Dr. Smith:

> In our long intercourse with Dr. Smith, I can only say that he has been uniformly desirous of accommodating those engaged in the steamship business, as far as he could, with a conscientious regard for the interests of the people. He has been uniformly courteous, attentive and efficient, discharging the duties of the office in the best possible manner, without committing a wrong of any description. The attacks which have been made upon his character and administration by some newspapers are wholly unfounded and unjustifiable. It is a matter for regret that some journals have permitted themselves to assail him indiscriminately without investigating the prevailing methods of conducting the quarantine establishment of the port. I think that all of the steamship men in New York will confirm my statement to the effect that Dr. Smith, in the printed criticisms upon him, has been outrageously slandered. If there had been the slightest crookedness, or wrongdoing, in the seven years of Dr. Smith's service, it must have come to public knowledge. The health officer

of the port is invested with extensive powers and can use them in a great number of directions. They have never been exercised, to my knowledge, in any way that could be termed improper. We have been agents of the North German Lloyd 26 years and I have been in charge 11 years, so I know whereof I speak.

Smith served in this post from 1880 to 1892. In those twelve years, from the official residence of the Health Officer, at Rosebank, on Staten Island, he could gaze across the Narrows as millions of the "huddled masses, yearning to be free," passed before his eyes. Now his own children were moving on in life. Frank had graduated from Yale in 1872, and Clarence in 1883.

In 1892, Smith had been married twenty-nine years. His children were grown and gone. A severe attack of bronchopneumonia had nearly killed him. The damp harbor air and the cold New York winters were probably not the best thing for a man with lung trouble. He was sixty-six years old. It was time for a change.

Mrs. Frances Lyon Smith around 1888. When she was Dr. Smith's fiancée, he worried whether she would wait for him. She not only waited and married him, but outlived him by twenty years!

SMITH FAMILY COLLECTION

After several years of travel in search of an agreeable climate, he settled in Redlands, California, a spot even today known for its charm and salubrious climate. There, he busied himself with real estate development and citrus growing, and was an active member of the Fortnightly Club, an intellectual discussion group.[6]

On January 18, 1902, a second attack of bronchopneumonia took his life. The first paragraph of his will stated, "I desire that all arrangements and expenses for my funeral be as unpretentious and inexpensive as is consistent with a due regard for propriety and decency."[7]

The ninth paragraph of the same will illustrates that concepts of honor and memories of the great war had not dimmed much in forty years:

> I desire and will that my son Frank shall have either my sword, sword belt, sash and other portions of my military uniform worn and used in the service of the United States during the War of the Rebellion, or those worn and used during my service as Surgeon-General on the staff of General John A. Dix, as he may choose. The choice not made by him I desire and will to be the property of my son Clarence. I charge upon my beloved sons that these relics shall be preserved by them, and remember that they were won by earnest endeavor and always honorably worn; during days that tested the faith of loyal men, or when peace had rewarded the perils and sacrifices of those who fought to preserve the Union, and one of the heroes of that war was the Governor of the State of New York.

(Dr. Smith's uniform as surgeon general of the State of New York, the original-hand-written manuscript of this diary, and his late 1890s surgical kit, are all held in the special collections of the A. K. Smiley Public Library, Redlands, California.)

His beloved Frances, who he had feared might not wait for him, outlived him by twenty years, dying December 31, 1922, in San Bernardino County, California.

The somewhat rigid and imperious persona that inhabits his diary seems to have softened over the years. Their grandchildren called him "Ampa Doctor" and Frances "Amma Doctor," and family tradition recalls them as cheerful, benign, and encouraging. The warmth of the family circle is often where all of us shine best.

NOTES: CHAPTER TEN

1. Medical Officer File, Record Group 94, entry 561, National Archives.
2. Anon., *History of Allegany County, New York, with Illustrative Descriptions of Scenery.* New York, F. W. Beers, 1879. Many entries.
3. Chadbourne, Paul A., ed., *The Public Service of the State of New York,* Vol. I, pages 424–28. Boston, James R. Osgood, 1882.
4. Anon., *Contemporary Biography of New York,* pages 436–38, photocopy. Publisher and date not recorded.

5. *The Allegany County Republican,* January 4, 1889.
6. Obituaries, *Redlands Daily Facts,* January 18, 1902, and *Redlands Daily Review,* January 20, 1902. See also widow's application for military pension, National Archives.
7. San Bernardino County Clerk's Office, Will #2086.

CHAPTER ELEVEN

Commentary

It would certainly appear that this diary was almost entirely a record of private thoughts, not intended for the eyes of others, and certainly not for publication during the lifetime of the participants. Many of the entries are quite damaging to the reputations of the officers that served with Smith—even the ones he liked—and it is also very likely that he would not have wanted his wife to see how he doubted her emotional fidelity before their marriage. Thus, we have the all-too-rare opportunity to see a man talking to himself, with both the honesty and possible self-deception inherent in internal monologue.

A first question that must be addressed is Dr. Smith *as a doctor.* The editor, during his forty years as a practicing physician, was often placed in a position where he was required to evaluate both medical students and fully licensed doctors. Judging one's peers is not easy and contains as many perils as rewards. Judging one's peers of a century and a half ago is fraught with even greater peril. However, the task is doable.

One possible guide is the hoary adage that describes the two things necessary for a successful medical practice: "Gray hair for a look of dignity, and hemorrhoids for a look of concern." While this suggestion is largely facetious, it calls to mind the need for a certain *gravitas* on the part of the physician, and the necessity of appearing compassionate. Better still, of course, is actual compassion, an active and informed empathy for the patient and his surroundings. Even better is empathy plus active and efficient techniques for lessening the patient's sufferings and increasing his chances of recovery. In brief, we can consider two factors: compassion and technical skill.

Taking compassion first, let us examine the evidence in this diary. At Harrison's Landing, Dr. Smith confronted a general to get his men a drier campsite. His diary frequently shows his concern for a patient's suffering and for the distress of the widows of the men who died. On several occasions, he walked in order to let a sick or weary soldier ride his horse. At the Nansemond River, he remarked, "My sick are pleasantly and comfortable provided for." He remarks on the suffering of the soldiers who have no tents and shows his pleasure when his men have deep beds of pine needles to ease their sleeping bodies. He comments on the burned and wounded Confederates: "a ghastly sight," and "victims of the dread carnage of war." After the battle of Goldsboro, he thought the military gain hardly outweighed the five hundred Union men killed and wounded. At Plymouth, his first act was to procure a comfortable house for his sick. There he also overcame his repugnance of prostitutes, to bring treatment and nutrition to one.

The other side of medical practice is technical competence. Compassion alone is useless unless it is accompanied by some activity that will cure or improve the patient, or at least reduce his suffering. There should be technical competence commensurate with what is generally known by physicians. Dr. Smith, of course, must be judged by the medical knowledge of *his* time, not ours. His diary gives us considerable evidence to answer the question. On the Peninsula, he fulminates at length on the fourteen regiments that were not provided with quinine; it seems clear that he knows "remittent fever" should be treated (or prevented) with quinine. He has definite ideas on what will facilitate recovery from typhoid. Though he disapproved of the activities that brought venereal disease to his fellow officers, he did not hesitate to treat them to the best of his abilities. One lieutenant with gonorrhea later sent a gift, presumably reflecting a cure. Smith seems to have done well when his hospital was inspected, and he passed the five-day examination for promotion to a higher rank of surgeon, when others failed. His descriptions of his amputation work seem accurate and informed. When he was the doctor for the Port of New York, he instituted a program of vaccinating immigrants as they left the European ports, rather than on arrival in the United States. From the evidence available, it would appear that Smith was above average in both compassion and technical competence. Even when he regarded his fellow Americans with a jaundiced eye, he did his duty.

What else can we learn from this journal? At least ten things come to mind. The first is the narrative of a war experience. Dr. Smith gives us fairly detailed descriptions of two battles—Kinston and Goldsboro—and of one siege, that of Washington, North Carolina. Further, he tries to relate the events around him to overall Union and Confederate strategy.

Second, his diary, plus the still-preserved answers to his promotional examination, tell us much about medical knowledge in 1861–63, and of Dr. Smith's high expectations of himself.

Third, we learn much of Victorian attitudes toward "fallen women" and the absolute dichotomy between good women and—the others. We are also witness to his dawning awareness that some of the not-good women were more victim than villain, which pitted his moral repugnance against the demands of Christian forgiveness and charity.

Fourth, we learn the rather surprisingly high incidence of venereal disease among the officers of the 85th New York and nearby regiments. Our diarist does not even mention the same problem among the enlisted men, although it is likely that such infections were even more prevalent with the soldiers.

Fifth, we learn of his susceptibility to sudden shifts of mood. Even on beautiful days, with combat far away, he often found himself wishing for the quiet of the grave, while in time of peril, he was just as likely to be optimistic and joyful as downcast and pessimistic. In his "blue" spells, he seemed specially vulnerable to thoughts of possible insufficient devotion on the part of his fiancée, Miss Frances Lyon.

Sixth, he reflects, to a remarkable degree, the Victorian concepts of honor. He worries himself to desperation over a totally unfounded accusation that he had stolen some army bedsheets; he frets that Miss Lyon's apparently innocent attendance at parties at home might cause gossip and damage his standing in the medical and political community.

Seventh, we see how much of the regiment's energy and time was devoted to internal quarrels, rather than to winning the war. (Review of many other documents in the Union court-martials indicates that his regiment was not alone in this serious flaw.)

Eighth, we are told the characteristics of several general officers whom Smith observed at close range: the steadfast bravery of John Foster; the bumbling cowardice of Francis Spinola; and the derring-do of Henry Naglee.

Ninth, we see his admiration of Maj. Gen. George B. McClellan gradually shift to contempt and scorn, as the terrible casualties mount and "Little Mac" fails at one crucial moment after another in his doomed Peninsular Campaign.

Finally, we see the difference between the inner world of a man and the face he shows to the outer world. Inside, he is filled with criticism and disdain, even of the men he most admired, while outside, he is productive and, from the surviving accounts, liked and admired by his regimental companions.

His apparent success in private practice, surgeon generalship of New York State, and as health officer of one of the world's busiest ports all suggest that his outer shell, that of a highly competent professional man and administrator, was a very real and enduring edifice.

Since most of us suppress our inner doubts, our internal carpings, our unexpressed annoyances at the frictions of daily life, and present, instead, to that outer world of necessity, of employment, of companionship, of family, some workable semblance of bonhomie and productivity, perhaps that should be the only standard by which we—and Dr. Smith—should be judged.

And by that standard, that yardstick of devotion and productivity, he earned the sobriquet given to him by a fellow officer: "a royally good man."

MCCLELLAN AND COWARDICE

A fter the Battle of Fair Oaks, Union major general George B. McClellan sent a telegram to Secretary of War Edwin Stanton, blaming the Union defeat on the weakness of the men in Brig. Gen. Silas Casey's division. This telegram, sent June 1, 1862, read, in part: "Casey's division, which was in first line, gave way unaccountably and discreditably . . . with the exception of Casey's division, our men behaved splendidly." Three days later, McClellan backtracked a bit, saying through his Assistant Adjutant-General that "It is difficult for him [McClellan] to decide what was the exact conduct of Casey's division." That same day, McClellan blamed the New York *Herald* for misquoting him. Casey, an old general with decades of service, complained as gently as possible, writing to McClellan's Chief of Staff (who was also McClellan's father-in-law!) on June 5, "In the New York papers of the 2nd instant I see that General McClellan reported to the Secretary of War that my division in some unaccountable manner, was driven back, losing artillery and baggage." After a detailed recital of the battle events, and his heavy casualties, Casey concluded, "You can well imagine that I feel much aggrieved by the remarks of the general commanding, but have that belief in his sense of justice which cannot conceive that he will fail to correct an error." The full text will be found in the *Official Reports,* Series I, Vol. 11, pages 749–56.

From 130 years away, this exchange of messages appears as a natural outgrowth of McClellan's colossal ego, his despicable unwillingness to accept blame, his blind ambition for the presidency, and his probable physical cowardice. Dr. Smith, who was actually there, is far more entitled to an opinion. On June 11, 1862, he wrote from Long Bridge, Virginia, to a friend at home, W. Van Nostrand.

My dear sir: Your favor of the 20th ultimo came to hand in
due time. Since that time, you know we have had a terrible collision with the Rebels. Much has been said of Casey's Division by
the jealousy of generals, chiefly, and correspondents, who are the
hanger-ons of these Generals & who were not on the battle-
ground of Casey's Division, nor indeed, dare be, with one exception: Buckley of the Herald, & he gives a very different story to
the public. It is sufficient for impartial men to know what they
will know, despite misinformation, that the battle commenced
between 12:00 and 1:00 P.M. and that the less-than-6,000 men of
Casey's command held a force, never estimated less than 40,000
men, until nearly 4:00 o'clock P.M., certainly three hours &
without a regiment to reinforce and sustain them, although
Couch's line of battle was less than 200 rods behind us; sustaining
a loss in killed and wounded of fully one-fourth the number with
which they went into battle. I remained under fire in the immediate vicinity of the ranks, dressing the wounded, until the overwhelming force had outflanked right and left of our line of battle
and wounded men were struck a second time while being dressed
and several horses had been shot down near the orderly who was
holding my own.

Consequently, I know the tenacity & bravery with which most
of the regiments of the division fought. The 103 PA broke early
in the action and rushed pell mell on Couch's line—they did not
receive or give a single volley—their conduct gave character to
the whole. The 85th in particular, fought well until enveloped by
the columns of the enemy. The character of the remarks by the
press & McClellan's first telegram has greatly discouraged the
brave men in this and other regiments composing the division.
No division has suffered half as much since they landed at Fortress
Monroe from neglect & exposure as this—they landed with
13,000 men. Today, cannot bring into line 5,000 effective men. If
ever a truthful history of this campaign shall be written, a dark
responsibility & disgraceful neglect will be laid at the door of
some of the managers.

My health is very poor. I have worked myself threadbare, in
trying to keep my department shipshape amid all the disadvantages of my want of means, help, et cetera. And now, after strug-

gling with my ailment [unnamed] through the dank swamps, pes-
tiferous malaria, weary marches, long days and nights of labor
with the sick & wounded [if] my health does not improve within
a few days, I shall return for a short time to see if the free bracing
air of my native hills will not restore me to myself. McClellan
waits for reinforcements. Unless the gunboats achieve a signal and
unexpected success, the battle of Richmond yet remains to be
fought. Signed W. M. Smith.

Other writers of the 85th New York shared Smith's feelings. Capt. Will
Clark, in a detailed letter to the *Ontario Repository* (Onondaga County, New
York), printed June 18, 1862, described the brave stand of the 85th, and
E. R. Stillman, late sergeant-major of the 85th, also defended the regiment
in an April 26, 1883, letter to the *National Tribune.* (Both letters courtesy of
R. E. L. Krick, Richmond NBP.)

An even more negative view of "Little Mac" was expressed by Maj.
Gen. Philip Kearny: "McClellan is no General, with all his talents. He has
not the remotest aptitude for war." This letter, printed in the Indianapolis
Daily Journal, October 12, 1864, expounded at great length upon McClellan's incompetence and political machinations.

DR. SMITH'S
EXAMINATION PAPERS

T he stereotyped picture of the Civil War doctor, partially intoxicated and doing nothing but amputations (and those not very well), is far from the truth. The entirety of Dr. Smith's written examination has been preserved and is presented here in order to give a more accurate perspective of the range of knowledge of a Civil War doctor, aspiring to the rank of Surgeon of U.S. Volunteers. The record begins with a two-page history of his experience and training, but this has been covered earlier in the book. The actual examination follows, with the questions in italics and the answers in plain type. My notes are in brackets.

Are there objections to the use of rivers on which large towns are situated? The refuse, vegetable and animal matter which finds its way into rivers upon which large towns are situated impregnates the water with their properties, which when taken by individuals communicates more or less the deleterious influence arising from vegetable and animal poisons. [The knowledge of bacteria in disease was a decade away.]

Describe the effect of warm and cold weather conditions. A low temperature is unfavorable to the development of diseases which have their origins in miasmatic influences. Diseases of an inflammatory character are most common at low temperatures. [Cold weather killed malaria-carrying mosquitoes.]

Such temperature as usually pervades in tropical climates is favorable to the development of disease to a much greater extent than that of temperate climates. A high degree of heat is, however, destructive of some poisons which are very active in producing disease.

Define a disinfectant and describe the several classes of disinfectants. A disinfectant is an article which decomposes or destroys or renders inert animal and vegetable poisons with which the atmosphere may be impregnated. I am not able to describe the several classes. The principle of these such as the chlorides have a chemical action on the poisons.

What is the minimum cubic amount of air which should attend each patient in a well-ventilated hospital? One thousand feet.

What were the causes of the last war with Great Britain and in what year did it take place? How long did it last, where and in what year was the Treaty of Peace signed and who were the commissioners? The right claimed on the part of Great Britain to search vessels under the flag of the United States and the impressment of seamen taken from vessels under that flag were the principle causes of the war.

Many vessels belonging to the merchant marine of the United States were confiscated by the British authorities for a violation of the edict of the English government forbidding neutral intercourse with French ports. This was a source of complaint on the part of the American government and in connection with the act of the British frigate Leopard in firing into the American frigate Chesapeake contributed in some degree to that exasperation of the American people, which resulted in the Declaration of War in 1812. The war lasted three years. The treaty of peace was signed in 1815. The names of the commissioners who signed the treaty of peace were Henry Clay, John Adams and John Randolph, but I am not quite certain of that.

Under what circumstances did the House of Hanover succeed to the British crown? Name the sovereigns of that house who have reigned in Great Britain. The House of Hanover succeeded by the extinction of the House of Stuart at the death of Queen Anne. George I of England, a German prince, was the first of the reigning House of Hanover on the English throne. George II, son of George I, succeeded to the throne. George III and George IV followed in regular order of succession. George IV died without legiti-mate male issue and was succeeded by William IV. At the death of William IV, the present reigning sovereign, Victoria I ascended the throne.

What are the signs of fracture of the acromial process? The shoulder is flat-tened—the prominence caused by the acromial process is absent; the patient is unable to raise his hand to his head and the shoulder appears as if fallen downwards and inwards.

The indications of treatment are to bring the fragment in apposition with the portion of bone from which it is detached, by raising the elbow and supporting it in that position. In luxation of the head of the humerus into the axilla, the prominence of the acromial process remains—there is a distinct depression beneath the acromion and the head of the humerus may be felt in the axilla by raising the arm from the side and pressing the hand well up into the axilla. In fracture of the acromion, the arm is not lengthened and retains its normal position. In the luxation referred to, the arm is lengthened, and the elbow thrown somewhat back and outward.

In what direction does luxation of the inferior maxillary bone occur and what are the signs and method of reduction? Luxation occurs forward. Signs—if luxated on one side only, there is angular deformity; the chin has the appearance of being thrown downward and forward and the mouth cannot be closed. The reduction may be effected by grasping with the hand that side of the inferior maxillary upon which the luxation exists, the thumb being placed in the mouth, on the inferior maxillary close to its ramus. The inferior maxillary should then be pressed firmly down until the condyle is sufficiently disengaged and then pushed backwards. In subluxation of the inferior maxillary, the condyle is not fully luxated, but rests on the anterior lip of the condyloid cavity. It is most frequently met with in the aged. [Treatment is much the same today.]

Describe the different forms of hydrocoele and the characters of the fluids contained in them and the treatment of each form. I do not recall to mind but three forms of hydrocoele—hydrocoele of the cord, of the tunica vaginalis and that form in which the effused fluid is external to the tunica vaginalis. When hydrocoele of the cord occurs, it is usually situated on the anterior portion of the cord, is circumscribed, and has the general appearance of a small tumor.

In hydrocoele of the tunica vaginalis, the testicle is situated in the posterior portion of the sac. The tumor is soft and somewhat elastic to the touch, giving the impression of a fluid content. When a light [a burning candle?] is held on the side of the hydrocoele opposite the eye, it is seen to be semi-transparent. The fluid contained in them is generally a colorless serum; sometimes, however, tinged with blood. Treatment: puncture of the hydrocoele and escape of the fluid contained is sometimes productive of cure. Generally, the injection of some stimulating fluid is necessary. Port wine is frequently used. Tincture of iodine is also used, with good effect.

What are the conditions on which secondary hemorrhage after amputation depend, and what are the best modes of treating them? Secondary hemorrhage may depend upon the imperfect application of ligatures—a too-early separation of the ligature from sloughing of the parts, or the imperfectly organized condition of the arterial plug, dependent upon the low vitality of the blood. If the hemorrhage arises from imperfect application of the ligature, the dressings of the stump should be removed and the artery secured. If from retraction of the artery, or the condition of its coats, this is impractical, the artery must be secured by ligature applied at the nearest practical point above. If hemorrhage occurs from sloughing of the stump, amputation higher up will in most cases be necessary.

In those cases which depend upon the imperfect and unorganized condition of the arterial plug, at the separation of the ligature, the general health of the patient must be the chief care of the surgeon. Active and vigorously supporting treatment will be necessary in those cases in which there is sloughing of the stump. [The concepts of bacteria and wound infection lay in the future.]

Describe one species in each class of the vertebrated animals. The fish is characterized by its ability to support life without access to the atmosphere. It is provided with a structure at the gills by which the elements of the atmosphere are abstracted from water, and which constitute its lungs. The brain in the fish is rudimentary; the spinal cord communicates with and appears to be a prolongation of the brain. Locomotion is performed by means of web-like appendages, situated at the termination of the vertebrae, on the back, and along the inferior portion of the animal. Reproduction is effected by means of ova which are deposited by the female and impregnated by contact with the spermatozoa of the male, which it deposits near the ova.

The lizards may properly be chosen as a type of this class. Many species of this class are amphibious. The brain of this class evinces development of an animal of higher order than the fish. The powers of locomotion of this animal are very limited, and is performed by means of organs situated inferiorly and having in some degree the structure and characteristics of the fin of the fish and the legs of the mammal. Reproduction is effected from ova which are deposited by the animal in situations favorable for the influence of sufficient heat for the development of the ovum.

The bird is the next highest order in the vertebrates. This class is endowed with organs and appendages which give it powers of locomotion superior to any other class. It is biped. Its brain evinces a higher order of development than the preceding class. Reproduction is effected by means of ova which, after being deposited, are subjected to artificial warmth.

The next and fourth class is the mammal. The type of this class superior to all other species is man. The superior development of his brain and the admirable adaption of all his parts to his numerous wants and to usefulness to his species is one of the principle characteristics of man. The distinguishing characteristic of this class is the method of reproduction. Impregnation takes place within the organs of the female and in which for a greater or lesser period the foetus is sustained. Subsequent to the perfect development of foetal life and when its independent existence is established by the delivery of the mother, the young of the mammal is supplied with nourishment by organs with which nature has supplied the mother. This endowment of nature is one of the chief and distinguishing characteristics of this class.

Enumerate the principle roots and grains from which alcoholic drinks are distilled in various parts of the world. Wheat, corn, barley and rye are the principal grains used in the preparation of alcoholic drinks in the United States and in Europe. There are other articles used in the distillation of alcoholic drinks, but I cannot now call them to mind. [Dr. Smith rarely drank.]

What is herpes? Give the symptoms, diagnosis and treatment. Herpes is classed among the eruptive diseases. Symptoms: the appearance of the eruption is attended with a stinging, burning pain in that portion of the skin affected. There is usually attending the eruption, more or less febrile movement. It has a tendency to spread and often covers considerable portions of the limb affected, or if on the body, has a tendency to extend around it. The eruption is bright red and crowned with a vesicle, which after the second day of its appearance, dries and forms [illegible]. Treatment of herpes: the bowels should be moved with saline cathartics—and emollient applications made to the affected part—if there is considerable irritation arising from the stinging and burning character of the pain, an anodyne may be given.

What are the rational symptoms, physical signs, duration, and termination of hypertrophy of the left ventricle of the heart? The patient complains of shortness of breath, there is a consciousness of unusual and stronger impulses of the heart. The impulse of the heart is stronger and more distinct. There is usually evidence of auricular valvular disease present. The duration is very uncertain. It may exist for many years, or suddenly cut short the life of the patient by inducing lesions of some of the arteries.

Give the etiology, essential symptoms, pathology, varieties, and proper treatment of dysentery. Causes—exposure, fatigue, and improper diet are among the most frequent causes of dysentery. [Again, the total absence of bacterial knowledge is obvious.] That exposure which subjects the individual to the influences of cold is most likely to give rise to the disease—if he is suffering from exceptional fatigue when so exposed, the liability is increased. Endemics of this disease are not infrequent, in which the influence of the above-mentioned causes are not observable, but in which miasmatic influences are believed to be the chief cause.

Symptoms: the disease is frequently announced by chills, a feeling of weariness, languor, and general lassitude. These symptoms, however, are most marked in those cases dependent on malarial causes—when arising from exposure to cold and wet, or excessive fatigue, the symptoms are more frequently secondary—the passage of bloody stools is always an early and most frequently the first symptom. There is often great and frequent desire on the part of the patient to go to stool, attended with severe tenesmus. The movements are generally scanty, of blood only, or mingled with hardened feces. There is usually more or less constitutional fever, the surface is hot and dry, pulse quick and tongue coated. The volume of the pulse will depend much on the cause, age, and habits of the patient. The pathology of dysentery: the mucous membrane of the rectum is the seat of the disease. The vessels of the membrane are greatly congested. The disease may be sthenic or asthenic and on this should in great measure depend the course to be adopted in treatment. If there is frequent desire to go to stool, attended with discharge of blood and great tenesmus, high fever, a full, quick pulse, the treatment may properly be commenced by giving a cathartic of Calomel [a toxic compound of mercury] and Oleum Ricini [castor oil]—generally the saline cathartics are best and of these sulfate of magnesia. Great relief is generally experienced after securing a free movement by these means. After the evacuation of the bowels, full doses of opium (one-half to two grains) should be given every four to six hours. If the tenesmus is great, it may be greatly relieved by injections into the rectum of starch, or some mucilaginous article, and laudanum. The dose of opium should, of course, be governed by the quantity of laudanum used in the injection. Other injections are often used with good effect. Nitrate of silver and acetate of lead in solution are sometimes used with great benefit.

The constitutional treatment [of dysentery] must depend on the causes and condition of the patient. As it occurs in the country, in sporadic cases, the treatment may need to be antiphlogistic [reducing fever].

In those localities where malarial influences exist, the disease not infrequently assumes a more or less remittent tendency. In these cases, quinine is of benefit. [Here, malaria and dysentery seem to be connected.] As the disease is usually seen among soldiers, a liberal and supporting treatment is necessary. The food should be un-irritating but nourishing. The use of the saline cathartics are admissible and necessary in all cases, when the relief of the portal circulation [the blood flow from the intestines to the liver] is desirable.

Describe the rational symptoms and physical signs of the first stage of phthisis [pulmonary tuberculosis], *also the pathology. Can it be cured in this stage? If so, how?* Symptoms: the patient is more or less emaciated, has indisposition to exercise, is easily wearied, there is hurried respiration on any unusual exercise. Cough is rarely absent and is generally short and dry, and the expectoration, mucous only. The general appearance of the patient will contribute to the diagnosis; the clear complexion, flushed cheek, eye sparkling with even more than wanted brilliancy in connection with the air of lassitude and weariness which characterizes the movements of the patient are indications of the disease. The appetite is usually unimpaired in the first stage, and the organic functions are generally undisturbed, so far as can be discovered.

Physical signs—there is dullness on percussion of that portion of the chest corresponding to the portion of lung affected. Auscultation reveals a roughened and interrupted respiration in the diseased portion of the lung. The respiration may be in part or wholly absent. In this case, the breathing is more or less bronchial.

Pathology—tubercule is present in the portion of the lung diseased. It seems to be infiltrated in and occluding the cells of the lung. It can be cured in this stage by supplying to the system those elements of nutrition in which it is deficient. This can best be done by making the diet nutritious. The fatty and oily compounds are believed to be the most efficient. Appetite should be promoted and digestion good. An abundance of fresh air, exercise and good food are essential.

Describe the rhomboid muscles. They arise from the ligamentum nuchae transverse processes of the fifth, sixth and seventh cervical vertebrae, and is inserted into the lower border of the scapula.

Describe the Quadratus lumborum—I cannot give the origin and insertion of this muscle.

Describe the Temporal muscle—it arises from the roughened line on the parietal bone above the squamous portion of that bone and is inserted into the coracoid process of the inferior maxillary.

Describe the deep palmar arch. It is the termination of the radial and ulnar arteries. It originates after those arteries pass from beneath the annular ligament and is in relation with and protected by the palmar aponeurosis and the tendons of the flexors in front and the extensor tendons behind.

Describe the hypo-glossal nerves. The function of the hypo-glossal is that of sensation. [Legibility is difficult here.]

Describe the thoracic duct. This duct is the receptacle for the reception and transmission of the chyle. [Chyle is a mixture of lymph and emulsified fats.] The duct is situated at the right side of the vertebral column and empties into the superior vena cava, near the point where the subclavian and jugular veins meet.

This completes the written examination. Dr. Smith certainly understood the basics of surgical anatomy. Microscopic anatomy and pathology seem totally absent. As to the bacterial and infectious diseases, he knew as much as any doctor in 1863, which is to say, practically nothing. There is no record of his "practical examination," in which he operated upon a live patient under observation.

APPENDIX C

SHIPS NAMED IN THE DIARY

The information presented here is derived from three sources: *The
Army's Navy Series,* Vol. III, Gibson, Charles Dana, and E. Kay Gibson,
eds., Ensign Press, Camden, ME, 1995; *Dictionary of American Naval Fighting Ships,* 9 Vols., U.S. Navy, Naval History Division, Washington, DC,
1959; and National Archives, Record Group 92, entry 1403, Records of
the Quartermaster, Water Transportation.

Arrow. A steam screw tug of fifty tons. She was appropriated from Southern
    owners in 1862 and chartered by the Union army in June of that year.
    While being used as a mail courier vessel, she was captured by Confed-
    erate partisans at the drawbridge at Coinjock, Virginia, on May 16,
    1863. She was recaptured by the Union a year later.
Butterfield. I could find no information on this ship.
Ceres. A steamer of unknown tonnage. She was probably used as a troop
    carrier in a raid against Elizabeth City, North Carolina, in April 1862.
    Later that year, a *Ceres* was reported on the lower Mississippi River.
    Ceres was the Roman goddess of agriculture.
Champion. Many ships bore this name. The likely candidate was a four hun-
    dred-ton side-wheel steamer mentioned in an 1862 expedition to the
    James River and in the assault on Fort Fisher, North Carolina, in Janu-
    ary 1865.
Commodore Hull. A 376-ton side-wheel ferry built at New York in 1860 as
    the *Nuestra Señora de Regla.* She was purchased by the U.S. Navy in
    September 1862, fitted with two thirty-pounders and four twenty-
    four-pounders, and assigned to the North Atlantic Blockading Squad-
    ron. After her service at the siege of Washington, where she was hit
    ninety-eight times by Confederate shells, she fought the CSA ram

Albemarle near Plymouth, North Carolina, on May 5, 1864. The original Commodore Hull fought Barbary Coast pirates at Tripoli and
commanded *Constitution* in her historic capture of HMS *Guerriere.*

Curlew. A 236-ton steamer built in Wilmington, Delaware, in 1856. She
was a Confederate Navy ship at Roanoke Island and was sunk defending the island against Burnside's successful invasion.

Dudley Buck. A 290-ton propeller steamer chartered several times during
the war. In addition to her service at North Carolina, she carried supplies to Sherman's troops at Savannah, Georigia, in December 1864. In
June 1865, she carried Union troops to Texas.

Eagle. She is mentioned in the *Official Records of the Navy,* Series I, Vol. 8,
pages 656–70, but without details.

Ellen S. Terry. A 260-ton propeller steamer, chartered by the Army from
February 1862 to May 1865. She made many runs between New Bern
and New York, and later brought supplies to Sherman's campaigns in
Georgia and South Carolina.

Elm City. This eleven hundred-ton steamer was one of the eight hospital
ships operated by the Sanitary Commission.

Emily. A steamer of unknown tonnage, she was captured with the *Arrow* in
the action described above. Her original charter date was June 27,
1862. In the *Official Records,* Series II, Vol. 6, Prisoners of War, Etc.,
there is a heated exchange of letters. A Union agent complained that
Captain Ford of the *Emily* was being mistreated at Richmond's infamous Libby prison; the reply by Robert Ould, Confederate Agent of
Exchange, denounced such an accusation as "an infamous falsehood."

Escort. A 458-ton side-wheel steamer, chartered by the Army in the spring
of 1863. She was purchased by the Quartermaster Department later that
year and was still on the books in late 1864. In addition to her heroic
service in the relief of the siege of Washington, she seemed to stimulate
misbehavior in her passengers. Court-martial records include Maj.
Henry Metcalf of the 58th Pennsylvania, who "did take off all his
clothes excepting his shirt and dance about the boat in an immodest and
indecent manner in the presence of officers and enlisted men . . . and in
the presence of a woman." He also spoke loudly of his recently deceased
colonel as "a damned old son of a bitch" and added, "I would go five
miles on my hands and knees to shit on the old cuss' grave." William
Ward of the 5th Rhode Island sneaked aboard the *Escort* in an attempt
to desert, while Robert Day of the 55th Pennsylvania disappeared for

three weeks from the *Escort* at Portsmouth, Virginia. He told his trial board, "I did not intend to desert. A man gave me whiskey and took me to a house of ill fame." Day's companion, Edward McGee of the 4th New Jersey Light Artillery, had the same excuse. Other men were convicted of theft and violence aboard this ship. After the war, *Escort* rejoined civilian life and carried groceries and passengers between New York and Connecticut and on the Catskill run. In 1897, she was run down and sunk in New York Harbor by the reckless action of the steamer *St. Johns.*

Genesee. One of the Navy's most modern ships, the eight hundred-ton side-wheel steamer was launched in April 1862. She carried a ten-inch Dahlgren gun, a one hundred-pounder, and six twenty-four-pounder howitzers. In the middle part of the war, she blockaded Wilmington, North Carolina, and Beaufort. Later, she was badly damaged at Vicksburg.

Halifax. There is little data on this steamer, other than her 1862–63 charter dates.

Hunchback. The unusual name is not explained. This five hundred-ton screw steamer was built as a ferry boat in 1852 and purchased by the U.S. Navy nine years later. The Navy added a one hundred-pounder Parrott gun (a fearsome weapon) and assigned her to the North Atlantic Blockading Squadron. In the invasion of Roanoke Island, *Hunchback* suffered severe damage in a close-range artillery duel with Fort Barrow. She served in many battles, both in the Carolina Sounds and on the James River. Wartime photos show several African-Americans in her crew. After the war, under the name *General Grant,* she worked for fifteen years on the New York to Brooklyn ferry run.

Huzzar. This 350-ton screw steamer was purchased by the army in October 1861 for $22,500 ($800,000 in today's money) and fitted with a thirty-pound Parrott gun and two rifled ten-pounders. After several years in the Carolina Sounds, she finished the war running between Pensacola and Apalachicola, Florida. Not mentioned in Dr. Smith's diary is the mutiny of the *Huzzar's* crew on November 28, 1862, while lying in the Neuse River.

Keystone State. This was a fourteen hundred-ton side-wheel steamer built in 1853. She carried four twelve-pounders as armament.

Lancer. Before the war, she was the *Duchess.* The Army Quartermaster Department purchased this four hundred-ton screw steamer for $46,000

in October 1861 and mounted a thirty-pounder Parrott gun and two
rifled field pieces on her decks. The *Lancer* was still in service in October 1864.

Louisiana. She was 143 feet long, with a beam of 27 feet; she drew 8 feet of
water. This steamer is described as a side-wheeler in one reference and
screw-driven in another. She was built the year before the war at
Wilmington, Delaware, and purchased by the Navy in July 1861. After
being fitted with three deck guns (an eight-incher, a thirty-two-
pounder and a twelve-pounder), she busied herself capturing Chin-
coteague Island. She spent the rest of the war patrolling the Carolina
Sounds. Her work at the siege of Washington, North Carolina, earned
this praise from Brig. Gen. John Foster: "The *Louisiana* had rendered
most efficient aid, throwing her shells with great precision." She ended
her days as a floating bomb, packed with gunpowder. Maj. Gen. Ben
Butler thought that such a vessel could destroy Fort Fisher, which
guarded the crucial Confederate port of Wilmington, North Carolina.
In a comedy of errors, the powder exploded later than expected, and
the effect was nil.

Massasoit. This 212-ton steam transport carried troops in many actions in
the Sounds, and evacuated civilians during the April 1864 Confederate
attack on Plymouth, North Carolina. She ended the war as one of the
ninety-nine ships carrying supplies to Sherman's advancing troops. The
original Massasoit was a Wampanoag leader who negotiated a peace
treaty with the Pilgrims in 1621.

Mercedita. This ship was completed at Brooklyn in late 1861. This thousand-ton screw steamer carried eight thirty-two-pounder guns and
could do over eleven knots. During blockade duty at Charleston, South
Carolina, she was rammed and badly damaged by Confederate iron-
clad *Palmetto State.*

Monitor. This is the ship that made history in her duel with the *Merrimack*
(CSS *Virginia*) at Hampton Roads, Virginia, on March 9, 1862. She
was all iron, with a revolving turret, carrying two eleven-inch Dahlgren
guns.

North Shore. I could find no information on this ship.

Ocean Wave. This was a 270-ton side-wheel steamer first chartered in March
1862. She carried troops on an April 1862 raid up the Pasquotank
River and in December of the same year carried the 1st New York
Marine Artillery Naval Brigade up the Neuse. She finished the war, still

carrying supplies, and ended her days in 1867, sinking at the dock at Mobile, Alabama.

Phoenix. This 154-ton steam transport participated in Burnside's expedition to Roanoke Island and the later capture of New Bern. In July 1863 she was still in service.

Princess Royal. This was a British blockade runner attempting to enter Charleston Harbor with a cargo of arms and ammunition. More ominously, she carried two powerful new steam engines, designed to drive iron-clad rams. She was captured by the USS *Unadilla,* commanded by Lt. Cmdr. Stephen B. Quackenbush, and became the USS *Princess Royal.* Under her new ownership, this screw steamer carried two thirty-pounders, a nine-inch Dahlgren, and four twenty-four-pounder howitzers, and quickly set about capturing other blockade runners.

S. R. Spaulding. This was a thousand-ton side-wheeler chartered in July 1861. After participating in the Roanoke Island expedition, she served as a hospital ship in the Peninsular Campaign, and returned to North Carolina for the rest of the war.

Sylvan Shore. This ship was chartered several times from 1861 to 1866, mostly in Virginia and North Carolina. She was a side-wheel steamer of 217 tons.

Thomas Collyer. This 446-ton side-wheel steamer was first chartered by the Army in March 1863. She served continuously in the Sounds until the end of the war.

Undine. In Roman mythology, an undine was a water spirit who could earn a soul by marrying a mortal and bearing his child. The Civil War *Undine* was a 110-ton side wheel steamer. Her records are confined to North Carolina service.

Whitehead. This ship was only a few months old when the Navy bought her in October 1861 at New York Harbor. This 136-ton screw steamer was fitted with a thirty-pounder gun (and later with armor plate) and spent the entire war in the environs of North Carolina. She fought in three battles against the dreaded Rebel ram CSS *Albemarle.* In addition to her role at the siege of Washington, she captured many small vessels in the tortuous waterways of the Sounds and nearby rivers. After the war, she was sold out of the Navy and spent her final seven years as the *Nevada,* carrying freight in the Connecticut area.

Dr. Smith's Descendants

Dr. Smith was married three times. His first wife, Adaline Martha Weeks, died after six years of marriage. They had one surviving child, Franklin Sullivan Smith, who married Clara Higgins. They had no children.

Generation 1

Dr. Smith's second wife was Emma Jane Spinks. This marriage produced one child, Clarence Melbury Smith. Emma died after two years of marriage. Dr. Smith then married Frances Lyon, who lived until 1922, twenty years beyond the death of her husband. They had no children, so all descendants are through Clarence.

Generation 2

Clarence Melbury Smith married Emily Maude Ball in 1896, and they had three children: William Melbury, Dan Clarence Andrew, and Mabel Emma.

Generation 3

The marriage of William Melbury Smith to Catherine Louise Gallagher in 1928 produced three children: William Melbury, Jr., Dan Sullivan, and James Francis. After a divorce from Catherine Louise, William married Ernestive Fetzer in 1954. They had no children.

In 1935, Dan Clarence Andrew Smith married Mary Repplier Cook in Redlands, California. They had nine children: Maria Bailey, Dan Clarence Andrew, Jr., Robert Leland Ball, Sidney Catherine, Cecelia Repplier, Susan Everett, John Lancaster, Edward Melbury, and Kathleen Mervale.

Mabel Emma Smith married Fitzhugh Preston Spalding in 1925 in Marquette, Michigan. They had two children: Emily Louise and Fitzhugh Preston, Jr.

Generation 4

William Melbury Smith, Jr., married Alice Louise Armantrout in 1964 at Laguna Beach, California. They had two children: Steven Melbury and Carolyn Louise.

In 1963, Dan Sullivan Smith married Sharon All Holmes. They had one child, Dan Sullivan, Jr. After a divorce, Dan S. Smith married Louise Higgenbotham in 1968. They had two children: Melissa Louise and Michael David.

Maria Bailey Smith married John James Patridge in 1957 in Redlands, California. They had six children: twins Carolyn Bailey and Susan Hunt, John Mitchell, Mary Repplier, Joseph Cook, and Christopher Lee.

In 1967, Dan Clarence Andrew Smith, Jr., married Joyce Ann Hardos in Redlands, California. They had three children: Theresa Diane, Joseph Andrew, and Alan Everett.

Robert Leland Ball Smith married Norma Elizabeth Ward in 1963 in Chula Vista, California. They had four children: Robert Leland Ball, Jr., Elizabeth Kathryn, Jeffrey Clarence, and Michael Alford.

In 1966, Sidney Catherine Smith married William Harold Sandstrom in Redlands, California. They had six children: Catherine Lynn, Susan Cook, William Edward, Brian Taylor, Kristen Marie, and Bradley Lawrence.

Cecelia Repplier Smith married James Patrick Donahue in 1965 in Redlands, California. This marriage produced three children: Kathleen Evarista, James Patrick, Jr., and Mary Repplier.

In 1968, Susan Everett Smith married John Michael McConneloug in Redlands, California. They had five children: Aimee Everett, Sara Elizabeth, Mary Carter, John Murphy, and Bridget Gaines.

In 1978, John Lancaster Smith married Brenda Sue Rafter in Riverside, California. They adopted two children: Emily Rafter and Sean Lancaster.

Edward Melbury Smith married Jeri Dee Abramson in 1999 in Redlands, California. They have no children.

Kathleen Mervale Smith married Kimbrough Lowe. After a divorce, Kathleen married Jeffrey William Anderton who has two children, Brian Jeffrey and Brittany Lynn.

Fitzhugh Preston Spalding, Jr., married Patricia Lynne Alvarez in 1961 at Pasadena, California. This marriage produced three children: William Preston, Richard Charles, and Cynthia Lynne.

Generation 5

Steven Melbury Smith married Mary Leclercq. They have no children.

Dan Sullivan Smith, Jr., married Donna Palazola. They have no children.

Michael David Smith married Keri McHale in 1999. They have no children.

Carolyn Bailey Patridge married Thomas Anthony Chabolla and they have two children: Sarah Patridge and Emma Antonia.

Susan Hunt Patridge married Daniel Jacob Misleh and they have three children: Benjamin Pfetzers, Anna Maria, and Zachary John.

John Mitchell Patridge married Denise Young. They have three children: Erin Nicole, Ryan Christopher, and Julia Suzanne.

Mary Repplier Patridge first married Bob Len Pritchett and they had one child: Megan Repplier. After a divorce, Mary Repplier married Brian Shortz in 1999.

Joseph Andrew Smith married Elena Alcober Serrano. They have no children.

Robert Leland Ball Smith, Jr., married Erin Murphy and they have two children: Chloe Anya and Everett Matthew Ball.

Elizabeth Kathryn Smith married Kevin Boyd Hight. They have no children.

William Harold Sandstrom married Kirsten Pasquinelli, and they have twin sons: Bailey Jensen and Holden William.

Kathleen Evarista Donahue married Michael Lee Kanapeaux. They have two children: Marie Evarista and Patrick Michael.

Aimee Everett McConneloug married Joaquin Lopez de San Roman Blanco. They have no children.

Bridget Gaines McConneloug married Jacob Andrew Peterson, and they have two children: Leah Taylor and Cody Mitchell.

William Preston Spalding married Kimberly Barbosa. They have two children: Tynam Nathaniel and Maria Nicole.

FEDERAL MISBEHAVIOR AT SUFFOLK, VIRGINIA

D r. Smith was not the only person distressed by the plunder and rapine of the Union soldiers. An Ohio private confirmed our diarist's observations.

Lafayette Baird was born February 27, 1841, in Tioga County, New York, and was with Company K, 67th Ohio Volunteers, at Suffolk, Virginia, when he wrote this letter to his parents. The date was October 27, 1862. The letter is from the files of Fredericksburg National Military Park, courtesy of Baird's great-granddaughter Joan P. Lowry. The spelling is as in the original.

I will make another attempt to write you a few lines after a march of some 50 or 60 miles and am still in the land of the living and am well as usual. We started Friday afternoon at 5 or about O'clock. and made a forced march to Black Water, about 30 miles. the way we went we got to our place of destination about noon, and we stoped after makeing a good reconoisance, and found no Enemy there. The only casuality. And the Band now puts me in mind of it, and I will name it. it was one of the cavalry men shot while on Picket. he was shot by a gurila or bushwhacker. he is now dead, I believe, by the sound of the Band that is playing the Death march. Father this march makes me almost disgusted, at the way this war is caried on or conducted on marches. more disgusting scenes never made themselves public, on any march I ever witnessed, than has this one. Poor people, robed of all or nearly all they had, and other thins commited toward them and on them to vulgur to mention. At the rich mans house you saw cavalry Sentinals stationed to protect them from

being interrupted in the least, and the poor have to suffer. I can
tell you, I cannot blame these poor much for arming themselves
to protect their own property, when they are interrupted as they
have been this time. it makes me feel to the bottom of my Heart
to see little Children of poor famalies standing in their homes,
and see the soldier dig the last hill of potatoes they have, and take
their Chickens from the roost, and all they have. and then have
the Vile and degraded soldier go into their houses and threaten
their lives if they do not give them some bread or what they have.
and nex to ill treat the women, as they did las Saturday. why was
they not Protected. aswer their Father was taken and put under
guard then goes these Vile specimen of Bruit, for I cannot call
them humane beings. they went to that Fathers house, and treated
his young daughter worse than a bruit and made threats of shooting her if she resisted them. and many things was commited that
would caus you or me to revenge in some way if posible. Oh parents the horrors of Civil war. it is surely reched to see the poor
famalies that have been made destitute of husband or father o
Brother by the conscript act. and to see our inhumane Soldier
enter their houses and take their last loaf of bread and the last cof-
feepot or Tea pot, and their Bead quilts and many other things
equal as useless to them. it might just as well be dispenses with as
not. I cannot blame the Gurila warefare that is caried on much
either, the Bushwhacking to protect their house and Homes. Parents let a true soldier look at this thing as it is and he will truly
shuder to think he is with those that will uphold such acts. It dis-
gusts me to that extent that I will never stay longer in such service
than to get out honerably. I am willing to draw with my comrades face to face to the armed for there to conquer or die but
will not stay with the army to lie still and rob the poor. I chose to
see this war close and am willing to do my share to execute to
that end if they will give us able and sufficint Generals. Those that
are true to the Cause in which we are fighting. May God be with
us in giving us such Generals. we have them and let us see them
put in power. may that time soon come when we whip or Give
up whiped. there is true and devotional Generals but they have
not the authority to execute the war in such a way as it ought to
executed. Father, I think J. C. Fremont is the man who ought to

be in General McClellans place. he made a proclamation one year ago in Missouri exually as meaning as President Lincolns, and I do sincerly believe if he had been left alone he would of had this war question settled in weeks passed and gone by. but I may be mistaken. but I long to see him placed in some high command. then I think the war will be Prosecuted some what earnester than it now is. so I think and write, but my opinion is nothing but a Privates, and it may not amount to much. I am anxiously awating to see such men as Generals placed in command as patrotic as the Private soldiers. I can tell you they are now trying men as Generals all to the expence of the Government, and to no good purpose. the poor private has to suffer the consequences and to suffer and die to try some traitor as a General in the Union army. Oh how we Privates do wish we had Generals who would work togather as the Southern Generals do, or have in these last few mooves in Virginia and Maryland. but no we cannot have our brave and Patriotic Generals where they can act without having Traitors over them. that you can see Parents as well as I can. and you ought to try and Give us good union men in both Civil and military offices. the Civil offices Gives the military, and influences them so please give us true union officers and we will do our part ably and as men and try to show ourselves men in all time we are permitted to stay on this Globe. I live in hopes now of seeing peace once more but it does not look much like peac yet, but we live in hopes still. we Privates Fight, have fought, and will still continue to Fight, if we can have able and competent leaders, but if not, we might as well give up and come home. I say what I think & these are my thoughts. I am well, may this few lines find you enjoying the same blessings.

Baird concluded his letter with a long plea for a pair of boots, a can of butter and a can or two of fruit, and a few comments about the high prices charged by the sutlers, but the burden of his missive was his disgust with Yankee rapists and robbers, and with incompetent Union generals.

DR. SMITH'S REPORT
ON THE 85TH NEW YORK

In February 1863, Dr. Smith was requested to submit a report on the medical history of the regiment. The full text is sixteen pages, and most of it repeats the history of marches and battles already in the diary. The medical high points are summarized below. (Original text courtesy of John Ball.)

December 1861 through March 1862, the 85th New York camped near Washington, D.C. The principal disease was pneumonia of the typhoid type. After the move to the Peninsula, north of Fort Monroe, they were sent to camp in low, marshy ground "by order of the general commanding." Many men were sick with intermittent fever, remittent fever, and bilious remittent fever, probably forms of malaria. Dr. Smith was promised quinine, but none was provided. Fifty-two men were left sick when the regiment moved north toward Williamsburg.

May 17, 1862, eight men were left sick at New Kent Courthouse. May 21, 1862, five men were left sick at Rose Cottage, near the Chickahominy River. May 25, 1862, the 85th camped in flooded ground near Seven Pines. Four men were sent to hospital at Antioch Church, and two officers to hospital at Savage's Station. June 4, 1862, they camped near White Oak Swamp Ford in a cold rain with neither coats nor tents. For several days, the only food was one square of hardtack per man.

June 28, 1862, they camped on the Jordan farm, on the way to the James River. In the preceding days, thirty-eight men and two officers were sent to the hospital ships on the James River. At Harrison's Landing, the regiment was assigned a camping spot, which was often underwater. Requests for a change were denied.

July 8, 1862, five men were sick in the regimental hospital and fifteen sick "in quarters." July 20, 1862, seventeen men were in hospital, and forty-two sick "in quarters," which might be a tent or merely meant the men were lying on the ground. July 21, 1862, the general commanding the brigade finally approved moving the 85th New York to a spot not underwater most of the time. The usual diseases were fever, jaundice, and scurvy.

September 10, 1862, they camped within the fortifications at Newport News. With improved food, the men's sallow, bronze complexions were replaced by the glow of youth. October 6, 1862, they camped at Suffolk, Virginia and engaged in heavy labor building fortifications. In a three-week period, 389 men (nearly half the regiment) were excused from duty for sickness, most with remittent fever (malaria) and diarrhea. A good supply of quinine quickly restored the fever cases. December 4, 1862, the regiment was ordered to march south; seventy-seven were left behind, too sick to march. In the Suffolk area, four men of the regiment died, several of malarial meningitis. Autopsy showed congestion of the arachnoid meninges and turbid fluid in the ventricles of the brain.

December 21, 1862, in the expedition to Kinston and Goldsboro, one man in the regiment was taken sick. Cool, dry weather was a positive factor. (The number of wounded does not appear.) January 11, 1863, two men were taken sick each day. The water supply was taken from the Neuse River.

Dr. Smith concluded his report in February 1863 with the remark that dysentery had been rare, while diarrhea was frequently seen. The definitions of these terms may have changed over the years.

SUGGESTED READINGS

Ball, John. 1996. *Escape from Dixie: The Experiences of Lt. John Lafler, 85th New York, Civil War Prisoner of War.* Williamsville, NY: Goldstar.

Barden, John R., ed. 1998. *Letters to the Home Circle: The North Carolina Service of Pvt. Henry A. Clapp.* Raleigh: North Carolina Division of Archives and History.

Barrett, John G. 1963. *The Civil War in North Carolina.* Chapel Hill: University of North Carolina Press.

Mahood, Wayne. 1991. *The Plymouth Pilgrims: A History of 85th New York Infantry in the Civil War.* Hightstown, NJ: Longstreet House.

INDEX

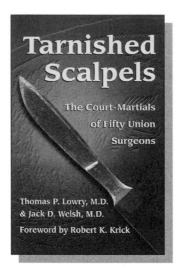